Building Cultural
Reciprocity with Families

Building Cultural Reciprocity with Families

Case Studies in Special Education

by

Beth Harry, Ph.D.
University of Miami
Florida

Maya Kalyanpur, Ph.D.
Towson University
Maryland

and

Monimalika Day, M.S.
University of Maryland
College Park

·P·A·U·L·H·
BROOKES
PUBLISHING Cº

Baltimore • London • Toronto • Sydney

Paul H. Brookes Publishing Co.
Post Office Box 10624
Baltimore, Maryland 21285-0624

www.brookespublishing.com

Typeset by Brushwood Graphics, Baltimore, Maryland.
Manufactured in the United States of America by
The Maple Press Co., York, Pennsylvania.

This book was supported in part by the Consortium for Collaborative Research on Social Relationships of Children and Youth with Diverse Abilities, Cooperative Agreement No. H086A20003, awarded to Syracuse University from the U.S. Department of Education. The opinions expressed herein, however, do not necessarily reflect the position or policy of either Syracuse University or the U.S. Department of Education, and no official endorsement by either should be inferred.

The case studies described in this book represent actual people and circumstances. In some cases, identities have been disguised; where they have not, written consent has been obtained.

The photographs that introduce Chapters 1 and 8 are courtesy of Jaideep Ghosh. All other photographs were supplied by the families in the case studies.

Excerpt on page 1 from "Poor Visitor" from LUCY by Jamaica Kincaid. Copyright © 1990 by Jamaica Kincaid. Reprinted by permission of Farrar, Straus and Giroux, LLC.

Library of Congress Cataloging–in–Publication Data
Harry, Beth.
    Building cultural reciprocity with families : case studies in
special education / by Beth Harry, Maya Kalyanpur, and Monimalika
Day.
        p.   cm.
    Includes bibliographical references (p.)
    ISBN 1–55766–377–7,
    1. Special education—Parent participation—United States case
studies. 2. Minority handicapped—Education—United States case
studies. 3. Parent–teacher relationships—United States case
studies. I. Kalyanpur, Maya. II. Day, Monimalika. III. Title.
LC3969. H377   1999   99–26306
371.9'04—dc21   CIP

British Library Cataloguing in Publication data are available from the British Library.

Contents

This case study presents the struggles of the family of a Salvadoran American young woman with cerebral palsy. The central issues challenge service providers to come to terms with their beliefs about independence, choice, and advocacy and to examine the needs of a student whose complex linguistic, cognitive, and physical attributes make her abilities very difficult to assess.

The vision of this family is one of full inclusion and a holistic view of an African American preschooler who happens to have Down syndrome. The family's struggle, led by Carissa's mother, challenges service providers to examine conflicting beliefs about equity and deviance and to reflect on the procedures by which children with disabilities are evaluated and placed in education programs.

In this case study, a Trinidadian American family concludes that their move to the United States was very beneficial to their son, once the family learned the ropes of advocating within the education system. Described as having mental retardation with some features of autism, this young man's strengths compete with his disabilities as he challenges service providers' and family members' views of his growing independence and cognitive potential.

This Palestinian American family responds with a mixture of faith and practicality to the changing needs of their charming, lovable, frustrating, growing-up son, who has mental retardation. Service providers will be challenged by the family's blend of a strong Moslem tradition with more American ways, as they assist the family with decisions that revolve around independence, individualism, and advocacy.

A single African American mother responds to God's call to adopt an infant with a disability. Full inclusion for this mother means including whatever educational approaches will support her goal of raising her daughter to be a Christian young woman, Down syndrome notwithstanding. Some service providers will be challenged by this mother's strong pro-life stand and by her preparedness to advocate for her daughter.

This case study describes the increasing cognitive and social development of a boy with mental retardation as he moves from elementary to middle school. Kyle's family reflects a blend of Chinese and American traditions and a winning combination of acceptance and advocacy. Service providers will be challenged to respond to the very individualistic approach of this family, who emphasizes that no one philosophy can fit all children.

This case study documents the transformation of an African American preschooler from the status of a "preemie" with developmental delays to that of a kindergartner in general education. Her parents' struggle to obtain all to which their daughter is entitled while keeping her from being relegated to a disability track will challenge service providers to review their assumptions about segregated services. Issues of equity and rights are central to the study.

In this tightly knit Dominican American family, the eighth of nine children has Down syndrome and is seen by his parents as "just like the others" yet "the center of the family." The case study describes Rafael's development as he moves from elementary to middle school. Service providers will be challenged to reflect on advocacy for a family whose sense of "rights" differs considerably from American views.

About the Authors

Beth Harry, Ph.D., Associate Professor, University of Miami, School of Education, Department of Teaching and Learning, Post Office Box 248065, Miami, Florida 33124-2040

Dr. Harry is a native of Jamaica and has lived and taught in Jamaica, Canada, Trinidad, and the United States. From a background in general education, Dr. Harry came into special education in response to the birth of her first child, Melanie, who had cerebral palsy. Prior to that, Dr. Harry taught elementary school in Jamaica; junior high school, high school, and community college in Toronto, Ontario, Canada; and in the School of Education at the University of the West Indies in Trinidad. After her daughter's birth, Dr. Harry founded and directed a private school for children with disabilities in Port of Spain, Trinidad. Dr. Harry came to the United States in 1985 and received her doctoral degree in special education from Syracuse University in 1989. Since then, she has focused on research and teaching related to the needs and perspectives of families from different ethnic backgrounds. Dr. Harry was an assistant professor of special education at the University of Maryland, College Park, from 1989 to 1995 and is Associate Professor in the Department of Teaching and Learning at the University of Miami, Florida.

Maya Kalyanpur, Ph.D., Assistant Professor, Towson University, Department of Reading, Special Education and Technology, 409 Hawkins Hall, Towson, Maryland 21252-0001

Dr. Kalyanpur's scholarly interests have focused on teaching and research related to the needs and perspectives of families from culturally diverse backgrounds. In 1997, she received a postdoctoral fellowship at the Beach Center for Families and Disability at the University of Kansas at Lawrence, where the work documented in this book was carried out. She serves as a consulting editor for *Mental Retardation* and *Critical Inquiry into Curriculum and Instruc-*

tion. She was a classroom teacher and director of a private school for children with disabilities in New Delhi, India, before coming to the United States as a graduate student. She received her doctoral degree in special education from Syracuse University in 1994.

Monimalika Day, M.S., Doctoral Candidate, University of Maryland, Department of Special Education, Benjamin Building, Room 1308, College Park, Maryland 20742

Ms. Day is a doctoral student in early childhood special education at the University of Maryland, College Park. She received her master's degree in child development in Calcutta, India, in 1989 and worked there for the next 3 years. She was the founder and administrator of a drop-in center for 300 homeless children. She also worked as a teacher at a special education center and assisted with starting a center-based program in one of the major hospitals in Calcutta. She came to the United States in 1992 and received a Certificate of Advanced Graduate Studies from Wheelock College in Boston. She joined the doctoral program at the University of Maryland in the fall of 1993. As both a researcher and a practitioner, she takes an active interest in promoting participation of traditionally underprivileged groups in mainstream society. Ms. Day received the Morris Frankel Graduate Award for academic excellence from the University of Maryland, Department of Special Education, in 1998. She also received the Naomi Hentz Scholarship from the University of Maryland, College of Education, in 1998 for promoting multicultural education. Her current interests focus primarily on action research with families of children with special needs, from culturally diverse backgrounds.

Introduction

This book presents eight case studies that are unique in one particular sense: The stories are personalized in a way that is not usually done in research-based reports. We wanted to offer a collection of case studies that would truly come alive rather than maintain the appearance of anonymity, which is usually used to protect confidentiality. Of the 10 families who participated in the research from which these studies emerged, we gained the permission of 8 to publish their stories; of those 8, 6 agreed to use their real names. One of the families who preferred to use a pseudonym described themselves as a "very private" family, and, although they were happy to have their child's story shared for the purposes of instruction, they considered the use of their real names too intrusive. The other family did not want their daughter's history of disability services to be made public because she has improved so much that she is now a general education student.

We believe that this range of perspectives illustrates well one of the main points of this book: Families differ on many dimensions, and it is the job of service providers and researchers to respect those differences. An interesting point to note regarding the issue of privacy is that privacy itself is a cultural value that may be more or less important to individual families. For example, for some people, rather than seeming an intrusion, the opportunity to tell their story is an empowering experience.

Our use of real names, however, stops at the families. We have used pseudonyms for all school district and community personnel and for any part-time employees of the project, such as students and job coaches. Names of locations, schools, and agencies also are fictitious.

THE CONSORTIUM FOR COLLABORATIVE RESEARCH ON SOCIAL RELATIONSHIPS OF CHILDREN AND YOUTH WITH DIVERSE ABILITIES: THE LONGITUDINAL FAMILY STUDY

The eight case studies reported in this book are the outcome of a 4-year research project funded by the U.S. Department of Education (USDOE), Office of Special Education Programs. The grant included five universities and was called the Consortium for Collaborative Research on Social Relationships of Children and Youth with Diverse Abilities. An explicit charge of the consortium was to support the effective inclusion of children with moderate to severe disabilities into the mainstream of the social life experienced by their peers and families.

The work with these eight families, which we called the Longitudinal Family Study, was one of several studies conducted at five universities under the auspices of the consortium. The consortium's approach to the research was guided by principles and practices of participatory research, which has been described by Meyer, Park, Grenot-Scheyer, Schwartz, and Harry (1998) in *Making Friends: The Influences of Culture and Development.* That book also includes reports of some of the findings of the Longitudinal Family Study.

The research in the Longitudinal Family Study was directed by Beth Harry, who was a co-principal investigator on the grant, with the assistance of three graduate assistants, Monimalika (Moni) Day, who was a doctoral candidate assigned to the grant during years 2–4; Faustina Quist, a master's student assigned to the grant during years 3 and 4; and Helena Davis, a master's student assigned to the grant during the first year. The team was racially diverse: Beth is Black, of Jamaican birth; Moni is Indian from India; Faustina is Black and is from Ghana; and Helena is Black, of Filipino and African American heritage. Another key member of the team was the Spanish–English interpreter, Cecelia Esquivel, who is from Chile and is a graduate student in social work at the Catholic University in Washington, D.C. Although this constituted the primary research team, data were also collected, from time to time, by undergraduate or graduate students and, in one case, by a school district teaching assistant, all of whom were employed as job coaches, participant observers, or tutors.

The other four co-directors of the consortium were also important members of the interpretive team. Because the consortium was collaborative in nature, findings from the five university sites were shared among the co-directors on a regular basis, as well as with the advisory board of the consortium on an annual basis. The sharing of findings resulted in considerable feedback and discussion among these various parties, and the interpretation of data and various aspects of decision making benefited greatly from these discussions. Particular mention must be made of Dr. Luanna Meyer, Director of the Consortium, and the other Co-directors, Dr. Marquita Grenot-Scheyer, Dr. Hyun-Sook Park, and Dr. Ilene Schwartz.

The second co-author of this book, Maya Kalyanpur, was not involved in the research for these case studies but is first author, with Beth Harry, of a companion volume, *Culture in Special Education: Building Reciprocal Family–Professional Relationships* (1999). The framework used to interpret parent–professional interaction in these eight case studies is derived from that publication.

In this book, we present eight of the case studies from the Longitudinal Family Study. Our purpose is to offer to personnel who are being prepared for careers in special education an opportunity to envision themselves working in a professional capacity with families from a wide range of cultural backgrounds and with children with varying types of abilities and disabilities. The companion volume (Kalyanpur & Harry, 1999) offers an analysis of the cultural beliefs on which special education policy and practice are based. Although this volume can be used on its own, a prior reading of the companion piece will offer a deeper understanding of the principles of cultural reciprocity.

GOALS AND ACTIVITIES OF THE STUDY

The purpose of the Longitudinal Family Study was to offer support to the families regarding their children's needs for social development and social activities, as far as possible, in inclusive environments. To accomplish this, we spent the first year of the project getting to know the students and their families. We interviewed various family members and other significant people in the students' lives, such as their teachers, therapists, friends, and individuals in the community who provided services from which our students might benefit. In addition to the interviews, we observed the students in several different environments, including their homes, schools, and various community situations. As we collected this information, we shared our learning with the families and, whenever possible, with the students themselves. In sharing our observations with the families, we sought their confirmation or correction of our impressions and further discussed with them ideas for ways that we could assist their children in developing their social identities and activities. Our goal was to offer assistance that would be culturally appropriate to each family because efforts that were not consonant with the families' values and wishes would not be helpful and would not last.

We spent the next 3 years of the project offering assistance that was agreed on in these discussions and evaluating the success of our efforts. A crucial point to be made is that decisions about how we would assist students were made on an ongoing basis and were constantly revised and reevaluated.

CHOOSING THE PARTICIPANTS OF THE STUDY

We must begin by explaining that the study had two cohorts of students. The first cohort comprised students in elementary and secondary schools, and this group participated in the study for the full 4 years, receiving social assistance from the project, as described previously. We recruited the second cohort, three preschoolers with disabilities, in the third year of the study, and our goals with them were simply to observe and understand the process that the families went through in developing inclusive socialization for their children. We did not conduct any interventions with that group. Five families described in this book are from the first cohort, and three are from the second.

In choosing the participants of the study, our intention was to include students of different age levels, with moderate to severe disabilities, who were placed in school environments that allowed some amount of integration with students who do not have disabilities. The first cohort were already in the school system, being served under Part B of the Individuals with Disabilities Education Act (IDEA) of 1990 (PL 101-476). In this county, the school system had traditionally placed students with moderate to severe disabilities in segregated special education centers. However, in the couple of years just prior to our study, the district had developed a program called "the LRE (least restrictive environment) program," which placed higher-functioning students in self-contained classrooms in general education buildings. Our initial seven students had recently been transferred from a special center to an LRE program; the four high school students were in one school, and the three elementary students were in another.

We chose these students by teacher recommendation. Having gained the permission of the school district and identified a secondary school and an elementary school that had an LRE program, we asked the teachers in the two schools to recommend students who were from diverse backgrounds, who the teachers believed would benefit from some social interventions, and whose families they believed would be interested in participating in the study. We sent letters to the families and followed up with home visits in which we explained the purposes of the study and gained the families' agreement.

In choosing the second cohort, we specifically wanted children who were already in inclusive environments and who were about to make the transition from Part C to Part B services. Because Part C has a stronger emphasis on community-based services, which allows for more inclusive environments, we anticipated that the transition to Part B would present much fewer inclusive options. Our purpose was to find out how families would negotiate this process and advocate for inclusion. A central focus was on each family's role in gaining access to and supporting the children's inclusion. We gained access to three families through the service coordinators of The Arc (formerly the Association for Retarded Citizens [ARC]), and all three responded positively to our invitation. Two of the children had Down syndrome, and the third had developmental delays, apparently resulting from premature birth.

Our group of participants turned out to be diverse on several dimensions. Table 1 shows the race/ethnicities and nationalities of the parents, as well as the ages of the students when the study began. The process of figuring out appropriate racial designators revealed the discrepancy between the way race is defined in the United States and the way it is approached in some other societies. In the United States, everyone is expected to opt for one race or another: Race is categorical. Among our participants, we had a range of definitions. For example, the Ignacio family (Chapter 8) described their race as *"una mezcla de africana, india, e hispañola"* [a mixture of African, Indian, and Spanish]. The *india* refers to the native

Table 1.   Participants in the study

Name	Age	Parents' race/ethnicity	Country of origin
Silvia Navarro	17	Indio/Spanish	El Salvador
Carissa Coates	2	Black	United States
Maldon Chappin	15	Black	Trinidad, W.I.
Maher Zaghal	17	Caucasian	Palestine
Brianna Roseboro	2	Black	United States
Kyle Lee	10	Caucasian/Chinese	United States
Theresa Marie Aldrick	3	Black	United States/ St. Lucia, W.I.
Rafael Ignacio	11	African/Indio/Spanish	Dominican Republic

peoples of Central America. For the Zaghal family (Chapter 4), we used the USDOE's definition of Middle Eastern peoples as "Caucasian." For four families, we used the term "Black" and treated nationality separately because "African American" includes the ascription of nationality, so a Black person who is not from America would not consider that term appropriate for him- or herself. The term "Chinese" is, of course, primarily a designation of nationality, but we believe that the term "Asian" is too broad to say anything specific about race (e.g., people from India are of very different stock from those from China, yet the USDOE uses "Asian" for both groups). For a fuller discussion of the meaning of such racial categories, see Harry (1992).

DILEMMAS IN WRITING THE CASE STUDIES

We started this introduction by explaining that the research conducted by the consortium was based on the principles of participatory research. We also stated that our explicit goal was to support the development of inclusionary social experiences for the students participating in the Longitudinal Family Study. Throughout the study, we did our best to adhere to these premises.

As a result of the principle of participatory research, our relationships with the families were much more personal than would normally be the case in traditional research. This, in itself, gave rise to certain considerations that we have discussed elsewhere (see Harry, 1995). With regard to these case studies, the quality of relationships with the study participants presented several implications, most of which took the form of ethical dilemmas.

To put it in a nutshell, the stories all had become too "real" to imagine writing them in the research tradition of anonymous cases using pseudonyms. The use of real names, we believed, would bring the stories alive and would be truer to the real families we knew. However, for the families, the idea of using of real names brought issues of personal privacy, of protection of confidentiality, and of the possibility of reprisals from service providers or others on whom families might have to rely for assistance. For the authors, the use of real names brought the issue of absolute accountability. We speak briefly of each of these concerns.

First, our suggestion to the families that we use real names and even photographs was well received by most. Some families were thrilled with the idea and even wanted to be sure that all family members got included in the photos. Others were fine with the real names but described themselves as camera shy. One family wanted to use the child's real name but not the family's surname, mainly because of the possibility of reprisals, and two families firmly preferred to use pseudonyms, seeing the use of real names as too intrusive.

The issue of privacy, however, still proved to be very real because there were some sensitive events related to individual students. On the one hand, we would have liked to include these issues because they would have been instructive for personnel who are being prepared to work with families of children with disabilities. On the other hand, we concluded that we should not include anything that we would hesitate to say about a student in front of him or her. In other words, we would not report or discuss a sensitive matter if the student would not know that it was in the book or would not understand it. We wanted to write the stories in a way that would be acceptable to the students themselves, if only they could read them.

The issue of confidentiality was a little different and usually related to materials such as conversations in meetings with administrators or documents that could be construed as "belonging" to the school district. Similar to this were accounts of interactions with or actions by service providers that would be embarrassing to or unduly critical of those individuals. Related to this were parents' concerns about how much criticism could reasonably be made without, as one parent put it, "burning bridges" that might be needed later. We resolved these issues by using fairly generic language wherever necessary and, obviously, by using pseudonyms for service providers, agencies, and schools. There were even some concerns that were important to the parents but that they did not want to say publicly, once more, because of fear of reprisals.

For us, as the authors of this book, the decision to use real names had one particularly powerful result: absolute accountability to the families for everything that we said! This is not to suggest that researchers do not always have the responsibility of being true to their data, but there was no question of our being able to let mistakes slide or to write anything that could be offensive to the families. Our approach to this was to send each family a draft of their child's case study and, through discussions or written responses, make as many revisions as were necessary to satisfy the family members' recollection of events, preference for types of language, desire for what should or should not be included, or any other details that concerned them. This slowed down our production process somewhat and also took up valuable time of the parents, but the result is a collection of richer and much more accurate accounts. Indeed, although we had kept careful logs, field notes, and interview transcripts, there still were actual and interpretive details that we would have missed or misrepresented if we had not been able to benefit from the participants' feedback and revisions.

We are very grateful to the families for their enthusiastic participation through all phases of this process, and we trust that this book will be an encouraging memento of our efforts with them. We say this with particular understanding that we know that whatever we tried to do for these students and their families simply was not enough.

REFERENCES

Harry, B. (1992). *Cultural diversity, families, and the special education system*. New York: Teachers College Press.

Harry, B. (1995). These families, those families: The impact of researcher identities on the research act. *Exceptional Children, 62*(3), 292–300.

Individuals with Disabilities Education Act (IDEA) of 1990, PL 101-476, 20 U.S.C. §§ 1400 *et seq.*

Kalyanpur, M., & Harry, B. (1999). *Culture in special education: Building reciprocal family–professional relationships*. Baltimore: Paul H. Brookes Publishing Co.

Meyer, L.H., Park, H.-S., Grenot-Scheyer, M., Schwartz, I.S., & Harry, B. (Eds.). (1998). *Making friends: The influences of culture and development*. Baltimore: Paul H. Brookes Publishing Co.

Acknowledgments

We acknowledge the contributions of members of the Consortium for Collaborative Research on Social Relationships of Children and Youth with Diverse Abilities to the interpretation of data on which the case studies are based. In particular, we thank the co-directors of the consortium, Luanna Meyer, Hyun-Sook Park, Marquita Grenot-Scheyer, and Ilene Schwartz, and the project director, Anne Smith. Thanks also go to Sari Biklen, Sharon Dunmore, Mary Fisher, Mark Larsen, Stacy Minondo, Cap Peck, Mara Sapon-Shevin, and Debbie Staub and also to all members of the Consortium Advisory Board, especially Robert Rueda.

We especially thank personnel on the project at the University of Maryland: graduate assistants Faustina Quist and Helena Davis and Spanish interpreter and translator Cecelia Esquivel. Although for reasons of confidentiality school district personnel are not named in the book, we thank the teachers who participated, many of whom went well beyond the research requirements in their efforts to assist us and the students. We also thank numerous undergraduate and graduate students who engaged part time in collecting data or in travel or job training of students in the case studies. We give special mention to Alicia Burnham, who participated voluntarily, without pay or university credit, as a tutor for one student over a period of 2 years.

Le dedicamos este libro a las familias de los ocho niños representados en los estudios individuales. Le damos las gracias por su participación en este proyecto y por dándonos la oportunidad de entender las penas y alegrías de tener hijos disabilitados. Esperamos que el libro contribuya en alguna manera a su satisfacción con nuestros esfuerzos, sabiendo que cualquier cosa que háyamos logrado a favor de sus hijos es, en todo caso, menos de lo que hubiéramos querido. Esperamos que parte de la satisfacción de estas familias con el libro venga de saber que las lecciones que hemos aprendido ayudarán en la educación de maestros/as de niños disabilitados.

We dedicate this book to the families of the eight children described in the case studies. We thank them for their willing participation in the project and for allowing us to gain a close-up understanding of many of the challenges and joys of their experiences with their children who have disabilities. We hope that the book will in some small way contribute to their satisfaction with our efforts, knowing that whatever we succeeded in accomplishing on their children's behalf was, in all cases, less than we would have liked to do. We hope that part of these families' satisfaction with the book will come from knowing that the lessons that we learned from them will be helpful in the education of future teachers of children with disabilities.

Building Cultural
Reciprocity with Families

Section I

The Posture of Cultural Reciprocity

That morning, the morning of my first day, the morning that followed my first night, was a sunny morning. It was not the sort of bright sun-yellow making everything curl at the edges, almost in fright, that I was used to, but a pale-yellow sun, as if the sun had grown weak from trying too hard to shine; but still it was sunny, and that was nice and made me miss my home less. And so, seeing the sun, I got up and put on a dress, a gay dress made out of madras cloth-the same sort of dress that I would wear if I were at home and setting out for a day in the country. It was all wrong. The sun was shining, but the air was cold. It was the middle of January, after all. But I did not know that the sun could shine and the air remain cold; no one had ever told me. What a feeling that was! How can I explain? Something I had always known-the way I knew my skin was the color brown of a nut rubbed repeatedly with a soft cloth, or the way I knew my own name-something I took completely for granted, "the sun is shining, the air is warm," was not so. (Excerpt from LUCY, Kincaid, 1990, p. 5)

Many of you may have had an experience similar to that of Lucy, the young Caribbean girl in the previous excerpt, when something you took for granted suddenly turned "all wrong"—and made you aware of what you had taken for granted until that point in time. It may have happened when, like Lucy, you visited a foreign country. You probably expected some overt differences, such as language, and you may even have prepared yourself by bringing a phrase book along with you. But then, during the course of your trip, you began to notice other differences that you had not expected. For instance,

1

you might have found that, when people talked to you, they stood a lot closer than you were accustomed to. Or that parents and children and grandparents talked to each other differently from what you grew up with. How did these experiences make you feel? Were you uncomfortable? Irritated? Threatened? Bewildered? Curious? Glad you had this experience because you learned about yourself something that you had always taken for granted? Would it have helped to have had somebody to explain what was happening and make you feel a little less out of place?

All of the things mentioned here, and many, many others, contribute to what we call *culture*. People who have lived all their lives within the dominant group of a society often think that they "have no culture"; they tend to think that culture is something that belongs to minority groups. The reason for this thinking is that people who belong to the group that holds power in a society usually do not have to define, explain, or contrast themselves to anyone because they belong to the group whose ways and rules are the "given" in the society. If you find that you think this way, then the easiest way to become aware that you really do have a culture is to visit another society or community. Another, though more abstract, way to become more aware is to question yourself carefully about what you value most in life, then ask from where you derived those beliefs. For example, a quick look at a famous phrase from the U.S. Constitution reveals a great deal about American culture: U.S. citizens have the right to "life, liberty, and the pursuit of happiness." These values are so deeply embedded in U.S. society that it may be hard to imagine that they are not necessarily universal values. Yet, if you think about it, you can quickly see that they are not the cornerstones of many societies.

Discovering your cultural stance and how it affects your interaction with families is what this book is about. It will give you opportunities to learn about yourself and to develop an awareness of your cultural identity, to learn to recognize the taken-for-granted values and beliefs that you hold and that make you think and act the way you do, and to use this understanding about yourself to understand others. You may ask, "What has this got to do with special education?" Everything, we believe.

For many families of children with disabilities, entering the culture of special education is like going to a foreign country. Just as each country has a dominant culture, so does each profession. The culture of a professional group may have several markers: language, style of dress, personal interaction patterns, status differentiation, laws and regulations, and, certainly, values and beliefs. To a great extent, these cultural markers are expressions of the various aspects of the national culture.

Special education in the United States is a product of American culture. There are certain core American values that have contributed to the way in which the field of special education has developed over the years, and they continue to be the underpinnings for current policy and practice. For instance, in the Individuals with Disabilities Education Act (IDEA) of 1990 (PL 101-476), the principle of parent participation is based on the value of equality and the expectation that parents and service providers should develop partnerships in the education decision-making process of students with disabilities. Similarly, the principle of due process of law is based on the value of individualism: the understanding that, in a culture where individuality is highly prized, people have rights to ensure that their individual interests are protected. Conversely, when families believe in social hierarchies rather than in social equality and consider professionals to be the experts and the holders of authority, the expectation that the family should partner with professionals can be bewildering. When families do not value individual rights because they believe that society is more important than the individual, the expectation that they will advocate for their children and assert their rights can make them quite uncomfortable. If they do not have someone to explain what is happening and make them feel a little less out of place, then they can end up becoming alienated from the process. As a result, the services that their children receive will be less effective, and nobody will benefit.

As a professional in the field of special education, you know the current recommended professional practices and you have the skills to implement them. This is what you learned in your professional training program. You may even have taken a course on working with families of children with disabilities and learned that collaborating with families is recommended professional practice or, at the least, a legal requirement. Perhaps you were taught the communication skills that you would need to build relationships and collaborate with families. However, as Skrtic (1995) pointed out, chances are that you probably did not have an opportunity to question why collaborating with families is considered recommended practice and is legally mandated. And chances are that, because you believe in equality, you would accept without question, even take for granted, the premise that building partnerships with families is good professional practice. Yet the professional preparation program that you have undergone also has taught you another value: The knowledge you have received is highly specialized and is valued more highly than a layperson's knowledge. It is most probable that you will not have been encouraged to note that the belief in equality and the belief in the superiority of expert knowledge are likely to come into conflict. In fact, it is very likely, if you have successfully undergone the process of becoming a professional, that, although you share many of the values that are embedded in the culture of special education, you may never have explicitly acknowledged them.

The reason that many of your values may be common to those that are embedded in special education culture is that most of the values of special education are mainstream values, or what Banks and McGee Banks (1997) called the *values of the macroculture*. This macroculture is a broad, overarching national culture that embodies core American values. By belonging to this national macroculture, you subscribe to all or some of these core values: They contribute to a part of who you are. But, as Figure 1 shows, subsumed under the macroculture are other, smaller, or *microcultural*, groups to which you might also belong. These microcultures are likely to reflect the values of the particular ethnic group or groups in which you grew up, and, of course, these microcultures may even overlap each other. However, Banks and McGee Banks took the concept of culture to a more personal level by pointing out that other aspects of your identity, such as your ethnicity, your gender, your age, your religion, and your professional training, also combine to create a cultural identity that is uniquely yours. Culture, then, is a broad concept that reflects a wide range of beliefs, practices, and attitudes that make up each individual. Figure 2 gives you a picture of what the various microcultural affiliations might be. Look at each of these figures in turn, and think about how they may apply to you.

This unique combination of micro- and macrocultures that makes up your cultural identity is what you bring to any interaction with families in the special education system. It affects how you respond or react to them, what you recommend to them, and why you might feel comfortable working with some families and not with others. If you and the family both believe in equality, then you will find it easier to collaborate with them because they are just as eager as you are to become partners. If, however, a family continues to defer to your authority or to avoid interactions with you, despite your best efforts to involve them as partners, then you might begin to believe it impossible to collaborate. Most significant, you may not understand why collaborating with this family is so difficult-unless you question the assumption, the taken-for-granted belief, that is embedded in your asking them to collaborate with you. To compli-

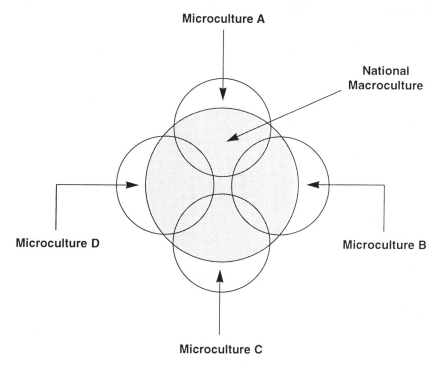

Figure 1.   Microcultures and the national macroculture. The shaded area represents the national macroculture. A, B, C, and D represent microcultures that consist of unique institutions, values, and cultural elements that are nonuniversalized and are shared primarily by members of specific cultural groups. (From Banks, J.A., & McGee Banks, C.A. [Eds.]. [1997]. *Multicultural education: Issues and perspectives* [3rd ed., p. 12]. Needham Heights, MA: Allyn & Bacon; reprinted by permission.)

cate matters further, you may not recognize that some of your own beliefs may be in conflict-that is, your belief in equality as well as your belief in expert knowledge. This conflict may be affecting your own attitude toward the importance of the family's input. Thus, you may want to see the family as equal to you, yet you may find it difficult to place as much value on their "everyday knowledge" as on your own specialized knowledge.

CORE VALUES THAT UNDERLIE

SPECIAL EDUCATION POLICY AND PRACTICE

In our book *Culture in Special Education: Building Reciprocal Family–Professional Relationships* (Kalyanpur & Harry, 1999), we

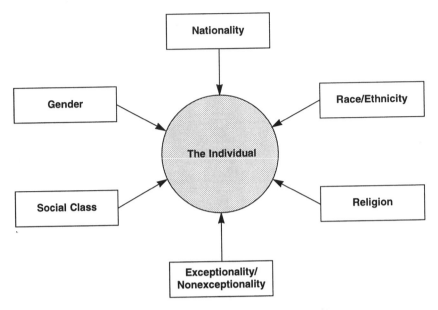

Figure 2. Multiple group membership. An individual belongs to several groups at the same time. (From Banks, J.A., & McGee Banks, C.A. [Eds.]. [1997]. *Multicultural education: Issues and perspectives* [3rd ed., p. 15]. Needham Heights, MA: Allyn & Bacon; reprinted by permission.)

identified certain American values that have influenced the way in which disability and disability services are conceptualized and implemented in the United States. You will need to turn to that book for a fuller explanation of the impact of these values, but for the purposes of analysis of the case studies in this book, we offer the following list of values for you to consider as you read the stories and examine your own reactions to them: individualism, independence, freedom of choice, equality/equity, expert knowledge, efficiency, and objectivity.

DEVELOPING A POSTURE OF CULTURAL RECIPROCITY

The purpose of this book is to introduce you to an approach to learning more about yourself and the process of collaborative interaction with families of children with disabilities. Different cultural beliefs and practices have been noted as a frequent barrier to effective interaction; therefore, some movement toward mutual understanding usually is required before people can begin to work well together. However, many researchers have noted that it is most often the people from the minority group who are required to understand or become acculturated to the ways of the majority group. Overall, this is probably a reasonable expectation. However, the process of acculturation takes time, and professionals who are hoping to make a difference for children must be willing to take the initiative in building a bridge between the cultures of diverse families and the culture of schools. To do this, we advocate that professionals initiate a two-way process of information sharing and understanding—a process that can be truly reciprocal and lead to genuine mutual understanding and cooperation. We outline four steps that are essential in developing what we have called a *posture of cultural reciprocity*.

Step 1: Identify the cultural values that are embedded in your interpretation of a student's difficulties or in the recommendation for service.
When you begin to identify the values and assumptions that are embedded in your professional practices, you are at the first step of our framework for developing reciprocal, empowering relationships with families. Let us offer you an example.

Imagine this scenario: You have recommended that a young adult with a developmental disability move out of the family home into a small group home or supported apartment. Ask yourself which values underlie your recommendation. You might find that your rationale goes something like this:

- Independence and individuality are highly valuable.
- Becoming increasingly independent is a mark of adulthood.
- At approximately the age of 21, moving out of the family home and establishing one's own home (alone, with friends, or with a spouse) is an essential step toward establishing adult independence and individuality.
- All human beings have equal value and should have equal opportunities.
- Young adults with disabilities should have the same opportunities as their peers without disabilities.
- A living arrangement that is as similar as possible to that of a young adult without a disability should be sought.
- This living arrangement will provide my client with greater opportunities to develop his or her independence and individuality.

By this analysis, you can see that there are two or three central values underlying your recommendation: Equity, independence, and/or individuality. The last two are closely intertwined because you might see individuality as an aspect of independence in that each individual should create a life of his or her own, according to his or her own wishes.

Now, use Figure 3, which we call your *personal identity web*, to identify those aspects of your identity that you think have contributed to your holding those three values. For example, you might look first at the aspects of *nationality and culture:* Did you derive your value of independence from the macroculture of the country in which you grew up? Did you also learn to value equity through the culture of the country in which you grew up? Or, to the contrary, maybe you grew up in a country where equity was not valued, which led you to desire it. Now relate this to your *ethnicity:* Was the value of equality supported by your ethnicity, such as being a Caucasian who grew up in a family who believed that all siblings have the right to the same opportunities in life? Or think of *socioeconomic status:* Was your belief in sibling equality supported by your family's having enough financial resources to provide for all family members' development? Did your financial resources also enable you to consider the option of establishing your own home as a means of achieving independence? You also might think about your own adult experience-let's say, *parenthood:* If you are a parent, then you might ask whether this has led you to believe that living on one's own is a good experience for your own child. Then, turning your attention to your *professional education,* you might ask whether you are a scientific rationalist/professional whose judgment is based on data that show improved quality of life for individuals who live in group homes.

By noting on your personal identity web several aspects of your identity-nationality/culture, ethnicity, socioeconomic status, parenthood, and professional education-you now have a more explicit understanding of the sources of your own beliefs. This has two important implications: First, you will see the relation between your own identity and your recommendation that your client move out of the family home. Second, by recognizing that your recommendation reflects your own cultural experience and identity, you see that you can be sure of its validity only within that framework. It may not, however, be valid outside that framework. It is not, after all, a universally held truth.

Now that you've had an example of the process entailed in Step 1, you might like to try the Introductory Exercise on pages 12–13. Alternatively, you can read on through the next three steps of our hypothetical example before trying your own first step.

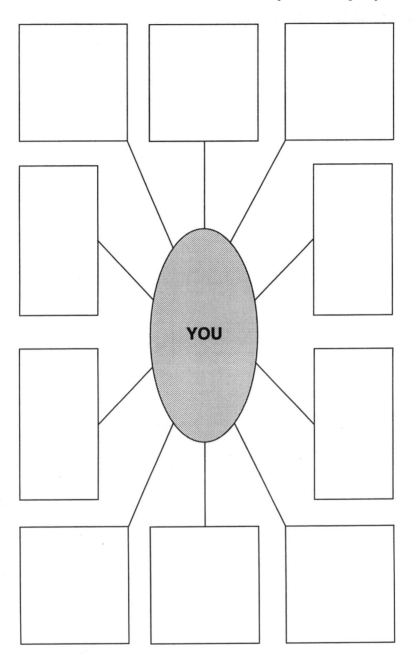

Figure 3.   Personal identity web. (From Banks, J.A., & McGee Banks, C.A. [Eds.]. [1997]. *Multicultural education: Issues and perspectives* [3rd ed., p. 14]. Needham Heights, MA: Allyn & Bacon; adapted by permission.)

Step 2: Find out whether the family being served recognizes and values these assumptions and, if not, how their view differs from yours.

Your approach to this dialogue must be marked by respect and a genuine desire to understand. Let us imagine that, in this example, the family does not want to consider a group home as a residential option for their young adult. Let us try a few possible explanations that they might give for their position.

First, moving out of the family home may *not* be normative for this family. The pattern may be for older siblings to continue to live with the parents until they get married, and maybe even after marriage. Therefore, the family may not see living on one's own as a milestone to adulthood and independence even for their children without disabilities. They may be more adamant about this regarding the child with the disability because they see that child as particularly vulnerable. They may see the chief marker of adult independence as the individual's ability to bring in adequate income to support other family members, or adult independence may be signaled by marriage.

You may also find that the family's view of equality is not the same as yours. They may see the family member with the disability as essentially *not* equal to the others in terms of having the same rights to independence. They may explain this in terms of the greater vulnerability of the family member with the disability, or they may even explain that they do not expect the siblings to be equal anyway because not all people are equal. Similarly, the family may explain that individuality is not highly valued and that it is more important to be a good member of the group.

Step 3: Acknowledge and give explicit respect to any cultural differences identified, and fully explain the cultural basis of your assumptions.

Remember how, when things went "all wrong" when you visited another culture, you wished you had someone to explain what was happening to you so that you would feel less out of place? Now, it is your responsibility to explicitly "put on the table" both your and the family's points of view.

By letting the family know why you made the recommendation, you explain to them what is happening and enable them to feel less out of place in their interactions with you. You explain that your recommendation is based on your belief in independence, individuality, and equality. You acknowledge that this belief reflects some key mainstream beliefs that are also part of your professional training. By placing these beliefs in the context of your own culture, you demonstrate your awareness that yours, or the mainstream's, is not the only way. Also, by offering this explanation, you are offering the family information about beliefs or practices that are valued in the mainstream of the society; as Apple and Beane (1995) would say, this information can become part of the family's *cultural capital* as they set about negotiating with mainstream professionals. At the same time, by asking the family what their point of view is, you are getting an explanation for what is happening from their perspective, which enables *you* to feel less out of place, too. This process creates a shared understanding that empowers both you and the family and creates an atmosphere of mutual respect.

Step 4: Through discussion and collaboration, set about determining the most effective way of adapting your professional interpretations or recommendations to the value system of this family.
Through your dialogue with the family, you may have found that although the family does not want out-of-home placement, they do acknowledge needing assistance in supporting the member with the disability. Your challenge, then, is to work out with the family a solution that respects their family system while bringing in the best that your professional knowledge and expertise can offer.

Your first steps would probably be to seek sources of additional income that could help the family achieve their goal. You would inform and assist the family in gaining access to any sources of financial aid for which they are eligible, such as Social Security Disability Income (SSDI), or you might focus on employment agencies that could assist the member with the disability in finding more appropriate employment. You might also need to seek sources of financial assistance that could provide home renovations that would make the plan more feasible for the family. You and the family might even decide to work toward creating a semi-independent arrangement within the family home.

There are many more potential outcomes of your interaction with this hypothetical family. Overall, this example is merely a beginning to illustrate what we mean when we speak of cultural reciprocity. Any of the interpretations that we have offered in this example might be inappropriate. Your examination of your values or those of the family and the sources of those values might produce an entirely different picture than the one we have depicted. This is exactly the point: There is no recipe for how your examination of yourself or your work with a family will transpire. By developing a posture of cultural reciprocity, however, you can ensure that every interaction with a family will be a learning experience for both you and the family and that any assistance that you offer will be within the realm of what is valued and feasible for that family.

This book contains the stories of eight families. As you read these accounts, we encourage you to apply the framework of the posture of cultural reciprocity to the situations that the families encountered with various professionals. Ask yourself, "What were some of the underlying values in the professionals' practices, and what values would I have brought to the situation?" Next, try to identify what the families' values were. After the first case study, "Silvia," we offer an interpretation of how the process of cultural reciprocity applied to our work with this family. After the other seven accounts, we suggest some brief interpretations and ask questions to prompt you to apply the process of cultural reciprocity. Our interpretations are by no means the only ones possible. You might find that you have a very different response to the stories, and, based on your personal cultural identity, you might identify other values.

By developing your own cultural self-awareness, you will be able to recognize the cultural underpinnings of your professional practice. This, in turn, will enable you to facilitate conversations with the families with whom you interact, toward identifying the values and beliefs that underlie their priorities, goals, and vision for their child. As you learn about yourself and the families with whom you work, the families will also acquire knowledge about the special education system that will enable them to make informed decisions about services. You will have developed reciprocal, truly collaborative relationships.

Be sure to read the Introduction on pages xi–xviii. It contains essential information about the unique dimensions of the study on which this book is based.

INTRODUCTORY EXERCISE

This exercise serves as an introduction to the process of cultural reciprocity. The following questions require you to work only on Step 1 of the process because you may not know enough about how the family really felt about the issues to imagine the rest of the process. If you think you do, however, then you might be able to attempt a hypothetical analysis of how Steps 2, 3, and 4 might have worked. If you can do only Step 1, do not be anxious, because each of the case studies in the book will give you the opportunity to try the process in more depth. For now, here's what we want you to do:

Recollect an episode or an interaction that you have had with a parent of a child with a disability (or a child suspected to be at risk) in which you recommended a particular course of action or service. Briefly describe the incident. Now, respond to the following questions:

1. Why did you choose that story?
2. What made you recommend that particular service?
3. Does your recommendation reflect a value that comes from your culture? What do you think it might be?
4. Use your personal identity web to identify specific cultural affiliations that affected your recommendations and your interactions with this family.

Section II

Case Studies in Special Education

The Ignacio family: Rafael with parents, brothers, cousin, and aunt

1

Silvia

"A Very Happy Person"

Silvia, Trinidad, Oscar, and Rosa

This case study presents the struggles of the family of a Salvadoran American young woman with cerebral palsy. The central issues challenge service providers to come to terms with their beliefs about independence, choice, and advocacy and to examine the needs of a student whose complex linguistic, cognitive, and physical attributes make her abilities very difficult to assess.

Silvia Navarro was 17 when we first met her. Her radiant smile and ready laughter, along with her frequently changing hairdos and attractive, light makeup, led her teachers to nickname her "Miss El Salvador." At school, her dark brown hair—sometimes permed, sometimes naturally wavy—was usually in a ponytail, but for special occasions such as a school party, Silvia wore it falling to her shoulders, pinned lightly with a colorful barrette, carefully chosen to complement the sparkling fabric of her dress.

Owing to her cerebral palsy, Silvia uses a wheelchair, with which she would often speed so fast through the school halls that her friend Asha would tell her that she ought to get a speeding ticket. Silvia's disability also causes her to have difficulties with her speech. When we met her, her Spanish was more advanced than her English, but she could carry on a conversation in either language. She always worked very hard to articulate clearly, and she readily repeated words or phrases until her listener understood. In English, Silvia tended to speak in one- or two-word phrases, whereas her spoken Spanish was much more fluent and her understanding of Spanish seemed appropriate for her age. Silvia has good mobility in her upper body and, despite some spasticity in both hands, she uses her left hand for fine motor tasks such as writing, typing, or painting. Her mother, Rosa, describes this youngest of her four children as *"una persona muy contenta"* [a very happy person].

All of our work with Silvia reinforced Rosa's very positive description. Not only did Silvia seem happy most of the time, but she also showed tremendous patience with difficult tasks. Silvia was in a self-contained special education class in a general high school, and her education program had a predominantly vocational emphasis, with a job placement 4 days per week. Our observations of this program revealed Silvia's determination to succeed at challenging tasks, such as steam-pressing clothes at the secondhand clothing store where she worked during the first school year and summer of our project. Similarly, her tolerance for frustration was evident during the two summers when project efforts to assist her in using public buses resulted in frequent inconveniences and delays, owing to faulty bus equipment and scheduling. Silvia smiled and kept on trying through all of these difficulties. The only time that we saw her appear discouraged was when her family received news from El Salvador, in the first summer of the project, that her grandmother had died. Silvia, in grief, missed 2 days of work that week.

Silvia's father, Trinidad, had been the first in the family to leave their native El Salvador to come to the United States to pave the way for his family. Some years later, Rosa came, leaving Silvia and her siblings in the care of their grandmother and aunt until they, too, could join their parents. Silvia came to the United States at the age of 11 years. When we met Silvia, she said that although she liked the United States, she liked her native country better because she had there many cousins with whom she had a lot of fun.

Growing up in a rural area of El Salvador, Rosa and Trinidad did not have the opportunity to attend school and learn to read and write. Both speak Spanish, and although they understand some English, they do not speak it. These features, however, did not deter the family from achieving their goals. Trinidad works in construction, which was abundant during his first years in the United States, and, according to Rosa, *"él trabajaba y trabajaba"* [he worked and worked] until he made enough money for the family to purchase a small house. The house had been abandoned for some time and, according to Rosa, had snakes living in it. Now the bright white cottage with its red-trimmed windows and eaves and its carefully tended flower beds lining the small, sloping garden, is undoubtedly the prettiest on the street. From the start, the house was perfect for them because the previous owners also had had a member with a disability, and they had built a ramp from the kitchen door out to the back garden. But throughout the 4 years of our project, Silvia's chair still had to be pushed up the slope from the street to the part of the garden where the ramp began. This daily effort took quite a toll on Rosa's petite frame, and when we met her she was having trouble with her back. Nevertheless, Rosa's smile was always cheerful, and her support of her daughter never wavered.

INITIAL RESEARCH WITH SILVIA AND HER FAMILY

In the first year, we focused most of our research efforts on observing Silvia at home, at school, and at the job where she was placed for about 4 hours daily from Monday through Thursday. We also interviewed Rosa and, on one occasion, Trinidad, but he rarely was available for interviews because of his varying work schedule. In our frequent visits to the home, Silvia's sister Doris and her brother Oscar were also included in interviews. Other family members, such as her sister-in-law Amelia and her cousin Patti, also were occasional participants in our conversations. Silvia's brother Luis was married and already living in his own home, so we did not see him often. At school, we interviewed Silvia's teacher and teaching assistant, her speech-language pathologist, and her classmate and best friend, Asha.

The information that we gained throughout this research resulted in four main thrusts for our efforts in the action research phase of the project, which began at the end of the first academic year—the summer of 1993. These efforts did not begin all at once; rather, we developed, reviewed, refined, and redeveloped our plans as we went along, based on ongoing evaluations by Silvia and her family members, teachers, home tutors, and work supervisors as well as from our own observations. Overall, our efforts over the course of the subsequent 3–4 years could be subsumed under the following four goals:

1. Increasing Silvia's work skills and opportunities along with her independence in using the bus to go to her summer job
2. Helping Silvia to pursue her friendship with Asha
3. Increasing Silvia's reading skills
4. Trying to assist the family in gaining access to appropriate benefits related to Silvia's disability

We detail each of these efforts in the sections that follow.

WORK AND INDEPENDENCE

As with the other high school students, the project's main focus in the summers was on employment. The summer jobs sometimes were organized by the students' teacher and sometimes by the project staff, the latter arrangements all being on the university campus. Payment for the jobs, however, came from an agency that had county funds for paying summer salaries to students with disabilities. In Silvia's case, her summer jobs all were arranged by her teacher and usually were a continuation of her academic year placement. In the first summer, Silvia continued in the job that she had had during the school year—working at a secondhand clothing store run by The Arc (formerly the Association for Retarded Citizens [ARC]). The project assisted by providing a job coach who also did travel training, as we had determined that this would be a useful goal for Silvia.

Silvia had proved herself an excellent worker during the year, and her summer tasks continued to be steam-pressing the clothes, putting on price tags, and clipping off buttons and placing them in a bag. Although the tasks seemed rather tedious, Silvia enjoyed the process of working. In the summer, it turned out that she needed practically no help with her work, and we were able to observe her tremendous determination, persistence, and good-natured approach to all of her tasks.

Giving Silvia opportunities for a wider range of social interaction was also a goal of the summer placements. Socially, Silvia was at first shy with strangers but always cheerful and increasingly friendly as she got to know people. Unfortunately, on the first summer job, there were not many opportunities for socialization because the few staff often were on separate lunch and work schedules.

In the second summer, Silvia's teacher once again arranged for her to continue in a job placement that she had started in the previous semester. This was at the county's Department of Social Services, where she was learning to remove boxes of files, copy the title of each file onto a master list, and replace the files on the shelves. Once more, we provided a job coach, Gail, whom, once more, Silvia hardly needed! Gail reported that Silvia had no trouble with recognizing and copying the letters but often could not discern where a first name ended and a last name began, a feature that most likely related to her lack of reading ability. This may also have been related to her unfamiliarity with English last names; Gail observed that Silvia enjoyed pronouncing the Spanish names. Gail would say the names with Silvia and emphasize the capitalization at the beginning of the name, and Silvia soon caught on. Silvia seemed to enjoy her work very much, although it required a great deal of repetition as well as considerable fine motor skills in handling the files and writing the titles. Her supervisor reported that her work was "always correct."

Socially, we were able to learn more about Silvia that summer because several of her co-workers took breaks and ate lunch together. Silvia got along well with them and, at first, enjoyed listening to their conversations but engaged in minimal participation. By the end of the summer, however, Silvia had become quite a vocal member of the group and joined the group's morning routine, which they called "typical question of the morning." By the end of the summer, co-workers reported that Silvia "joined right in" with their discussions. As the job coach gradually faded out her presence on this job, Silvia's female co-workers were very helpful to Silvia in the area of toileting, where she needed help getting from her chair to the toilet.

In the third summer, Silvia's teacher once more arranged for a continuation of her school-year job, this time at the public library. This job is described in more detail in the section "Learning to Read" because her tasks were specifically tied in to the progress that she was making in reading at that time. That summer job was the most enjoyable for Silvia socially because she had worked there during the school year and was well known and welcomed by all of the staff.

Travel Training

When we began to plan for Silvia's summer job the first year, the issue of transportation was paramount. Because the family car was not in working condition, everyone except Silvia traveled mainly by public transportation. We suggested to Rosa and Silvia that we try to have Silvia use the bus, too, and they were quite enthusiastic about the idea. We planned that the job coach would do as much of the travel training as possible, but Erin, Silvia's first summer job coach, who was one of our graduate students, was able to provide travel training only 3 of the 4 days of Silvia's job. Before we knew it, Rosa had come up with her own idea of engaging a neighbor to help on the other days. The project was able to pay the neighbor for these services.

During both summers, travel training proved an exciting but frustrating challenge for Silvia. The project had arranged with the city transportation system to put a bus with a lift on Silvia's route on the appropriate schedule. On the very first day, Silvia and Erin used the recommended route, which entailed a two-block walk and then riding on two buses. The first ride presented a very helpful bus driver and no problems. The second driver, however, could not get the lift up and had to wait for another driver to help him. This driver also did not know the street that Silvia needed, and Silvia and Erin got off two blocks too soon; Silvia arrived at work 20 minutes late, hot and tired, but still very enthusiastic.

Erin soon learned that Silvia was both skilled and motivated in her work. Despite her limited use of her right arm and hand, Silvia persisted and succeeded well with her tasks, hardly wanting to take a break. Thus, her first day went well at work but ended with tremendous frustration on the bus ride home. Erin's's notes for that ride read as follows:

> The trip home was a little more difficult. The wheel lock on the bus [for Silvia's chair] did not work properly, and the wheelchair kept rolling forward as the driver stopped the bus. He had to stop about three times to try again to get the lock to hold. This made us late, and we missed our connecting bus. We had to wait until 2:30 for the next bus. The next bus arrived, and the lift did not work. It was hot, we were tired, and the bus driver tried for only 5 minutes to get this lift to work and it did not. He told us that we would have to wait for the next bus and *hope* that it had a lift. We waited until 3:15 for the next bus to arrive. The lift worked, and we got on the bus. We rode about 10 minutes and we were home. It was a long day. It took about an hour and a half for us to get home . . . all in all, we did get to work. Silvia did work, and she was still excited. She did not become frustrated—much—but we will look for new avenues or new directions for transportation. (June 28, 1993)

The next working day, Rosa recommended a different route, which involved a longer walk but only one bus. Erin's notes for that day reveal the ongoing challenges of public transportation for Silvia:

> I picked up Silvia at her house. We have a new bus route. This time we're only taking one bus instead of two. We have to walk a little farther—about six blocks—but it's easier than trying to transfer and take two buses. So we walked six blocks and Silvia led the way, and we walked through winding streets and back streets to get to our bus stop. We had one major problem today. We were walking down the street and a *large, loud* Doberman ran up and started barking and running around in circles. The dog scared both of us to death. We stopped and waited. Silvia was scared, but I told her to be calm and just stop and wait and maybe he would leave. So we stopped and waited, and he left. He went back in his yard, but then he barked and we continued. We crossed the street and went over and the dog came out of the yard again and came over to where we were and started barking again. We stopped, then he turned around and left. We then continued, very nervously, on our way to the bus stop. After we arrived at the bus stop, we waited about 15 minutes for the bus. (June 30, 1993)

Over the course of the next 6 weeks, Silvia's travel experiences continued to have recurring difficulties, such as imperfect wheel locks and late buses. On one more occasion, they encountered a lift that did not work, this time resulting in Silvia's not being able to get off the bus:

> The day started off fine, and we were early leaving for work. When we arrived, we could not get off the bus. The bus driver could not get the lift to work, and we were stuck on the bus. The bus driver's telephone did not work. He had to get off the bus and go across the street to the mall to call the office. We had to wait 35 minutes on the bus for the repair van to come and repair the lift so that we could get off, and then we arrived at work 30 minutes late. Throughout the entire ordeal, Silvia did not become frustrated; she remained calm and had a good attitude. (July 21, 1993)

The end of that same day showed that things did go well sometimes:

> The ride home was uneventful. We met a bus driver who recognized Silvia from days before, and he was happy to see her. He joked with her and kidded her, and she laughed and talked to him.

At the end of that first summer, Silvia said that despite the difficulties, she loved traveling by bus and would try again the next summer "if they fix the buses."

The next summer, she did try again but with very similar frustrations. The difficulties with buses were identical to the previous summer's, despite a great deal of communication with the supervisor in charge of scheduling buses for people with disabilities. Gail, Silvia's job coach that summer, was very assertive in following up with the metro transit department. In the second week, when she called because the accessible bus did not show up as promised, a supervisor came out to the bus stop, went over the schedule in detail with Gail, and promised that there would be no more scheduling mistakes during the rest of Silvia's 6-week program. The scheduling of the accessible buses did improve, but there continued to be recurring problems with late buses and ineffective wheel locks and lifts.

Nevertheless, Silvia persevered and became quite independent; the job coach's assistance gradually, though not totally, faded out. Gail worked systematically on fading her support and on teaching Silvia accommodations such as getting on the bus alone with a written note naming the stop at which she had to get off, just in case the driver did not understand her speech. For the first week, Gail traveled on the bus with Silvia both to and from work. By the second week, she saw Silvia onto the bus then drove behind the bus to the next stop. Next, she followed the bus but waited a little distance from the stop to observe Silvia getting off independently.

Finally, the great day came when Silvia was enjoying her independence so much that she told Gail not to drive beside her from the stop to her house (about three blocks) but to stay out of sight so that Silvia could wheel along in her chair entirely on her own. Gail, thinking this a wonderful development, agreed and followed about a block behind Silvia and out of her sight. On arrival at Silvia's home, however, both Gail and Silvia experienced considerable chagrin. Seeing her daughter arrive home without an adult in sight was too much for Rosa, who reprimanded them both. Rosa felt that this was too dangerous because Silvia would be vulnerable to loiterers on the street. We all agreed that this would have to be the limit of Silvia's independence, for the time being at least.

Some positive social aspects of the travel training were evident toward the end of the second summer. There were a couple of individuals who now recognized Silvia and greeted her pleasantly or chatted briefly at the bus stop. The afternoon schedule tended to have a more consistent driver, who soon came to know Silvia, and one day, when she succeeded in independently releasing the latch for the wheel lock, the driver applauded, exclaiming, "All right! Now, you just need to do that every day!" Silvia experienced great pleasure from these social exchanges.

In the third summer, however, both Silvia and Rosa believed that the public transportation was too stressful and unpredictable and really not worth the effort. For Silvia's job that summer, which was at the public library—a couple of bus exchanges away—the job coach, Faustina, transported Silvia to and from work in her car.

LEARNING TO READ

Approximately 10 minutes into the first interview with Rosa, she suddenly made a statement that was to become a central theme in our work with Silvia—the family's wish that Silvia learn to read. Rosa said that Silvia loved El Salvador because of the cousins there with whom she was close. She said that she had promised Silvia that she could visit El Salvador that summer if she learned to read. She continued,

> *Ese problema tengo yo, que ya está grande y no sabe leer nada. . . ¡Eso es lo que yo quiero, que ella aprenda a leer, porque sin sabe leer no sabe nada . . . ! Yo le digo a ella, porque ella es la única que está conmigo, y soy la única que salgo con ella a veces a varios lugares, y digo si tú sabes leer, todo está bien porque yo no sé nada.* [This is what I'm worried about, that she is grown and she can't read anything. . . . This is what I want, that she learn to read, because if you don't know how to read you don't know anything . . . ! I tell her because she is the only one who is with me, and I am the only one who goes with her to various places, and I say if you can read, then everything will be alright because I can't read anything.]

Rosa further noted that Silvia was able to read only materials that she had been taught and had practiced at school.

Approximately 30 minutes later, Silvia arrived home from school and our first interview began. Because the focus of the research was to be social development, one of the first questions was which extracurricular activities she participated in at school. She mentioned going to physical education and to the media room. Then I asked whether there was anything else she would like to do at school that she does not do; I was expecting more information on school-related social activities. The conversation proceeded as follows:

Silvia: I like it to do—I like aammmm, read?
Beth: To read? Okay. In your class you don't read much?
Silvia: No . . . I working. *Trabajo* [I work].
Beth: *¿Y no dices a la señorita que tú quieres leer?* [And don't you tell the teacher that you'd like to read?]

Silvia:	*Sí.* [Yes.]
Rosa:	[joins in] *En vez de trabajar* [instead of working].
Silvia:	*Yo digo a la señorita. . . . No, no oye.* [I tell the lady. She doesn't hear.]
Rosa:	*Ah, no te entiende. Oye, pero no te entiende.* [Ah, she doesn't understand you. She hears, but she doesn't understand.]
Silvia:	*No, no entiende.* [No, she doesn't understand.]
Beth:	*¿Por qué?* [Why?]
Silvia:	*Hablo rapidito inglés.* [I speak English too fast.]
Beth:	*Dígame en inglés* [tell me in English], "I want to learn to read."
Silvia:	I wanna learn to read.
Beth:	*¿Y ella no entiende esto?* [And she doesn't understand this?]
Silvia:	*No. Ella dice . . . ¡no sé!* [No. She says . . . I don't know!]

This was in December 1992. The research progressed, and that winter and spring we observed Silvia at school, interviewed her teachers, and attended her annual individualized education program (IEP) conference in April. These observations made it clear to us that reading was not a focus of Silvia's education program. The IEP conference highlighted this issue.

Silvia's Annual Individualized Education Program Conference

In April 1993, we attended the first of four school-based conferences for Silvia. At this conference, Rosa raised the issue of reading: How, she asked, can Silvia graduate from high school if she cannot read? The teacher began her response by explaining that Silvia would receive a High School Completion Certificate, not a High School Diploma. Then the teacher led into a very thoughtful discussion in which she outlined the following factors that could be having an impact on Silvia's progress in reading.

First, because she had never attended school until she came to the United States at the age of 11, Silvia was off to a very late start. Second, in her first few years of schooling, it seems likely that there was very little emphasis on literacy skills for her because she was placed in a "special center" for students with very severe disabilities. Third, her limited command of English would have made it very difficult for Silvia to profit from the functional reading in English offered in that program. Fourth, Silvia may have experienced some confusion between the two languages, including the possibility that as English was introduced there was a slowing down of her mastery of her native language. Fifth, Silvia's own learning difficulties, possibly a learning disability related to effects of her cerebral palsy, could be retarding her progress in learning to read. Consequently, the teacher explained, although Silvia's program did include some reading every day at school, the general focus of her program was more functional and work oriented. The school personnel believed that this was appropriate because Silvia would be eligible for only 3 more years of schooling.

Rosa accepted the explanations but reiterated that she wanted the school to continue to try to teach Silvia to read. Silvia agreed emphatically, stating that this was what she wanted most in school. The team agreed that despite the difficulties outlined, reading should be noted as a primary goal on Silvia's IEP. It is important to note, however, that there was relatively little time for instruction in reading because Silvia's daily schedule included 50 minutes of English four mornings per week, approximately 40 minutes of math three mornings per week, and approximately 2½ hours of vocational training four days per week (on Fridays, that 2½-hour block was designated for "community activities"). At the end of each day, there was 30 minutes of various electives, such as physical education, domestic skills, computer lab, or recreation/leisure activities. In that year, Silvia replaced the last 30 minutes with an English as a Second Language (ESL) class, which she attended but did not like.

Our research team believed that Silvia's lack of instruction in developmental literacy made it impossible to interpret her lack of reading as a sign of cognitive deficit; it seemed clear that for different reasons at different times she had really never been taught the essentials of reading. We would never know whether she could learn to read if someone did not try to teach her. Most important, we believed that if there were to be any chance of her making progress in that area, the instruction would have to be intensive, structured, and individualized. Furthermore, the likelihood that Silvia's potential for academic learning had been grossly underestimated was reinforced by another crucial point discussed in that IEP conference—the inadequacy of any attempts that had been made at formal evaluation of Silvia's learning potential.

Our research into Silvia's records had revealed that, like Rafael, the other Spanish-speaking student in our project (see Chapter 8), all psychological assessment of Silvia had been conducted in English. Assessment in the native language is, of course, a requirement of the law, and I had raised the issue with both the teacher and Rosa, who had not been aware of this. The teacher pointed out that it actually had been 4½ years since Silvia's last assessment, which made the entire situation doubly out of compliance because the law requires a full evaluation every 3 years. When I explained to Rosa the importance of this legal requirement, she expressed great concern, and I advised her to request that a new evaluation be conducted in Spanish.

Thus, at this annual meeting, Rosa raised the question and was assured that a request for a Spanish evaluation would be submitted immediately. However, the school personnel commented that because of a backlog in the school district, these assessments were "very hard to come by," and they expressed the expectation that they would get a very slow response from the school district. Just as they said, despite two inquiries made by Rosa over the course of the next year, the assessment that was requested at the end of April 1993 was finally conducted in the fall of 1994—18 months later. The results and implications of that assessment are discussed after describing the beginnings of our project's efforts to assist Silvia in her goal of becoming literate.

Reading Instruction as a "Social" Goal

Despite Silvia's and Rosa's concerns about Silvia's reading, we did not initially make this one of our project goals for two reasons. First, it was a while before our project team realized that we would simply have to accept that literacy should be seen as a reasonable goal to be included in our plans for Silvia's "social" development. Our definition of *social* did not include activities that we thought of as primarily academic. Furthermore, we believed that the IEP conference in the first year would have started the ball rolling for more appropriate assessment and educational planning for Silvia. As the foregoing sections have described, that summer we targeted employment and travel training for Silvia, and in the fall we began our efforts to support Silvia in pursuing social activities with her school friend, Asha. It was not until the next summer that the research team made the commitment to reading as one of Silvia's goals.

Throughout our first 1½ years of efforts related to work and social activities, Silvia's intelligence and perseverance became increasingly evident. We saw a young woman who was determined to catch up to the best of her ability, after a very late start. We observed her classroom instruction and noted some features that convinced us that that the classroom-based reading program would not make Silvia literate. First, the approach was group oriented rather than individualized to Silvia or to other students. Second, it was described by her teacher as an adult program, with some phonics and sight words and some language-experience approach. It seemed to us to be a largely functional approach that introduced some phonics clues but did not emphasize decoding or analytic reading skills, depending, rather, on considerable repetition and an understanding of contextual clues. The teacher acknowledged that, at Silvia's age, it generally was considered too late to use a "developmental reading" approach—in other words, to teach the mechanics of reading "from scratch" as one would to a young child. It seemed to us that this was the only way that she would ever learn to read. We still did not see reading as a "social" goal; however, we decided to target it simply because it seemed evident that Silvia would benefit from the opportunity and because she and her family wanted it so much.

"Es Duro, Duro, Duro . . ."

Rosa reported, *"Dice que es duro, duro, duro . . . y a veces llora y se enoja . . . ¡pero le está gustando!"* [She says that it's hard, hard, hard . . . and sometimes she cries and gets angry . . . but she's enjoying it!]

In the summer of 1994, we arranged for 7 weeks of tutoring by a doctoral student, Lisa, to be conducted twice per week for 2 hours each session. As it turned out, Lisa was to be the first of four tutors paid by the project over the next 1½ years.

Lisa's goals for Silvia were 1) to improve reading skills through both phonetic and sight-word approaches; 2) to work on language development, articulation, and writing; and 3) to introduce her to basic computer skills. Lisa set up a structured schedule that included a range of activities, such as putting pictures in a sequence and telling the story, through which she learned that Silvia needed to learn the English words for sequencing concepts such as first, next, last, beginning, finally, and so forth. She also worked on basic phonics, which not only prepared Silvia for decoding but also developed her awareness of correct pronunciation, such as the endings of the words *brown* and *black,* which she had previously pronounced as *brow* and *bla.* Lisa's report emphasized that this was very important because "now that she is learning how to read words, she may not always recognize the word if she has been saying it differently in her speech for several years." She also worked on spelling simple three-letter words and high-frequency words from the Dolch list (a standardized list of sight words graduated by difficulty). Silvia practiced these through games such as tic-tac-toe and other board games. They also worked on reading texts, which had to be mainly children's-level books because even the high-interest/low-vocabulary books that Lisa could find were still too difficult for Silvia.

Lisa's report at the end of the summer concluded that Silvia had made a good start and definitely should profit from continued intensive instruction. Lisa described Silvia's high level of motivation, pointing out that even though the only working space that they had was in the family's living room, where there were many distractions, Silvia "gave the instruction her full attention." Perhaps the most powerful theme in Lisa's report was the interdependence of English language development and reading in Silvia's progress. She emphasized that Silvia's development of English needed to go hand in hand with her reading; for example, speaking in complete sentences was essential so that she could learn to recognize the correct pronunciations, as mentioned previously, as well as the structures of English sentences and structural words such as articles, prepositions, and conjunctions. Another strong theme was Silvia's need for intensive speech-language therapy, which she had received for two 30-minute sessions per week at school in the 1992–1993 school year but had not been receiving in the 1993–1994 year.

We had planned to find a computer to lend to Silvia but, to our surprise, discovered that Rosa had taken the initiative and bought an old Macintosh for $50. Lisa was never able to do much with the computer because there were many problems with it, but this would become much more central later.

By the end of the summer, both Rosa and Doris, Silvia's older sister, were very impressed with Silvia's progress and were adamant that reading become a focus of her school program. Doris, in particular, had begun to talk to the teacher and to Silvia about the components of Silvia's program. Doris's conclusion was that there was far too much emphasis on employment skills, field trips, and, when she was in class, Silvia's engagement in "teaching other students," which we believe referred to some amount of informal peer tutoring between Silvia and another student. Doris wrote a letter to the Spanish-speaking counselor in the school, asking him to help get Silvia's program changed to include more academics. In reply, she received a telephone call from the school psychologist, who told her that they were soon going to conduct the required reevaluation of Silvia but expressed the opinion that perhaps the family was expecting too much of Silvia. Doris was incensed. Rosa, meanwhile, was becoming nervous about Doris's increasingly vocal advocacy because she feared that if school personnel became offended, there might be reprisals against Silvia. As she put it, *"Cuando uno reclama algo, alguna cosa, a veces se portan mal con, con los alumnos. Y me da miedo a mi que. . . ."* [When you complain about something, sometimes they take it out on the students. And I'm a bit afraid that. . . .] Rosa ended her sentence with a shrug.

Despite her fears, however, she was fully prepared to attend a meeting that had been promised after the reevaluation was completed.

Silvia's Reevaluation

In October 1994, the promised bilingual evaluation was conducted and was to be reported to the family in a specially convened meeting. The assessment had been done by a private contractor, who would not attend that meeting; rather, the findings would be reported by the English-speaking school psychologist. The teacher asked the psychologist to meet with the family prior to the official conference to give them a fuller understanding of the findings. This did not occur, however, and the official conference was held in the first week in November, attended by the classroom teacher, the school psychologist, Rosa, Doris, and Beth. Doris served as the interpreter for Rosa.

In reporting the assessment findings, the psychologist began by summarizing the history of Silvia's previous psychological assessments since her arrival in the United States. Her first assessment had been done in the Washington, D.C., school district in November 1986. It was reported only as "nonverbal testing" done by someone from the "bilingual office." The second testing, done in 1989, was reported in more detail and consisted of the performance section only of the Wechsler Intelligence Scale for Children–Revised (WISC–R; Wechsler, 1974) and the Bender Gestalt Test (Bender, 1946). This report generated some discussion between the psychologist and Beth because it seemed to suggest that these tools were appropriate in light of Silvia's lack of English skills. Beth pointed out that because Silvia did have verbal skills in Spanish, which were not tested, the lack of verbal testing put her at a disadvantage. The psychologist also stated that the performance section of the WISC–R is less biased and is more appropriate for testing "native intelligence." This was not true for Silvia because her motor difficulties made the performance tasks on both the WISC–R and the Bender Gestalt very difficult for her; the psychologist admitted that this was true. The result of that second assessment was that Silvia was designated as "multihandicapped," which, the psychologist explained, included physical, cognitive, and speech-language disabilities.

The psychologist's report of the recent assessment gave a very different picture and highlighted the following: The test used was the Wechsler Adult Intelligence Scale–Revised (WAIS–R; Wechsler, 1981), conducted in Spanish. Silvia scored 76 on the verbal section and 65 on the nonverbal, giving an overall score of 70. This placed her in the borderline mentally retarded range, with evidence of multiple needs in speech-language, visual motor, and cognition. Her academic skills had been tested on the Woodcock-Johnson Psychoeducational Test Battery (Woodcock & Johnson, 1977), with a resulting reading comprehension score of 1.7 and a word recognition score of 1.4 (grade-level equivalents). The teacher observed that Silvia had made progress in reading since that testing but noted that a repeat of the testing would not be valid if done sooner than 1 year from the date of the last testing, so she asked Rosa's permission for that retesting. Furthermore, the teacher noted that she would give Silvia informal tests to continue assessing her progress in the interim.

On the basis of this most recent assessment, the psychologist concluded that although increased reading instruction would not be harmful, the family should not place high expectations on this goal. The teacher explained to the family that the functional and work skills focus of the program was appropriate because of Silvia's advanced age. The teacher asked whether Rosa was questioning Silvia's placement in this program, to which Rosa replied that she was not against this program but wanted more intensive academics included in the program. The teacher agreed that it would be possible to modify the program to include 1 hour of reading instruction in the mornings and another hour or 30 minutes in the afternoons, after Silvia returned from her job placement. The family asked whether the instruction could be individualized, and the teacher said that she would do so as much as possible but that it would be mostly small-group instruction. The family agreed to this. There was also discussion about the possibility of instruction on the computer, to which the teacher replied that she would very much like to do this but that math and reading instruction on the computer required a great deal more one-to-one instruction than she could guarantee.

Home Tutoring: In Your Own Backyard

One aspect of our research that quickly emerged as a key theme was "in your own backyard," meaning that we soon found that the best way to accomplish our goals was to seek help in our own establishment rather than to pursue more far-flung sources. This strategy worked well in planning Silvia's tutoring because, faced with limited funds for paying for tutors, we had come up with the idea of offering students course credit for tutoring. Thus, during the fall semester, the project continued its reading support to Silvia by arranging for Annie, an undergraduate student in special education, to earn extra credit by working with Silvia at home one afternoon per week for the semester. Annie followed up on Lisa's guidelines from the summer, including sequencing activities, basic phonics, and the Dolch word list. Annie also worked on the computer with Silvia in a variety of ways. For example, after reading a story, Silvia would tell Annie about the story in her own words in complete sentences, and Annie would type her narrative into the computer, leaving some key words blank so that Silvia could fill them in. Annie also followed up on reading assignments sent by the teacher and assisted Silvia with her homework.

The year drew to a close, and reports from Annie and from Silvia's classroom teacher and our own observations concluded that there was no way that we could stop now! Annie could not continue in the January semester, owing to the pressure of work in her graduating year, and it was not until the end of January that we were fortunate enough to find a graduate student, Alicia, whose program had no room for extra credits but who offered to work voluntarily with Silvia.

When we succeeded in making the arrangement with Alicia, I visited Silvia's home to tell Rosa and Silvia about the new tutor. Upon entering, I saw a young woman sitting on the couch reading with Silvia. Faced with a brief lag in our project support for Silvia's literacy project, Rosa had once more acted on the "in your own backyard" principle and made her own arrangements. The young woman was Silvia's 17-year-old cousin, Patti, a junior in high school, whom Rosa had engaged for $15 for a 3-hour session with Silvia once per week. So, for part of that semester, Silvia had two tutors. Although we did not get reports from Patti, Alicia reported that Silvia was "benefiting from some specific strategies introduced by Patti." One thing that was different in Silvia's work with these two tutors, however, was that the extreme tolerance and good-naturedness that Silvia displayed with the university tutors was not so consistent with her cousin. Rosa reported that sometimes when Silvia got tired or frustrated, she got angry at Patti and told her to go home. Once, she said, Silvia got so frustrated that both of the girls ended up crying. To the contrary, Alicia's report of Silvia was that she was consistently good natured, and "she never, never lets on that she's tired."

Lessons Learned from Silvia

There were many features of Silvia's learning style that gave us extended food for thought: In particular, we came to realize just how difficult it is to assess the learning abilities of a student with an educational and linguistic profile as complicated as Silvia's. The lessons that we learned in this regard convinced us that we can place no faith in an assessment that is conducted in one or even a couple of sittings by a stranger and with standardized materials.

One example of this was a lesson that we learned about the difference in Silvia's recall abilities in spelling orally versus by typing. Alicia began her work with Silvia by testing her orally in spelling to determine what she had retained from the past 6 months of tutoring. Alicia had assumed that spelling the word out loud would be easier for Silvia than typing it because that would complicate the task by adding a motor component. Her first tests of Silvia's memory of the Dolch list, however, showed that she had "tremendous difficulty" with recalling most of the words. Alicia noted that as Silvia attempted to spell the words out loud, she was spending much of her time trying to recall which parts of the word she had already spelled, thus losing concentration on the total word. When Alicia changed the strategy and dictated each word for Silvia to type on the computer, she correctly typed 29 of 38 words from the same list.

Another feature of Silvia's learning related to the pace at which new reading should be introduced. Alicia found that it was better to introduce Silvia to a book and return to that book several times in a sequence than to keep introducing new books each week. Even in short-term testing, Silvia would recall the last but not the first part of a text based on a series of simple, illustrated statements, such as, "I like to jump," "I like to play with the dog," and so forth. However, Alicia noted, "If I use the same book or if I leave it at her house for like 2 weeks or so and we keep reading it and we keep going over the vocabulary, she knows the book." There could be numerous interpretations of this feature, none of which we could be sure was correct. For example, the difficulty could be a deficit in comprehension or in memory, but in either case, what caused this? It could be a genuine cognitive deficit in the sense of an impaired ability to learn and retain material. It could be a result of Silvia's not having experience with the concepts and therefore not enough of a cognitive framework on which to build new information. It could be an inadequate English language base on which to retain new information. It could be that the effort of decoding the text distracted her attention from comprehending and storing the information in memory and that with repeated readings and increasing familiarity with the words, overall text comprehension became easier.

A third observation that indicates the complexity of the reading process was Silvia's frequent tendency to make what we called "logical mistakes," such as reading "shop" for "store" and "dish" for "bowl." Either Silvia knew the meaning of the word upon seeing it but replaced the written word with a synonym upon saying it out loud, or she may have understood the context of the sentence and simply substituted an appropriate word.

Alicia was very inventive in her work with Silvia. Every session included music as Alicia taught Silvia to read the words of a song, which she would then sing along to Alicia's accompaniment on the guitar. This aspect proved very enjoyable for Silvia and filled the small living room with a cheerful atmosphere that other family members also enjoyed.

Perhaps the most important aspect of Alicia's work with Silvia was on the computer. After very little practice, Silvia was able to use the mouse with her left hand, but the programs that were available for the 8-year-old computer that her mother had bought for $50 were too text based for Silvia's level. What we needed were programs that relied more on pictures or icons. Alicia proved a tireless and dedicated volunteer. Dissatisfied with the limitations of the old computer, she considered many avenues for getting a new one, including writing letters to a newspaper and making appeals to local government officials, and finally succeeded once more through the "in your own backyard" strategy in getting her own relative to donate a used but much more up-to-date computer.

Alicia's work with Silvia continued from February until December 1995. For most of this time, she devoted weekly 3-hour sessions to home tutoring. She also took Silvia to the library to extend her literacy skills.

During this period, Silvia made great progress in reading and in using the computer. In the 1994–1995 school year, Silvia's job placement was at the local library, and the teacher was able to arrange this placement as a summer job for her also. One of the project graduate assistants, Faustina, was assigned as her job coach for the summer, but we began by having Alicia do a job assessment. Silvia's job involved preparing donated paperbacks to be entered into the library's database and stacking children's books alphabetically by author and reshelving them. Silvia was able to demonstrate independently each step of the process: applying the library logo and the date due stamp, the barcode labels, and the library stamp on the spine of each book. Silvia's limitations were related mainly to her limited reading ability because she could not follow the written instructions for setting up the database for the barcodes.

At the end of May 1995, after working with Silvia twice per week for about 4 months, and about 9 months after we first began Silvia's tutoring, Alicia reported on Silvia's progress as follows:

> Much more consistent . . . steady. She knows her A to Z sounds, she knows her short vowel sounds, consistently, about, I could say 95%. . . . Sounds with consonants 95% of the time. I don't need to worry about that. But every book she picks up, it seems like, you know, she's gaining more, she's got more sight words under her belt. And it just has been an explosion. And I don't know what it was. I can't tell you exactly when it was—the day she exploded—but it's there!

That summer, Silvia and Rosa visited El Salvador, and Silvia's tutoring slowed down for a while. Alicia's progress report in December was a bit more cautious, reporting that Silvia had slipped a bit in her memory of phonics and that she still did not show that she could consistently pronounce words applying her knowledge of phonics: "Her dominant reading strategy is still sounding out each letter of the word and then putting them together but finding smaller, more familiar words within larger words, such as 'key' in 'monkey.'"

By December 1995, there was one more key development noted by Alicia—the increasing involvement of Silvia's family members in her learning. Alicia's relative's donation of the Macintosh and its more sophisticated software was just the catalyst needed for family participation in the project. Alicia's notes stated,

> It should be noted that, since the computer has been set up in the home, Silvia has successfully instructed many members of her family in using the computer for typing letters (cousin Patti) and playing games (brothers Luis and Oscar). Silvia's brothers have also taken an active role in helping her by making several attempts to buy games and other educational software as well as taking a great interest in learning about how to use and work the computer.
>
> I've been using Kid Pix . . . a drawing program . . . that provides commands and speaks in Spanish as well as English. . . . During one session in which her mother and one of her cousins were present, Silvia repeated after the computer in English and then switched to Spanish and repeated the drill. While this occurred, I was able to hear both her mother and her cousin repeat the letters both in English and then in Spanish at the same time as Silvia. It appeared to be fun for all. . . .
>
> Since the introduction of the computer, the family has expressed a desire for Silvia to further her education as well as commenting that they are proud of her accomplishments and are glad that she is learning how to read and write in English. (December 21, 1995)

Although Silvia's progress in reading was a source of great delight and encouragement to all, there was another goal of the project that was a source of constant frustration for her family, her teachers, and our research team: attempting to advocate for much-needed social welfare benefits for Silvia and her family.

SILVIA'S FAMILY AND
THE SOCIAL WELFARE SYSTEM

>*Nosotros vamos a una parte, vamos a otra, ¡y nada. . . ! Yo oigo en la radio, dicen, "No estás solo!" "Tienes ayuda!" que llame aquí, que llame allá, el ciego, el patojo, el aquí, que allá. . . . ¡Es mentira! Bueno, pero nadie se muere, ¡nadie! Y Dios está con uno. Sí, de veras. Porque mucha gente me ayuda con cositas, con ropa, con lo que sea, pero me ayuda.* [We go from one place to another, and—nothing. . . ! I hear them saying on the radio, "You aren't alone! You have help!" That you should call over here or over there, the blind, the destitute, this one here, that one there. . . . It's a lie! But it's okay, you don't die! And God is with you. Yes, really. Because many people help with little things, with clothes, with whatever it is, but they help me.]

Trying to obtain social welfare benefits for Silvia was *"un gran dolor de cabeza"* [a big headache] for Rosa and her family. The first time that we came to appreciate the size of this headache was when we took Rosa and Silvia to a meeting with a local agency that had written the family a letter advising them to make an appointment to apply for assistance for Silvia's physical needs.

The man conducting the meeting began by asking about the history of Silvia's condition. Rosa recounted the story of Silvia's high fever in her first year of life and the resulting paralysis. This was the second time that I had seen how painful this story was for Silvia to hear (at a school-based annual review conference, Rosa had been asked to tell this history). On this occasion, Silvia grew more and more unhappy as her mother spoke, struggling to stifle her tears. The interviewer, nevertheless, proceeded with his questioning for details of the history.

Then, the strangest thing happened. After all of this ordeal for Silvia, the man asked a few more questions about her current status at school and, upon learning that Silvia still had 1 more year in high school, suddenly informed us that this application was coming too early because she would not be eligible for the benefits offered by this office until she was about to make the transition from school to work. We were incredulous, asking why the family had been invited to the meeting, and the man replied that he really did not know the source of the error but that there was no assistance that he could offer her until she was headed for a job. He said that the file would be "closed temporarily" until the year that she was to leave school, at which time the family should apply again.

Another inexplicable foul-up occurred when a social worker from another agency (the family could not tell me which) came to visit the house to determine with which specific physical needs her department could help Silvia. Once more, a very strange thing happened: Both Rosa and Silvia reported with the utmost conviction that the woman, upon seeing Silvia's bed, advised them that her department could certainly help the family by getting her a bed better suited to her needs. According to both Rosa and Silvia, the woman advised them to sell the old bed, and the department would get them a new one. Rosa did so, and, according to Doris, the result was that her father "had to sleep on the floor for almost 6 months" until the family could buy another bed. The social worker, when contacted by Silvia's teacher, told her that she had never given that advice. When I interviewed Rosa and Silvia, I suggested that they must have been mistaken because there was no translator present, but they both were vehement in their understanding of what had happened. Our conversation went as follows:

> **Beth:** I still think they didn't understand. Or she didn't understand.
> **Rosa:** *Aquí estaba Silvia. . . . ¿Cómo me dijo ella, Silvia?* [Silvia was here. . . . What did she tell me, Silvia?]
> **Silvia:** Sell the bed.
> **Beth:** Sell the bed?
> **Silvia:** Yeah. . . . Sell the bed and they buy another bed. . . . A special bed.
> **Rosa:** *Vaya, no es mentira. Es verdad. . . . Y también me dijo que llevara al Social Security . . . a la oficina . . . para cosas de ropas y otras cosas para Silvia. Me dijo que fuera. Eso me dijo la mujer.* [You see, it's not a lie. It's the truth. . . . And she also told me that she would go to Social Security . . . to the office . . . for things like clothes and so on for Silvia. She told me that she would go. That's what the woman told me.]

Social Security Disability Income

As mentioned at the beginning of this case study, in the first 2 years of the project, Silvia's family was having a very hard time financially because there were no jobs available for Trinidad, and the family was worried that they may not be able to continue paying their mortgage. For a while, their oldest son, Luis, and his wife and 1-year-old boy came to live with them to help pay the mortgage. Some family members, however, wondered whether this was in fact helping his family; they suspected that their owning a house was one of the reasons that the family could never receive any social security benefits. This was an idea that was frequently discussed by family members, that perhaps the Social Security Administration saw the family as "too rich" to be eligible for benefits. Another fear held by the family was that their legal resident status might be taken away if they pushed too hard to obtain benefits.

Silvia's teachers, throughout the years of our project, consistently went "beyond the call of duty" in trying to obtain support for Silvia. The effort to obtain Social Security Disability Income (SSDI) benefits had been initiated by the teacher, who contacted the appropriate department and asked for the papers to be sent to the family. She also requested that the department telephone Rosa to explain the details of the application. This telephone call, however, never occurred, and the SSDI personnel said that it had proved difficult to get a Spanish-speaking person to call at a time when Rosa had said she would be home. Eventually, the papers were filled out and sent in, and the teacher accompanied Rosa and Doris to a meeting at the SSDI office. Doris reported that they were told that because Luis had sponsored Silvia to come to the United States, he had to be responsible for her for 2 years before she became eligible for benefits. By the time we were discussing this with the family, in September 1994, Doris explained that the 2 years had passed and that the application had been approved. According to Doris,

> They sent a letter saying that they approved everything and that they were gonna start sending the money since May. . . . Then they sent another letter saying that they denied it. So, you know, how can they first send something saying that they'll approve it, and then they deny it?

Silvia's teacher once more attempted to get clarification on the issue. The information that she was given by the SSDI office was that her brother's sponsorship required him to be responsible for her for 3 years, not 2, and that there were now new regulations pending that might extend that requirement to 5 years. The teacher had also learned that there were some exceptions to this, but none applied to Silvia, such as that the wait period would be waived if the disability had occurred after entry into the United States. The teacher succeeded in securing another appointment for the family to discuss the matter with the SSDI office.

By this time, Silvia had gained another helper, a social worker from The Arc, who we hoped would help to provide more continuity in her family's ability to obtain services for Silvia and take the pressure for advocacy off the teacher and the research team. The provision of this case worker was another effort that had been initiated by Silvia's teacher early in 1994 but that had also proved a frustrating process because The Arc's promise to provide the case worker took a year to come through.

The SSDI meeting arranged by the teacher was held in the middle of June. The Arc case worker (who was very eager and empathic but spoke no Spanish), the research project's interpreter, and Beth accompanied Rosa and Silvia to a meeting with the SSDI authorities. Between the need to make room for Silvia's wheelchair to pass and the small entourage that followed her, our entrance seemed to cause quite a stir in the crowded office. The conversation with the SSDI staff member immediately created some consternation among our group, as she began by stating that she could find no record of a file on Silvia and that we would probably have to make another appointment. Rosa immediately became very assertive, stating very firmly that the file was right here in this office because this was where the previous meeting had taken place and the file *was* here. The tone of Rosa's voice was very effective; the staff person then rose from her seat, went over to another cabinet of files, and in a matter of minutes returned with the file. She then proceeded to explain several complicated requirements and exceptions regarding Silvia's eligibility. The staff member said that although there were exceptions that would have allowed Silvia to be eligible, the bottom line was that Luis, the brother who had sponsored her, was "earning too much money." The file indicated that, in his original application, he had declared an annual income of approximately $12,000. When we asked what the official cut-off income level was, the SSDI staff member could not locate that information because "her computer was down." As the interview continued, however, Rosa became more and more assertive, insisting that she give us more information. Finally, the staff person informed us that a parent with one child would not be eligible if he or she earned more than $1,326 per month ($15,912 annually). At the time that Luis had applied for this benefit for Silvia, he was not yet married, so she seemed to imply that because he had no children at that time, the income requirement would have been even lower. Thus, his $12,000 should have been enough to support himself and Silvia.

The meeting ended with the agreement that Rosa would ask Luis to submit a new statement of his income within 30 days, and a new application would be made. However, when Rosa made this request to Luis, both Luis and Trinidad were very hesitant to pursue the issue. They perceived the entire situation as placing the family in jeopardy of being victimized if they asked for too much. After much discussion, they decided that they should not go any further with the application because they believed that they "wouldn't get it anyway" and that they might "lose their green card" if they pushed too hard.

In the years that followed came the federal government's withdrawal of noncitizens' eligibility for social welfare benefits. Consequently, 3 years later, an update interview with the family revealed that Silvia's SSDI benefits had never come through. However, she was now eligible for citizenship and had applied. As always, nothing in this kind of effort would go smoothly for Silvia: Her application had been returned three times because of faulty fingerprinting. It seemed that something about Silvia's thumbs made the fingerprinting process difficult, but Rosa had been assured that the final set that she had taken were all right and that the application would go forward. Finally, in September 1998, Silvia received her U.S. citizenship, and her family expressed the hope that all of the "promises" now would be kept.

BEST FRIENDS

One of our key goals for Silvia was to assist her in developing "a social life." Silvia had told us that her best friends were two cousins— one in New York and one in El Salvador. The distance between them, however, certainly limited Silvia's ability to enjoy these relationships, although her mother told us that the family telephone bills were quite astronomical as a result of Silvia's attachment to these cousins! Although we recognized that the majority of this family's socializing typically was done with extended family members, it was also usual for the young adults to begin to form their own relationships outside the family as they matured. We believed that assisting Silvia in socializing with chosen friends was appropriate. Rosa was comfortable with this idea.

In the second year of the project, we observed that Silvia was particularly friendly with a classmate named Asha. Asha, then 20 years old, had come with her family to the United States from India when she was about 12. She was a very sociable young woman who had no physical disabilities and was classified as having mild mental retardation. The two girls had told our project personnel that they wished that they could go out together outside school, and both Silvia and Rosa responded eagerly to our suggestion that we help the girls to do this.

We contacted Asha's family, explaining the project and asking their permission to pursue this idea. The family gave permission on the condition that the girls be accompanied by Moni, who is also from India and who was the project's graduate assistant. Asha's mother commented to Moni that her chaperoning was important because Silvia's family "might not understand our ways."

Silvia's mother, conversely, was very open to any suggestions regarding our ideas for supporting the girls' friendship because, she said, she wants Silvia "to be happy." For example, when we discussed the problem of transportation for Silvia to visit Asha, Rosa said that she would find a way to get Silvia to her friend's house and exclaimed, "Well, I'll take her in a taxi if I have to!" However, the visit did not prove possible because the entrance to Asha's house had several steps up a slope and was not accessible to Silvia's wheelchair. As it turned out, we succeeded in getting the girls together for a trip to the mall and one visit by Asha to Silvia's house. Plans for a movie, however, did not materialize, owing to continuing difficulties with transportation and also with what seemed like an increasing difficulty on Asha's part to be available. We suspected that Asha's family's reluctance to her pursuing these activities was a central issue. In the end, our attempts in this aspect of Silvia's life did give us a great deal of information about her friendship with Asha, although we concluded that we were not able to affect the course of the friendship by providing more opportunities for socializing.

Through our interviews with and observations of the girls, we noted three aspects of their friendship that seemed very important. First, it was evident that their friendship was reciprocal and fun filled and that they shared many interests typical of American teenagers. Second, they saw themselves as mutually compatible in a way that they were not with their other classmates. Third, the girls seemed to share a kind of cultural affiliation because of their common experience of having come from other countries and being "outsiders" in the United States. We briefly describe these features as we came to see them in our discussions and visits with Silvia and Asha.

"My Friend. I Like Her"

It was clear that these two young women simply enjoyed each other's company. They emphasized that they were understanding of each other. As Asha put it, "She knows about me—what I like, what color I like, what kind of subject I like, she knows everything." She added, "By a good friend, I mean she understands the feelings." Silvia's characteristically briefer explanation was, simply, "My friend. I like her."

The mutual acceptance shared by the two friends was evident in their lighthearted teasing of each other. Moni's field notes on their trip to the mall together are full of examples of this. Upon leaving Silvia' s house,

> Asha asked Silvia, "How are you going to go?" Silvia replied, "In my wheelchair. You have to push it, Shanti!" And she laughed. Asha responded, "Oh my God!" and put her right hand on her head. She also laughed.

Silvia's use of Asha's home name, "Shanti," indicated their closeness because Asha was never called by this name at school; Asha's teachers were not even aware of the name.

Their friendship was very reciprocal. Silvia described Asha as someone who was "nice," was "funny," and helped her. She also described the reciprocity in this, however, by saying that Asha pushed her wheelchair while she carried Asha's books. Similarly, Asha said that Silvia tends to speed in her wheelchair but she also waits for her: "She always waits for me. You know, she is a very good friend. She's sweet." They talked to each other over the telephone at least two to three times in a week and sometimes exchanged gifts.

One particularly striking feature of the friendship was the "teenage" interests that the young women enthusiastically shared. When asked what they would like to do together, both promptly listed activities typical of American teenagers: They wanted to spend the night at each other's homes and go to the mall and to the movies. Asha, however, explained that overnights to Silvia's home would not be permitted by her parents because this was not something that she had ever done; Silvia would not be able to visit Asha's home at all because of the steps up to her house. On their trip to the mall, the young women toured stalls selling hair ribbons, videos, posters, earrings, and computers, and both purchased earrings. When Moni had to go to the rest room, Silvia went along to freshen her lipstick (Asha was not allowed to wear makeup, however). Information on their parents' views of them were also very typical for their age: Both said that their parents thought that they spent too much money on shopping, Silvia's mother said that Silvia was "too coquettish," and Asha complained that her parents did not understand her interest in Michael Jordan. Asha also said that her parents thought that her room was a mess but that she did not care. Both girls also told us that their fathers were more indulgent with them than their mothers. Silvia's father, however, was stricter than her mother about anything that related to "guys."

One of their main interests *was* "guys." On their trip to the mall, the friends delighted in telling Moni tales of the various "guys" who had caught their attention at school, but the most engaging was their report of an occasion at school when they had wanted to see the face of a young man who was standing with his back to them. To see him, Silvia purposely bumped into him with her wheelchair. He turned around and asked whether she was okay, and Silvia apologized, laughing, as she and Asha looked him in the face.

Asha's crush on Michael Jordan was a high point of her life. The walls of her bedroom were covered with posters of Jordan, and she had made a scrapbook about 6 inches thick on her hero, on which she claimed to have spent $900. Silvia's friendship with her schoolmate, José, also was a point of great interest, and, on their trip to the mall, when her mother and sister were teasing her about a telephone call from José, Asha expressed surprise and disappointment that Silvia had not yet told her about this telephone call.

There was also a serious side to the friendship. The two friends shared common concerns about their futures, although Asha was the more vocal on such matters. In her interviews with Moni, Asha expressed many concerns about the transition to the world outside school: What was next for her, what kind of job, what kind of husband? Silvia did not discuss those concerns with Moni, and Asha expressed the opinion that although Silvia did not talk much about the future, she might be "worried" about it.

Because the outing to the mall was the only social activity that we were able to achieve, we were gratified that it did bring the friends great satisfaction. Three times during the outing, Asha exclaimed, "This is great!" Silvia's mother, meanwhile, wishing to express her delight that her daughter was having this opportunity, initiated and closed her interactions with the researcher and with Asha's father with the exclamation, *"¡Silvia está contenta!"* [Silvia is happy!]

Different Yet Similar Backgrounds

On the one hand, these girls were from very different backgrounds. Asha's family were of an entrepreneurial class from India, whereas Silvia's family were of rural, working-class status from El Salvador. The native languages of the two families were of entirely different origins, as were their religious affiliations—Asha's family is Hindu, and Silvia's is Catholic. On the other hand, there were ways in which the girls were very similar. Within the U.S. context, they both belonged to ethnic minority groups, they both were immigrants, they both were interested in and enjoyed many aspects of American teenage culture, and they both had been identified through the school system as "individuals with disabilities."

Family Identities   Both girls were very much influenced by their relationships with their parents, siblings, and extended family members. Their conversations with each other showed that they were very aware of American social norms but very respectful of their own and each other's family traditions. For example, Asha wished that she could spend a night at Silvia's house but did not complain about her mother's not allowing it. Both she and Silvia seemed to accept that differing family practices would constrain their relationship.

Similarly, on matters of adult independence, the friends seemed to balance their two worlds. Although Asha's conversations with Silvia often revolved around "guys," she did not talk of hoping to have a boyfriend because this was not acceptable to her family. At that time, her family was in the process of arranging a marriage for her, as they had done for her sister. Asha expressed satisfaction with this plan and also explained that when the time came she would be able to meet with her proposed husband and decide for herself whether he would be someone who would value love above money and would appreciate her efforts at housekeeping and child care. If he did not, then she would not agree to marry him. Meanwhile, Asha was very aware of the contrast between single versus married status for a woman in Indian culture. She viewed her current age as providing freedom that she would lose when she married, such as changes in her clothing and jewelry. According to her, "This is the age to enjoy. This is the age to spend time yourself, you know. When you get married, you have to take care of the kids, you have to take care of family."

When Silvia spoke to us about Asha's plans for an arranged marriage, she did not express any surprise, although this tradition differed greatly from her own. Indeed, although the families were similar in their expectations for parental supervision of the daughters, the attitudes toward marriage and courtship were very different. In contrast to the tradition of an arranged marriage in Asha's family, the idea of a spontaneous and informal courtship was very acceptable in Silvia's family; her mother and sister often teased her about José's occasional telephone calls, but Silvia insisted that he was "just a friend" and became embarrassed by their teasing.

In terms of future residence for Silvia, Rosa and Silvia expected that Silvia would remain in the family home after she became an adult, as her two older brothers and her sister had done. Furthermore, both brothers had, at different times, lived in the family home with their new spouses and first infants. Silvia had been a joyful participant in the upbringing of those two nephews. On the question of marriage for herself, she responded, blushing, that she did not think that she would marry, despite her mother's statement that "maybe she will!"

Overall, these young women understood and respected their families' values and traditions. They enjoyed as much as they could of their shared U.S. experience but understood each other's situation. They understood, for example, that their parents had moved to the United States in the hope of providing more opportunities for their families, in particular, these daughters. Silvia's own journey to the United States had been under extremely adverse conditions, and she was grateful to Luis for being the one to make her status legal by sponsoring her U.S. residence. On one occasion, when Luis argued against her going to a weekend camp, she hid her disappointment; fortunately, her mother clarified to Luis that the conditions of the camp were safe and accessible for Silvia, and she was allowed to go. In a similar vein, Asha's family's resident status had been facilitated by her uncle. Asha said, "The reason [her father] came was because I want to learn, I want to have the opportunity."

The Immigrant Experience   The separation from their home countries was an important feature shared by these young women. They both talked about extended family members whom they had left behind and whose presence had allowed them more freedom and a more varied social life. Silvia specified that one of her best friends was a cousin in El Salvador and that her grandmother had been very special to her before she died.

Asha referred to racial and cultural features of the American experience that supported the mutual attraction between Silvia and herself. She suggested that their being outsiders was an important aspect of their affiliation. When asked for an example of why Silvia seemed more "understanding" than her other classmates, Asha replied that

> Colors, like black people, white people, it doesn't matter. As long as they're friendly, you know. . . . But when I talk to my classmates . . . they don't talk. They don't say "hi." You know, they run away from you. So I don't like it that way, so I just talk to Silvia. We have fun.

Asha speculated that part of the reason that she became friends with Silvia but not with the others in the class could be that "some American people are different. But maybe because Silvia came from another country—Salvador? Because I had one friend that came from that country also, and she's nice." When asked to explain the "difference" in Americans, Asha replied, "Maybe they know everything about something, but we don't."

Despite their "outsider" status, both Silvia and Asha spoke of the United States as a country that had provided them the opportunity to realize their potential. Asha talked about the great opportunity that she had to prove how much she could learn in spite of the "learning problem" that she had. Silvia, meanwhile, said that she enjoyed school and that her mother said that she would not return to El Salvador because there was "no opportunity" for Silvia there. Both spoke of their teachers as being very supportive and caring and of school as a place for both learning and socializing.

Impact of Disability

Silvia's and Asha's disabilities, both in their home countries and in the United States, gave their friendship another shared experience. It was not, however, the mere fact that both had disabilities; rather, it was a combination of many aspects related to disability.

First, immigrating to the United States from countries where schooling was not readily available for students with disabilities meant that both of the girls had been excluded from school in their native countries. In the United States, both students began school in the county's special centers for students with severe disabilities. We have already explained the inadequacy of the psychological evalua-tion that resulted in this placement for Silvia. At approximately age 15, both girls were moved to a self-contained special education classroom in a general education building, as part of the county's creation of the "LRE" program mentioned in Section I.

The self-contained classroom meant that, apart from the general education ESL class that they attended, these students were limited to regular contact with only 12 other students. Our observations of the classroom indicated that Silvia and Asha were perhaps the most advanced students in the class. This seemed to be one factor in how they came to be attracted to each other, as both girls described their other classmates as being "boring" and unable to converse with them.

Both students were very aware of their disabilities, but only Asha spoke openly about this issue. She described her disability as "the learning problem I had," especially in India, where, she said, "I was not smart enough to learn anything." In the United States, how-ever, she found that her doctors, teachers, peers, and even she her-self were surprised at her knowledge about Michael Jordan. Conse-quently, she viewed her Michael Jordan scrapbook as an "opportunity to show it to the world."

Overall, Asha was quite philosophical about her disability:

> Not many people have hearing. They have that hearing problem. Eyes—they don't have eyes. All that problem, but still, I think, you know [it] doesn't matter, I can learn it or not. The only thing [is], I can walk, learn, do everything.

Asha constructed a positive view of her disability by comparing herself with others whom she perceived as worse off. Silvia, con-versely, seemed to emphasize her similarity to those without dis-abilities. For example, Asha told us the following story about Silvia:

I said, "How do you feel in a wheelchair?" Because I want to know, you know. See, we are all walking, running . . . so I want to make her happy, and I ask her, "Are you okay?" She said, "Yes." I asked her, "How do you feel about sitting in the wheelchair?" She said, "It's fun. So I don't have to run."

Asha also reported that she had teased Silvia about "speeding" in her chair, telling her that the teachers would give her "a ticket" if she kept it up. Silvia's response was to compare her usage of the wheelchair to other people's walking, so that her "speeding" through the halls would be the same as other students' running through the halls. Thus, argued Silvia, whereas other students would "get a ticket" for running, she would get one for "speeding" in her chair. In this way, she emphasized the normalcy rather than the difference of her mode of mobility.

In contrast to Asha's open discussions about disability, Silvia never initiated conversations regarding her feelings about her disability. Home observations revealed that she was very sensitive regarding her physical limitations and tended to remain silent whenever her disability became the topic of conversation. As mentioned previously, this was particularly poignant in meetings with school or agency personnel who asked for details of Silvia's history, which caused Silvia to become acutely uncomfortable.

The only way in which the girls' disabilities influenced their relationship negatively was in logistical matters such as transportation and in the increased protectiveness of their parents. Indeed, the barriers to their friendship seemed to be a combination of logistical issues and cultural and familial concerns: First, the inaccessibility of Asha's house, and, second, transportation limitations because Silvia's family had no consistent transportation and Asha's father, who did most of the family driving, was frequently away on business. Asha's brother could have transported them, but Silvia's father was not comfortable with this. Furthermore, we suspected, as mentioned previously, that Asha's family had some reservations about the appropriateness of this cross-cultural friendship.

Overall, our efforts to support Silvia and Asha's nonschool activities offered them only a brief period of social independence. The girls' friendship continued at school, nevertheless, and after Asha's graduation, they kept in touch on the telephone for a while. At that time, Silvia informed us that plans for Asha's marriage were under way. However, 2 years later, Silvia reported that she was then out of touch with Asha; she could not really say why, but just "didn't have her phone number any more."

VISIONS OF THE FUTURE

Silvia graduated from high school in 1996 and began working at The Arc soon after. We are not quite sure how this decision was made. Our work with three other families of students in Silvia's class informed us that the usual approach was for the teacher to give the families a list of agencies providing postschool services, and it was the families' job to choose the one that they wanted.

In the update interview with the family in 1998, Silvia, characteristically, said that she was quite happy at her job at The Arc, where her main task was packing eggs into egg cartons. Demonstrating how carefully she handled the eggs, she emphasized that she never dropped or broke them. The Arc bus picked up Silvia at 6:30 A.M., and she returned home at approximately 5:30 P.M. Silvia said that she enjoyed working there, and her only dissatisfaction was with the rate of pay. Her biweekly pay slip showed that she had earned $6.45 and had paid $.49 FICA, leaving her with a net income of $5.96 for a 2-week period.

During that visit, Silvia's family expressed their dismay and bafflement that Silvia could be earning so little. When asked whether Silvia still had a caseworker from The Arc, they said that her previous caseworker, who had been very good to her, had left. The family were not sure whether Silvia had been placed at The Arc under the "Day Program" or under the "Supported Employment" option. They had, however, spoken with a staff person at The Arc, who said that they planned to give Silvia a better position soon and pay her by the hour, but that was a year before and there had been no change. As they said, this was very unfair because how could Silvia ever have any independence—anything of her own—if this was all she could earn? Silvia had told her supervisor that she might quit the job if she could not earn more, but the supervisor replied that if she did that she might not be able to get The Arc services any more. We promised the family to do whatever we could to find out what Silvia's prospects at The Arc really were and to determine whether better alternatives for employment could be found.

Silvia still received no social welfare benefits, but the family hoped that Silvia would soon be eligible for SSDI because her application for citizenship had been sent in. The family had benefited somewhat from some provisions made by an agency (no one in the family could recall which agency it was), which had made modifications to Silvia's bathroom and had built a lift and a ramp from the street up to the garden. The lift, however, was not very reliable and sometimes got stuck when it rained. One day, it had become stuck while Silvia was in it, and it took several family members to lift out the wheelchair with Silvia in it. Consequently, Silvia was afraid to use it and, instead, had become quite adept at wheeling herself up the far side of the garden, which had a gentler slope. The family said that the people who had actually built the lift and ramp had left them no paperwork at all, so they did not know how to contact them for repairs.

We asked Rosa, Silvia, and other family members what their current hopes were for Silvia's future. Luis, who had been Silvia's sponsor for resident status in the United States, wrote the following:

> For the future, the family hopes that Silvia will be able to get better pay on her job and be able to buy the things she wants. Now that she has her citizenship, she should be able to get better jobs and benefits that she has been denied for not being a citizen. The family would also like for Silvia to be able to get more tutoring so that she can better herself and become more independent. Silvia likes the U.S., but often she wishes that she could visit the rest of the family in El Salvador. My parents often worry about how much longer they are going to be able to keep paying for the house because of expenses going up and them getting old. They always think about what's going to happen to Silvia. When they can no longer work, they want Silvia to have a decent and safe place to live. As for me, being her oldest brother, I want the very best for my sister.

I asked Silvia what she hopes for in the future. Our conversation went as follows:

Silvia: Work! Make more money! Work like with clothes—you know—like pants and underwear and stuff.
Beth: You mean, like in a clothing store?
Silvia: Yes.
Beth: Why would you like that?
Silvia: More people! Help them buy things.
Beth: Okay. And what else do you hope for?
Silvia: Go out! Like movies, store, park. I go by bus.
Beth: You'd like to go by the bus? Even with all the trouble we had, you'd try again?
Silvia: Yes! I try again! Maybe my sister-in-law (Amelia) go with me.
Beth: Okay, great! Do you have any other friends now that you could go out with, too?
Silvia: Yes. A friend at work [giggles].
Beth: A girl or a boy?
Silvia: A boy [giggles].
Beth: So, is he cute?
Silvia: Mmm . . . so-so!

Beth: Have you told your mom that you'd like to go somewhere with him?
Silvia: Not yet. But I will. She will say okay.
Beth: What about dad?
Silvia: That's the problem [giggles]! But maybe someone go with us!

We must emphasize the unfinished nature of this story—indeed, of all of the stories in this book. A couple of months after our update interview with the Navarros, Beth spoke with Rosa on the telephone. She said that Silvia was very despondent as a result of there being "nothing to do" in her "job" at The Arc. Most days, she said, there was so little to do that Silvia could go to sleep there if she wanted to. Rosa said that they had inquired of The Arc personnel for information regarding trying to get Silvia into a community college program, where she could continue learning. Rosa emphasized that Silvia had not forgotten what she had learned through her reading tutoring but that there was still a lot for her to learn and her reading was still very hesitant. The Arc, she said, had promised to send the papers for Silvia to apply, but so far this had not happened. As far as Silvia's social life was concerned, there was practically nothing, so the quality of her daily activities, whether work or school, was crucial. Beth promised to do her best to find someone who spoke Spanish and who would bring the family the relevant information regarding college possibilities for Silvia.

APPLYING THE POSTURE OF CULTURAL RECIPROCITY

In this section, we assist your learning of the posture of cultural reciprocity by illustrating how we think that it worked with Silvia's family. We do not do this in such detail with the other case studies because we want you to work out your own interpretations, but we believe that an extended analysis of how we perceive our work with the Navarros will provide one solid illustration of how you might proceed in analyzing the seven stories that follow.

Before turning directly to Silvia's story, we make some general comments about the way we approached the families. Note, however, that these comments relate to the families of the five students with whom we worked for all 4 years of the project—Silvia, Maldon Maher, Kyle, and Rafael. With these students, we attempted "action research" efforts intended to assist in the students' social development. Thus, the challenge of cultural reciprocity was central to everything that we did. Our research with the families of the three preschool students, Carissa, Brianna, and Theresa Marie, was entirely observational. Our efforts at cultural reciprocity were more passive with these families because setting goals and implementing interventions were not a part of the process. We simply had to be culturally sensitive enough to understand and respect what we were learning from the families.

From Cultural Sensitivity to Cultural Reciprocity

Remember that the explicit charge of our research project was to assist families in providing opportunities for social development for their children who had disabilities. Our project defined social development in terms of an inclusive framework—that is, in environments and situations that typically would be experienced by their peers without disabilities and in the company of such peers. Our approach was to begin by finding out, through interviews and observations, what social goals the families held for these students and what opportunities we could find or create for pursuing these goals in inclusive home or community environments.

Making plans with the parents emerged from a dialogue that usually moved from broad to specific goals. The types of goals that parents stated initially were very broad and reflected particular principles rather than specific goals. Several parents said, for example, "I just want him to have a normal life like his brothers and sisters." "I want her to be like the others [siblings]." "I just want him to be happy." "I want him to have his own life." "I want her to be more independent." In response to these statements, we tried to come up with suggestions that might fit within the family's scheme of social activity and general value system. In most cases, the families responded positively to our suggestions, and we tried out the ideas, working out all details of planning with the families and evaluating the success of these efforts through ongoing discussions with them and with all of the personnel involved. Nothing that we set out to do was set in stone; everything was "a work in progress."

A central premise of the work was cultural sensitivity, which meant being able to respect and respond supportively to the families' beliefs, values, and communication styles. Needless to say, this came about most easily in cases in which our own beliefs, values, and communication styles were closest to those of the family. For example, in working with Maldon's family, with whom Beth shared both a cultural and a personal history, I usually felt as though I were in my own living room. Cultural sensitivity was a given. With the other families, I shared a range of commonalities and differences: With some, my own preference for an informal, personal interaction style was well matched, and the area that was more challenging was particular beliefs, for example, regarding individual rights, parental advocacy, or inclusion. In other cases, my beliefs were very much in tune with the families', but I had to work within a more formal approach to personal interaction than came naturally to me.

The fact that we needed to approach different families differently soon became evident. For example, both Kyle's and Maher's families' carefully planned schedules, somewhat more formal home organization, and occasional out-of-town travel by a parent required ample advance planning for appointments. With Rafael's and Silvia's families, by contrast, the parents' less predictable work schedules, along with their extended family systems' spontaneous and frequent socializing, made advance planning close to impossible. Consequently, we seldom requested an appointment with the Navarros or the Ignacios more than a couple of days in advance and, upon arrival, were fully prepared to include visiting family members in the discussion or to have the "interview" completely change course by virtue of some unexpected event.

Being culturally sensitive, however, is not quite the same as being culturally reciprocal. We believe that it is possible to be sensitive—recognizing and respecting differences—without truly reciprocating—that is, learning from the family while also having the family learn from us. As a professional, I may understand and respect what you say yet never be truly influenced by your perspective. By "being influenced," we do not mean necessarily changing our own beliefs; we may never do that. We do mean, however, being able to bend so as to work effectively within the family's framework of values.

As you read through our interpretation of our work with Silvia's family, you may ask to what extent we consciously used the posture of cultural reciprocity. The answer is that we really developed our reciprocity instinctively, as a part of gradually becoming more in tune with the family. The fact that our approach to the research was essentially reflective and heuristic allowed for this reciprocity to develop naturally. On the one hand, we believe that this is good—an indication that the principle of reciprocity was already internalized in our thinking. On the other hand, had we been more conscious of each step of the process, we might have come to our understandings sooner. For example, as you read our interpretation, you will notice that it took us a while to fully grasp the Navarro family's perspective on literacy. Had we been quicker to appreciate their focus on this area, we would have targeted it sooner.

In this commentary, we show how we, as researchers, began by making assumptions about Silvia's needs that were based on our own cultural framework as American professionals. As we came to know the family better, our awareness of our different perspectives grew, and as we shared these differences with the family, we were able to develop assistance that was more "in sync" with those perspectives.

We offer the following interpretation to assist you in becoming more aware of how subtle, often implicit cultural assumptions can affect our interactions with families. However, our comments are by no means exhaustive, and there may be many other ways of seeing the same events. Also, we do not try to address all of the issues that are embedded in this case study. We invite you to approach our comments critically, with a view to exploring your own interpretations and thinking about how the posture of cultural reciprocity might have proceeded for you, had you been working with Silvia and her family.

Step 1   When we applied the posture of cultural reciprocity in our interactions with Silvia's family, we became aware that although we all had agreed that "independence" was an important goal for Silvia, our research team had been focused primarily on our own interpretation of what that meant. What were the beliefs on which this focus was based? First was the belief that, as a young woman of almost 18, Silvia should be preparing for adulthood. What did *adulthood* mean? From the perspective of American society, it meant paid employment, social independence with freedom of choice of friendships, and the ability to pursue some social activities independent of her family. Where did these values come from? Almost certainly from the cultural norms of mainstream America.

Where did our belief that Silvia should aim for the same kind of lifestyle as mainstream American youth come from? Probably from our belief in equity and individual rights. These were essential American values that were deeply inculcated in our professional training as special educators. On what basis did we set about identifying specific objectives that would represent the overall goal of independence? From our professional knowledge about transition planning for adulthood, we knew that it was time to start employment planning, travel training, and social relationship building and that Silvia should make good progress in these areas before graduating from high school.

Thus, in our initial attempts to target the goal of independence and to provide Silvia with age-appropriate ways of attaining that goal, we set about finding her a summer job and a job coach. Through this job, we targeted work skills, social skills on the job, and the use of public transportation. We also focused on socialization and having friends outside the family as an equally appropriate goal toward independence for a teenager. We envisioned assisting Silvia in attaining her expressed desire to extend her friendship with Asha into a typical teenage relationship, whereby they would meet outside school, "hang out" at the mall, and go to the movies together. This emphasis also reflected an individualistic focus: Sylvia's having the option of public transportation and increased opportunities to make friends on her own would enhance Sylvia's self-esteem and sense of autonomy.

Both Rosa and Silvia responded eagerly to all of our suggestions regarding these goals. But there were two other goals that it took us 1½ years to incorporate finally into our portfolio of action research for Silvia: learning to read and obtaining SSDI benefits.

On the issue of literacy, both Rosa and Silvia had told us in our first encounter that this was what they wanted most for her. Although we assisted Rosa in raising this issue at Silvia's annual IEP conference, we did not see it as an appropriate goal for our project because we identified it as an academic rather than a social goal. We also did not think of literacy development in terms of independence. Examining our slowness to revise our view of the importance of this issue, we noted a couple of sources of our belief system. First was our professional education: As special educators prepared for working with students with moderate to severe disabilities, we were accustomed to focusing on community-based, functional curricula by the time students were 16 or so. Thus, the curriculum that the school was providing Silvia seemed appropriate to us. Part of the rationale for this is that the student has only a few years left in school, and it is crucial to target skills that can be mastered in that time and that would be useful upon leaving school. Second was that we interpreted our "social" charge in terms of recreational socializing or friendship building and simply assumed that literacy was beyond the purview of the project.

Regarding Rosa's expressed concerns about Silvia's eligibility for SSDI benefits, once more, this was a goal with which the school was already assisting and that we saw as having little to do with either social development or independence.

Step 2   In our conversations with Silvia and Rosa, we began to become aware of these differences in our shared goal of independence for Silvia. Rosa's objection to the job coach's allowing Silvia to go part of the way on her own and her decision, in the third summer, that all of the trouble with public transportation just was not worth it sharpened our understanding of her point of view: Rosa viewed giving Silvia an opportunity to learn how to travel by herself on a bus as a good idea that she would readily support, but, as far as she was concerned, it was an opportunity, not a goal. Similarly, when efforts to extend Silvia and Asha's friendship did not materialize as we had envisioned, Silvia's mother seemed to accept it with resignation. Although she had enthusiastically endorsed the idea, she could accept the eventual outcome because 1) that had not been a primary goal for her, 2) she quickly discerned that Asha's family had been reluctant about the relationship and were unlikely to overlook the cultural differences between the two families, and 3) she knew that Silvia would continue to have friends within her family network.

We knew that Rosa was just as concerned as we were about increasing Silvia's independence. However, we came to see that she approached this goal in terms of literacy acquisition. If Silvia learned to read, then she would not be dependent on family and friends to read for her when they went out together. In fact, by learning to read, she would have a skill that her parents did not have and that would be useful for the whole family. Similarly, Rosa's concern for Silvia to obtain SSDI benefits was closely tied to independence—financial independence, which she hoped the SSDI allowance would enable. She hoped that, like her other children, Silvia would one day get married. But regardless of whether she did, she should have a source of income that would contribute to her independence. Because her siblings were expected to—and would—look after their sister when the time came, Silvia's having her own money would lessen their economic burden. This goal, too, would help the whole family. In contrast to her attitude toward the travel and friendship plans, Rosa was much more persistent and assertive in reaction to any efforts toward Silvia's learning to read and obtaining SSDI benefits.

Step 3 Step 3 was a gradual process that occurred through conversations with Rosa, Silvia, Doris, and Oscar. With regard to SSDI, we really cannot say when we began to become involved in these efforts. This seemed to creep up on us gradually as we became more and more aware of its importance to the family and of the fact that the school personnel simply could not do it all. Regarding the issue of literacy acquisition, however, we changed our view very explicitly after listening to Rosa and Doris express their disbelief that Silvia was going to graduate from high school without learning to read. Suddenly, we became aware that this was a cultural oxymoron for them! Their definition of *school* was a place where you learned to read, and, after all, the lack of this opportunity was why neither Rosa nor Trinidad could read. How could it be that their daughter was going to school and would graduate yet not be able to read? All of the others—Luis, Doris, and Oscar—had graduated from American high schools and were fully literate in English.

This was the point at which we spent a good deal of time discussing with Rosa and Doris the different interpretations that we had of what could and should constitute schooling. As we explained to them more of the special education system and its goals, they understood that schooling that included students with disabilities had different goals than did traditional schooling and that Silvia's graduation certificate would not be a full diploma. They had been told this before, at the first annual IEP conference that we attended for Silvia, but like many new ideas, it took a while for them to absorb it. As they came to see the reasoning behind the kind of schooling that Silvia was getting, so did we come to be persuaded by their conviction that Silvia was capable of learning to read and that no stone should be left unturned until she had had all possible opportunities.

Step 4 Through this discussion, our charge as action researchers became much clearer to us: Our research team came to see that literacy was, indeed, an aspect of independence for Silvia. In light of the importance of this decision, whether literacy was a "social" goal became immaterial. We would simply accept that a major focus of our efforts for Silvia would have to be on literacy. This also meant a greater advocacy role for us, either in trying to persuade the school to increase their emphasis on reading in Silvia's curriculum or, at least, to give the family more support in advocating for themselves. Our discussions with Silvia's family resulted in a commitment to providing tutoring for Silvia, as well as assisting them in presenting their case to school personnel.

Questions

1. *The meaning of independence:* How would you have reacted to the issues related to independence that we have outlined? Are there additional issues that would concern you, such as planning for Silvia's future residence? Using your personal identity web (see Figure 3 on p. 9), explore the source of your reactions.

2. *The importance of friendship:* In our outline of our cultural reciprocity process with this family, we briefly mentioned Rosa's reactions to our efforts in this area. But what about Silvia's views? As far as we knew, Silvia did not express great disappointment when our efforts did not have any lasting effects. We suspect that she must have been disappointed, however, because the idea had come from her and Asha, and years later she

continued to wish to go out with friends. Different cultures have different definitions of friendship, as well as different values placed on friendship. How do you define *friendship* and its importance?

    a. Using your own definition, put yourself in the position of working with Silvia's family, and identify what you think might be some of the issues for you.

    b. If you had been the person attempting to support the friendship between Silvia and Asha, which particular values would have affected your response?

3. *Intergenerational differences:* The foregoing question leads us to the issue of differences between Silvia's wishes and Rosa's on certain issues. Besides her socializing with Asha, Silvia clearly was more invested than Rosa in regard to enjoying some independence in travel. The idea of riding in her wheelchair out of sight of the job coach was all hers, and she was delighted with the feeling of independence that that little jaunt gave her. But Rosa would have none of it! How do you react to this event and to the issue of intergenerational conflict generally? As researchers, we accepted that despite Silvia's age, her parents were still in charge of her and that their wishes had to be respected. If you were a professional working with Silvia, how would you attempt to pursue the posture of cultural reciprocity with the family on such issues?

4. *Psychological assessment and educational placement:* It is evident that Silvia underwent an inappropriate and disadvantageous process of assessment. What biases do you think might have prevented some professionals from seeing the inappropriateness of the assessment that she had gone through? How would you have reacted in this situation?

5. *Educational programming:* When Rosa and Doris made it clear that they wanted literacy to be a primary goal for Silvia during her high school years, more important even than work, how would you have reacted? Using your personal identity web (see Figure 3 on p. 9), identify the sources of your responses, then work through the process of cultural reciprocity with Rosa and Doris.

6. *Obtaining SSDI benefits:* Obtaining SSDI benefits for Silvia was a central goal for her family. We believe that the obstructions that they encountered in their efforts related to a range of problems: language difference, their own lack of knowledge of the system and of their rights within it, changing laws, and lack of personal accountability on the part of some of the social welfare

personnel handling the case. What is your reaction to the family's continuing difficulties with this aspect of the system? How do you see the rights of people who have resident status but not citizenship in the United States? Using your personal identity web (see Figure 3 on p. 9), examine the sources of your own reactions to these issues.

7. *Researcher responsibility:* When we began this project, we knew that one of the challenges would be to offer assistance that would empower families to learn how to help themselves so that they would not become dependent on a project that would, after all, last only 4 years. We believe that we attempted to do this to the extent possible. Yet, on withdrawing from the project, and even 4 years after its official completion, we wished—and still wish—that we could have done more to leave more lasting effects. After reading the story of our work with this family, offer a critical analysis of our efforts from the point of view of their usefulness and longevity for the family. What could or should we have done differently?

2

Carissa

A Family with a Vision—on a Mission

John, Carissa, and James, Jr.

The vision of this family is one of full inclusion and a holistic view of an African American preschooler who happens to have Down syndrome. The family's struggle, led by Carissa's mother, challenges service providers to examine conflicting beliefs about equity and deviance and to reflect on the procedures by which children with disabilities are evaluated and placed in education programs.

> She's the little red engine chugging up the hill. . . . She's extremely
> bright, inquisitive, independent, adorable, cute as a button. . . . She's
> charming, engaging. She captivates people. She can wrap people
> around her little finger. . . . She has a great way of finding things out,
> and her problem-solving skills are really good. . . . She's a creative
> thinker. (Ruth Coates, Carissa's mother)

An example of Carissa's creative thinking at age 6 reveals the type
of thinking skills that any child needs to get around the restrictions
of childhood. It was late at night, and Ruth was cleaning up the
kitchen. She noticed that Carissa was hanging around as if waiting
for her to leave, so Ruth purposely left the kitchen to watch what
Carissa would do. Taking a bottle of soda from the counter, Carissa
went to a darkened corner and opened the bottle as quietly as she
could. Her mother came out and asked Carissa what she was doing.
Carissa's reaction was immediate: Holding the bottle up to her
mother, she announced, "It's for you, Mommy!"

When Carissa was born, the day before Valentine's Day in 1992,
she was diagnosed as having Down syndrome. This birth was
Ruth's third cesarean section, and she told us that as she was emerging from the anesthesia,

> I heard them talking, and it didn't sound good. The nurse was talking
> to my husband, using strange medical terms that I hadn't heard before,
> such as "Simian creases," "flat occiput," and "hypotonic." I also heard
> talk about "dusky coloring," "not breathing on her own," and "heart
> defect." My immediate reaction was that I was supposed to be there to
> have a baby, and I didn't see a baby. I figured they must be talking
> about my baby. My first words were, "What's wrong with my baby?"
> They didn't hear me the first time, so I said it louder. The nurse re-
> sponded, saying that I had a "beautiful little girl." That statement
> seemed inconsistent with what I had heard her saying before, and I
> said, "So what's all this stuff you're talking about?" At that point, my
> husband pointed out that I hadn't seen the baby yet. So they wheeled
> me to the neonatal intensive care, and they told me that a cardiologist
> was on the way and that the baby might need immediate open heart
> surgery.
> When I saw Carissa, I saw a beautiful little girl. What I saw was no
> reflection of the description I had heard. . . . She opened her eyes, our
> eyes locked, and the only way that I can describe it is to say that I was
> overtaken by, I believe, a peace from God. It was as if her eyes were
> telling me, "It's going to be okay: maybe hard, but okay. I'm in here,
> help me out." I later interpreted that to mean "to my potential." She
> did pretty well: They got her stabilized and she continued to do well,
> and after 8 days we took her home.

This was the little girl whom Ruth had longed for, but, 2 weeks
later, the power of professional convictions about Carissa's diagno-

sis began to sink in for the Coates family when a leading geneticist explained to Ruth and James that, on the basis of Carissa's diagnosis, Carissa would not graduate from a general high school. Several years after that pronouncement, Ruth told us,

> What makes it so frustrating is that I recently talked to a new parent whose child is 5 months old. She had the same doctor, and his report is the same exact words as mine was 3 years ago. He set it up on the first word processor ever, and he's still using it. . . ! When my sons were born, no one tried to predict whether or not they would graduate from high school or go to college!
>
> And this has been a recurring theme with providers, whether it be from the medical or the educational community, that Carissa would be defined by her diagnosis. Unbeknownst to me, this was the first hint I would have of what lay ahead, which was to force the point that Carissa is not her diagnosis but her prognosis.

At first, the hurt engendered by professional pronouncements, along with a total lack of information from the hospital authorities, made Ruth feel like she should run away to a desert island where she could protect her daughter from the kind of hurt that promised to be an inevitable part of Carissa's life. To the contrary, however, Ruth's determination and strong grasp on reality quickly won out, and, with the absolute support of her family, she set out on a path of advocacy for her daughter and for other young children with disabilities. As she said, "The information void . . . the lack of information, the lack of support, sent me on this—this chase." Before long, Ruth's view of Down syndrome became clear:

> I think we've got to continue to find out that basically it doesn't really mean anything. I think it's going to be like beauty being in the eyes of the beholder—that Down syndrome is really in the eyes of the beholder.
>
> We made a decision early on, in the first several weeks of her life, that the Down syndrome was not going to have any more control over our lives than we allowed it to have. That we were going to be like stubborn, bratty kids and say, "No. No, you will not control my every waking moment. No, Carissa will not be able to throw her toys around or throw her clothes on the floor because she has Down syndrome. No, she *will* learn, it may take a little longer, we may have to be a little creative." Actually, the burden is on us, not the person who has the disability. The challenge is for us to figure out new and different and exciting ways of working with them and supporting them. And, so, Carissa is learning how to help Mommy around the house. You know, she puts things in the trash, she wipes up if she spills something, she gets the paper towels and she knows how to wipe it up. When she takes her coat off, she knows to hand it to me, and the next step will be hanging it up when she can reach the hanger! You know, she took her coat

off one day and threw it on the floor and walked away. I said, "No, no young lady! Come back here and you pick up that coat!"

CARISSA AND HER FAMILY

Carissa was 2½ when we met her in the fall of 1994. Our first visit to the Coates family's attractive suburban home assured us of the welcoming nature of this family.

It was a Saturday morning, and the large family room to which Ruth led us was dominated by a sports event on the large-screen television set. However, it was just about time for Carissa's brothers to set off with their father for their football and basketball practice, so we were quickly introduced, and Ruth told the boys that it was time for them to turn off the television and get ready to leave. James and John responded promptly and cheerfully. Their ready cooperation was something that we observed on all of our visits to their home and was a notable example of one of the basic house rules set by James and Ruth: The parents give an instruction only once, and compliance is expected.

The extensive array of formal portraits and informal photographs that lined the far wall of the family room spoke of the powerful family ethic that characterized this African American household. The portraits included Carissa's immediate family: her parents; her brothers James, then 13, and John, then 8; and Carla, their stepsister, who was then in her 20s. Other family members were also very much in evidence, and we were particularly pleased, on later visits, to have the pleasure of meeting one very prominent person among the portraits—Carissa's great-grandmother, then in her late 80s.

James Coates works with the postal service, and Ruth is a middle manager for a trade association. Our interviews all were with Ruth, and we met James several times but always briefly at home, at school district meetings, or at our project's social activities. Ruth's description of her husband fit perfectly with the image that we had of him—"the invaluable Mister Mom, a rock of stability." James's central roles in the family circle are evidenced by a range of activities, from cooking to leading a daily family devotional hour.

The Coates family adheres to a traditional Christian faith yet is unafraid of new ideas. For example, the unconventional approach that characterized Ruth's search for inclusive services for Carissa extends to her view of medical protocols. This is evident in the many hours that she contributes on a voluntary basis to the work of a neuronaturopathic geneticist/virologist, assisting him with setting up a college of complementary medicine. Ruth explains that the term *complementary* indicates an array of medical protocols, versus a strictly Western approach, and represents a pioneering approach to medical treatment that is embraced by the Coates family. Ruth described her family as built on "a strong foundation of faith that is our family's underpinning. . . . This is what allows us to have confidence in venturing out."

As we settled in to our first visit, Ruth seated us comfortably on the sofa, then curled up on the floor in the midst of a wide scatter of Lego pieces, plastic numerals and letters, and other accouterment of a 2-year-old's life. Carissa, active, persistent, and bubbling with enthusiasm, was only too willing to comply with her mother's requests that she demonstrate some of the knowledge that she was gaining at the church-affiliated child care center that she attended. Her demonstration included sight recognition of several colors, letters of the alphabet, and names of animals. Using signs and a few words, Carissa sang nursery rhymes, her favorite being "Itsy Bitsy Spider," complete with the appropriate gestures. She recited the Pledge of Allegiance with her right hand on her heart, ensuring that we also had our hands on our hearts before she began. Throughout the performance, Ruth sang and signed along with Carissa, following her and prompting her when necessary. After the performance, we cheered Carissa and she joined happily in our applause.

We learned that Carissa communicated extensively using gestures, signs, and a few words. At that time, she had an expressive vocabulary of about 70 words in sign language. Her parents had opted for a total communication approach, and the entire family uses signs and spoken words when communicating with her. James, Ruth, and the two boys all had attended classes in sign language and consulted books on sign language whenever necessary to extend Carissa's vocabulary. As we were leaving her home, Carissa pointed to a maple leaf displayed on a wall near the main hallway and said, "I did dat." Quite surprised at her three-word utterance, we were reinforced by this simple statement that our first impressions of Carissa were correct: She was motivated, persistent, and proud of her accomplishments.

Carissa's brothers are very fond of their little sister. However, before Carissa was born, they had been so adamant about wanting another little brother that John had threatened to lock himself in his room and never come out again if the baby turned out to be a girl. When John was later reminded of this, he quickly responded, "I changed my mind!" Carissa won them over on their very first visit to her in the hospital. Ruth told us that the boys' bonding with

Carissa began when her husband bent down to say something to her and she hit him; the boys have been in love with her ever since! They get along remarkably well. The boys have loved her from the very beginning. And they really take good care of her. They have a tolerance level. You can tell when it gets met" [laughter].

They are also very protective of their sister: During a home visit, a service provider commented that "Carissa does great for a child with all of her problems!" James immediately turned to her and said, "Carissa doesn't have any problems." The family structure reflects a clear pattern of older sibling authority and responsibility, and we often noticed James giving directions to Carissa and John, especially during mealtimes. The brothers are also proud of Carissa's achievements and often help her to learn her colors or numbers, asking her questions and prompting her if necessary. Ruth believes that the boys became more compassionate and caring toward all people after Carissa's birth. The following story indicates Ruth's watchful approach to her sons' perspectives on disabilities:

> James went to a football camp this summer, and John and I went to pick him up on the last day of camp, and so we were sitting in the stands and John whispered to me, "Mom, there's a person with Down syndrome sitting behind us!" And then he said, "Look, Ma!" So I said, "Well, John, it's rude to look right now. I'll look in a few minutes." But I really wanted to see if he really knew what he was saying. . . . So when I looked around, I said, "Oh, John, you were right!" There was a little boy. And I said, "How did you know he had Down syndrome?" And he said, "Well, 'cause he has eyes like Carissa." I said, "Well, John, what does that mean—having Down syndrome?" And he was like, "I don't know."
>
> We've always talked about it, and James, one time, last semester in school, he found a paragraph in one of his school books that gave a definition of Down syndrome. It was a very old book, and it referred to it as Mongolism and told a little bit about how it happens, about the chromosomes and everything. . . . He handwrote it out of the book and brought it home to me. He said, "Ma, I brought this home for you so you could read it, in case you wanted to know." He was educating me about Down syndrome, which is fine. All in all, I think that maybe it's time for me to revisit what their perceptions are about Down syndrome.

Since that time, James, at age 15, did a research report on Down syndrome and at 16 made this the topic of a class speech. In his research report, James's thesis was, "Just because a person has Down syndrome, that doesn't mean that he is different. He's just a person like you or me." He went on to state,

For me, it has been hard and even beyond belief that a member of my family has Down syndrome. Before Carissa was born, I had no idea of what Down syndrome was, nor had I ever heard of it. There have been times when I've been frustrated and wondered how long we would have to take care of Carissa, but our family really got strength from our church and prayer. I believe that with continued prayer, therapy, and love, Carissa will lead a full and productive life.

ENSURING INCLUSIVE ENVIRONMENTS FOR CARISSA

The "information void" that characterized the initial period after Carissa's birth did not, in retrospect, last long. A nurse who was part of Ruth's health maintenance organization (HMO) also had a daughter with Down syndrome. The telephone number that she gave Ruth started the ball rolling and led the Coates family to The Arc (formerly the Association for Retarded Citizens [ARC]) in the county in which they lived. Part H services as mandated by the Individuals with Disabilities Education Act (IDEA) of 1990 (PL 101-476), now Part C of the IDEA Amendments of 1997 (PL 105-17), came quickly after that.

From the very beginning, Carissa's life experience was in the inclusive environments that are natural for any child. Her first non-family care was provided by a home-based child care provider. At first, Ruth had found it difficult to decide to return to work but was soon guided by the thought of what she would have done if Carissa had not had a disability and what she had done after her sons' births. Then came the challenge of finding child care; Carissa was on an apnea monitor when she slept, and between that and her diagnosis of Down syndrome, Ruth found that child care providers were not very responsive. As she said, "Some were direct, some were diplomatic," and Ruth, obviously, was not interested in a provider who would not be comfortable with accepting Carissa.

Soon, however, Ruth remembered someone who she thought would do the job. James's mother, having been diagnosed with terminal cancer, had come to live with Ruth and James when Ruth was 7 months pregnant with Carissa. One of the members of her church, Mrs. Hill, had come to visit and had said, "Oh, by the way, I do child care." As soon as Ruth recalled this, she called Mrs. Hill, went to visit her, taking Carissa along, and, according to Ruth, "She fell in love with Carissa, and that was it." Mrs. Hill was afraid that she might not have all of the knowledge that she needed but was willing to try. Reflecting on this, Ruth commented that perhaps seeing the child was a key aspect; the other providers with whom she had spoken had made their excuses after a telephone call, never having seen Carissa. Mrs. Hill provided a nurturing, family-style environment for Carissa from the age of 3 months to 2½ years.

Soon after Carissa's second birthday, Ruth made a strategic decision. Convinced that an inclusive educational environment would be best for her daughter, Ruth decided that she needed to place Carissa in a general preschool where she could receive special education services under Part C of IDEA. As she put it, she figured that if she could keep her out of a segregated environment, then she would never have to extricate her from it! Until that time, Carissa had been receiving home-based early intervention (Part C) services; the providers alternated their visits between Mrs. Hill's home and the Coates family's so that Carissa's family members could participate. Mrs. Hill participated eagerly in the activities suggested by the providers, and she soon realized how much she already knew: The activities that were appropriate for Carissa were basically the same as those for children in general. Realizing that Part C, with its community-based emphasis, would no longer provide services after Carissa's third birthday, Ruth decided to ensure that there would be a precedent for Carissa to receive services in an inclusive educational environment.

Ruth began her search for a preschool program by calling a number of child care centers that advertised a lot of advantages, but she quickly found out that the ads were geared only toward typically developing children. Although the providers all stayed within the law, by not refusing to take a child with a disability, they, nonetheless, made it an unattractive option by saying things such as, "Well, she could come but we don't have the resources to do anything special," or, "We've never done this before, so we don't know if it would work."

Finally, it dawned on Ruth to call the church-affiliated child care/preschool program that John had gone to and that Ruth knew was a very caring, nurturing environment. Once more, she realized that this was the program that she would have chosen if Carissa had not had a disability. The director of the child care center was extremely warm and encouraging even though the center had never had a 2-year-old with a developmental delay as extensive as Carissa's. So Ruth and Carissa went to visit the program, and Carissa adapted so well that Ruth left for a while, and Carissa had a wonderful day. Ruth gained another confirmation of her 2½-year-old's adaptable and adventurous spirit.

In an interview with Mrs. Wilson, the director of the child care center, we learned about the positive approach of this program. The program had previously had children with identified developmental delays, but this would be their first child with Down syndrome. Mrs. Wilson brought Carissa's communication needs to the attention of the pastor, and it was quickly agreed that the church would go ahead with a plan to introduce their teachers to sign language, which was something that they had been considering anyway. Carissa's teacher, whom Mrs. Wilson described as having a "Christian spirit [that] just shines out," was enthusiastic, and Mrs. Wilson described the entire effort as follows:

> I honestly believed the Lord had opened all the doors on this. I don't give our center any credit. I just say that we were here, available, and we asked what we could do and this is what has happened thus far. . . . I don't take this—this is not a job. This is the charge the Lord has given me.

Mrs. Wilson told us that the only concern that the staff initially had about Carissa was that she may have been harder to potty train than the other children. Their fears were unfounded, however, as Carissa was one of the first children in her group to be toilet trained.

THE LITTLE ENGINE THAT COULD

When we started observing Carissa in her preschool program, she was in a class with two teachers, one aide, and 11 other children, none of whom had any defined disabilities. The school district, under Part C of IDEA, had readily agreed to provide Carissa with site-based services of special education, physical therapy (PT), occupational therapy (OT), and speech-language therapy. Carissa had also been receiving private speech-language therapy from a local college from the time she was 15 months of age.

As we observed Carissa's preschool program, Ruth's perspective on the power of an inclusive environment became evident. Carissa participated with enthusiasm in the classroom activities and on the playground, and it was easy to see that her greatest learning strength at that time was imitation. Using signs and single words to communicate with her teachers and peers, she initiated interactions and responded happily to initiations from others. The children in the group all had been introduced to some sign language, which was used with the entire group throughout circle time and whenever Carissa was being given instructions. Moni's observation notes on the circle time illustrate Carissa's participation:

> They began with the prayer song "Our Father," followed by the pledge of allegiance, then "We Love Our Flag, Our Beautiful Flag," and then

"Two Little Hands Go Clap, Clap." They sang another prayer song something like "This Is the Day the Lord Has Made." The children were standing on their feet at this time. Carissa was swaying, clearly enjoying the music. She fit right into the group, since some children were singing and others were not, so Carissa did not stand out in the group in any way. Occasionally . . . from her lip formation, I could make out that she was trying to say, "This is . . . ," when they were singing, "This is the day." The teacher asked Carissa what song she wanted to sing. . . . Carissa pointed her thumb towards her heart. The teacher said "'Joy'? You want to sing 'Joy'?" Carissa nodded and the teacher started singing, "I've got the joy, joy, joy down in my heart." Along with the entire group, Carissa pointed her thumb to her chest with gusto and started shaking her head to the rhythm. (September 7, 1994)

Two of Carissa's peers, Shawna and Tom, shared a special relationship with Carissa. Shawna asked for Carissa when Carissa was late and was visibly upset when Carissa did not show up. Moni's observation notes on another visit provide a snapshot of the relationship between Carissa and these peers:

Carissa's mother walked in through the classroom door and smiled at me. . . . Carissa [following behind] peeked through the door, and then she stepped back, probably because she saw me. Her mother called her, and she came in slowly, hiding her face. She was probably feeling shy because of my presence. Shawna walked up to Carissa and pulled at her jacket, trying to open the buttons. She was not able to open it and pulled Carissa's mother's hands, and her mother unbuttoned the jacket. Carissa was wearing a purple hat, which Shawna then took off. Ruth told Carissa to go to the bathroom, and Shawna followed. I did not follow them since I thought Carissa may feel shy or embarrassed. After a while, Shawna called for help, and Carissa's mother went in and helped Carissa. Shawna went near the tables, and she picked up a red chair that had Carissa's name on it and put it near me. Then she went back to get her own chair with her name on it and put it diagonally across from Carissa's. Shawna seemed more animated . . . and more physically active after Carissa's arrival. . . . After her mother left, Carissa walked to the door and was looking around, and Tom went up to her and gave her a hug. (January 20, 1995)

We also noticed that Carissa performed differently when she interacted with people who were not acquainted with her abilities. For example, during one classroom observation, Carissa was playing on the floor with blocks alongside a peer, Tina. Tina stacked a few blocks, and Carissa broke her tower with a purposeful hand movement. This happened twice, and Tina shouted at her and said, "No, go away," and pulled the blocks closer to herself. The teacher, who was new, reprimanded Tina and instructed her to share. She also asked Carissa to say that she was sorry, but after a few requests she gave up when Carissa did not comply. This teacher was not aware that Carissa was able to sign and maybe even say, "Sorry," so she allowed her to get away without apologizing.

Carissa also spent a lot of time observing her peers and imitating their actions. This was especially evident in our observations of her on the playground. For example, during one of Moni's observations, she observed Carissa watching, then imitating a child who climbed backward up the slide. Carissa did not imitate blindly, however, and the following notes indicate her ability to engage in careful judgment as she attempted her imitations:

> Carissa stood and watched some children climb up a jungle gym. These children are bigger than her in size—they are probably 4-year-olds. There were three steps or iron rods to climb, then they could reach out to hold on to the rod at the top and swing from there. Two children were playing, then a third one joined them, and then all three left. Carissa had been watching. She ran to the equipment, climbed the first two steps, holding a rod on the side. Then she reached for the bar on top with one hand while holding to the metal rod on the side with her other hand. She couldn't quite make the top rod. Then she got down, climbed up the two steps again, came down, walked backward, and looked at the equipment for a while. Then she turned and left. (November 12, 1995)

Carissa was a busy, active participant in group activities, always with consistently appropriate behavior. Our videotape of her during the preschool's Christmas celebration in December 1994 illustrated her ability to judge which behaviors to imitate. She was sitting on stage in the first row, Tina was on her left, and there was a little boy on her right. Tina was very jumpy, and she kept getting off her seat, standing up, skipping about, and turning around. She was clearly being disruptive, and, finally, the teacher picked her up and made her sit on her lap. The celebration lasted for an hour, during which time Carissa's participation was totally appropriate, singing along with "Jingle Bells" and playing the tambourine. She seldom got distracted by Tina and imitated only a couple of her behaviors, such as turning around twice to see the children at the back when Tina had done so and getting off her chair once in imitation of Tina.

The natural evolution of peer interaction among the children was a source of great encouragement to Ruth. She believed that this was the most effective aspect of Carissa's instruction. Summing it up, she said,

The kids did a great job of figuring things out on their own. Some approached Carissa from a mentoring standpoint, others responded to her in age-appropriate ways. The wisest of the adults in charge minimized their direct intervention. As far as the related services were concerned, I really preferred a "train the trainers" model, where the specialist providers would teach the regular providers how to include the special services into the classroom routine for all the children. Some providers were more open to doing this while others were quite resistant to the idea. . . . There was one provider who was fluent in sign language. She did a marvelous job of facilitating Carissa's performance in the classroom by blending in and casually addressing all of the children so that Carissa didn't "stand out."

Overall, Carissa's placement at the preschool confirmed all of Ruth and James's beliefs that "the environment we put people into *matters!*" When Carissa turned 3 in February 1995, her family was determined that inclusive environments would continue to be the norm for this "little engine" who had readily demonstrated her ability to do many things that people thought she could not do. According to her mother, "We are often accused of being in denial. We finally decided, 'Yes, we are in denial.' Carissa should not be denied any right and privilege in her life. We 'deny' anything that caps or pigeonholes her abilities." Accomplishing the vision of a happy and productive life for Carissa had been easy enough at the beginning of her educational career. The subsequent years, however, proved to be more of a battle for the Coates family.

TRANSITION FROM PART C TO PART B

It was amazing that [inclusion] was relatively easy to be done under Part H [now Part C]—with natural environments and services that were community based. But then when the child turns 3, there are basically no alternatives. You have to really create one. . . . Primarily we're talking about the age span 3–5. It makes absolutely no sense that they'll consent to community-based services from birth to 3, then only provide this segregated setting from 3 to 5, and then we'll try to transplant the child back to the community. (Ruth Coates)

The Ruth Coates whom we met when Carissa was 2½ bore no resemblance to the person who once had contemplated escaping to a desert island. On the contrary, the lack of information at Carissa's birth and Ruth's interactions with professionals had motivated Ruth to immerse herself in an understanding of the law and her rights as a parent of a child with a disability. As well as talking with many other parents, Ruth had consulted a local advocacy organization, whose lawyer had worked closely with her. By the time we met her, she was prepared to invoke due process if necessary to accomplish the family's goal of an inclusive and appropriate education for Carissa. She told us,

> What we're doing right now—what we envision doing for the immediate future—is really the vision that we have for her life. Just as she is [now] going to school and being supported in the community environment, that's what we'll have to look at for her employment. That will always be. I really need to focus on what the supports are and to advocate and fight for the supports that are necessary. . . . So we're going to have to watch for the moment and put the emphasis on, as far as I'm concerned, on . . . an inclusive placement. So whether that continues to be public or private and what the supports are, I haven't been able to figure that out. And I finally convinced myself—'cause I have a tendency to try to plan everything—I'm just going to keep the vision and keep the goal. And then work methodically through it.

When we began learning about Carissa and her family, it was coming up to "transition time." Ruth was fully informed about the differences between Part B and Part C services, as well as the timing of the services. She explained the issue as follows:

> What we're moving into is transition. Okay, Carissa will be 3 in February, we have a [conference] coming up just 2 weeks from now just to establish eligibility under Part B, which probably won't be a problem! She'll be eligible, and then shortly, we'll be having the IFSP/IEP [individualized family service plan/individualized education program] . . . you know, to go over—transition—to establish her Part B services. Although all that has to be done, you have to start the process within 90 days of them turning age 3, but we don't suspect there will be any change in her program until the fall, though she probably won't get services this summer. I'm not really sure if they'll treat her officially as if she's under Part H or Part B this summer, but chances are it'll be Part B, so I wonder if she'll get the services that I want for her. We've been thinking ahead a little as to what we're going to do this summer, and we have some options and some programs.

The process of negotiating with the school district proved an arduous lesson in professional versus parental perspectives on disability. The transition conference (from IFSP to IEP) was to be held in May, at the Special Center that offered preschool special education services. Prior to the conference, Ruth's description of her feelings was,

> I've been psyching myself up. It's like I'm an athlete in training or a soldier in basic training! Trying to be sure that I can keep my emotions and everything intact and go through this very deliberate process and

not be intimidated or drawn off course by some of the strange things
that someone might choose to say.

Ruth's performance at the conference, however, revealed not the
slightest indication of this inner turmoil. To the contrary, by her demeanor, this mother could not have been distinguished from any of
the five service providers seated around the table. The process of
the meeting was a lesson in special education protocol, every aspect
of which was conducted in such a way as to indicate an absolutely
rational procedure leading to decisions based on scientific facts.
The only deviation from this was that the placement recommendation ultimately arrived at by the school district bore no obvious
connection to the previous 60 or so minutes of discussion! Let us
explain.

The meeting began with a suggestion from Carissa's special education teacher that because she and Ruth had already talked in detail about the desired goals for Carissa, the team should simply
summarize those goals and move directly to the question of what
Carissa's placement would be. This suggestion was overruled by the
administrator, who said that the team must have a correct record of
all of the goals and the reasoning behind them.

Thus, the first hour or so of the meeting was spent on the following procedure: Working from a list of specific developmental
goals identified in the school district's handbook, the team compared each goal with Carissa's current level of performance and discussed whether specific goals were seen as "realistic" and "functional" for Carissa. The goals included items such as a vocabulary
of 900 words, which would be expected of a child of 36 months;
recognition of 13 or more letters of the alphabet, which would be
expected of a child of 60 months; and so forth. Carissa's age at that
time was 39 months.

The central difference in perspective between the providers
and Ruth was dramatic and consistent: For the former, the issue
was whether Carissa could be expected to attain the recommended
goals within the following year, with the implicit understanding being that this would determine in which kind of educational environment she would be placed. Their focus was the potential product of Carissa's education in each of the domains addressed. For
Ruth, the issue was the *process* by which Carissa would learn whatever she would learn. For example, when the administrator asked
whether learning the letters of the alphabet had any "functionality"
for Carissa, Ruth replied that Carissa was currently learning the letters of the alphabet within the context of group activities in which

all of her peers engaged and that this was appropriate for her to aim for, regardless of whether she would achieve it, "which no one could know at this point." On the question of functionality, Ruth explained that when she and Carissa went shopping, Ruth pointed out letters as they related to objects in the store. She saw this as a process of teaching Carissa the applicability of her school learning.

Another prominent feature of the discussion was what any observer could readily identify as a game of "yes, but . . . ," engaged in by the providers. For example, the speech-language therapist who had evaluated Carissa had sent a report, but a different therapist attended the meeting. The report stated that Carissa's language comprehension level was at the 30- to 33-month level; some members responded by suggesting that Carissa may be learning much of this by rote. Yet another feature was a tendency to focus on which professional area should be responsible for which goals. For example, when the discussion came to a motor goal of throwing a ball a distance of 5 feet, several minutes were spent discussing whether this was a responsibility of the teacher or of the physical therapist. It was concluded that this goal is a physical education skill, which then becomes a PT task if it is related to the child's ability to move her body.

The discussion of goals lasted for more than an hour. Beth's notes on the meeting included the following comment:

> Throughout all this detailed discussion, Ruth's facial expression and tone of voice never wavered. Her tone was such as I would expect from a professional who held strong opinions but who was relatively detached from the implications of the process. She showed no signs of impatience or frustration; rather, she seemed to accept the rules of the game and showed tremendous skill at holding to her opinions while also acknowledging [providers'] views. For example, when the comment was made about the rote learning, Ruth responded, without a change of facial expression, "Yes, I know exactly what you mean. . . . There is that possibility. . . . However, the way I see it is that when I was a child, I learned a lot of information by rote and later realized how it was applicable." (May 24, 1995)

The purpose of the entire process was to arrive at a decision about Carissa's educational placement. Finally, the chairperson, satisfied that the goals had been addressed adequately said that the next decision would be how much special education time would be needed to accomplish these goals. The subsequent discussion among the providers confirmed that Carissa did need a special education preschool environment with specified time allotments for speech-language, PT, and OT consultation. For these services, the team concluded, Carissa would need a specific number of hours weekly, which was what the special center program offered. Beth's observer comments read,

> I was taken aback at the tone and focus of the discussion. I felt as if the purpose was to "prove" that the mother was being unrealistic in her goals. I was trying to figure out where this was going and was beginning to realize that the game was to prove Carissa's limitations as much as possible so as to negate the appropriateness of the mother's wishes for continued inclusive placement. . . .
> The "quantification" of the specific number of hours weekly seemed to come out of nowhere. . . . No one had tried to specify how many hours it would take to address the goals that had been listed for Carissa. . . . What it really seemed to mean was that the program that exists offers that many hours per week, so that's where they'd send her. (May 24, 1995)

The team did offer another option: If Ruth wished, Carissa could stay at her current preschool and be bused to the special center in the afternoons, where she could have a homeroom "so she could be part of a group there" and also be pulled out for her therapies. Ruth, however, explained that she believed that this would send a negative message to Carissa, that, after being fully accepted in her community preschool, she would be sent to

> A program where she'll learn that she has limitations and expectations won't be as high, and where she won't be able to see typically developing behavior models. . . . I'm concerned about any message I am sending to her—you have to go to this special place because there is something wrong with you.

The team's recommendations provided the only point at which Ruth's tone changed somewhat. Allowing herself a smile and a tinge of irony, she said, "Now that we've *quantified* the amount of special education service she needs, why not let's think about whether there are some innovative ways in which it could be provided?" She asked whether OT and PT services could be delivered by itinerant therapists or whether the district would consider paying a special education graduate student from the university to provide on-site consultation. The administrator replied that community-based services could be possible up until age 3 but not after. The school district's perspective was clear: To summarize, the least restrictive environment (LRE) after age 3 is the public school. The school that Carissa was in then was a private school. The family has the right to pay for private school if they wish, but because the county did not provide a general preschool program that would constitute the LRE for a preschooler, the special center programs or inclusion into a program such as Head Start would be the LRE that the county could provide.

Ruth's response was equally clear: Head Start or a similar county program would not be appropriate because they were either location based or income based to serve low-income families. Carissa's family did not qualify for either. Furthermore, the public preschool program that was suggested served children who were at least 1 year older than Carissa, so it would not be chronologically age appropriate for her. Ruth concluded that because the district did not provide an appropriate general education program, the only appropriate LRE available was Carissa's current private preschool.

At that point, the meeting had finally come to the moment that had been anticipated by all: The administrator asked whether the family would like to consider going through the appeals process because the team did not have the jurisdiction to make such a decision. Ruth nodded, saying, "It does seem a shame to have to go to all that trouble, but we don't have any choice." James, who had been present but silent throughout the foregoing discussion, nodded, saying, "Obviously. No problem."

The foregoing meeting was held near the end of May, and the process of appealing the district's recommendation took all summer. Ruth requested that the county continue serving Carissa at her current placement until a decision was reached. Rather than go directly for an official appeal, Ruth took the route of individual negotiations with school district personnel, moving up the administrative ladder as necessary. The initial responses that she received were not very encouraging. She summed these up as follows:

> Basically, they said, "We tried that in the 70s and it didn't work. . . . " "We don't do that, and we don't have to do that. That's the way we interpret the law. What we've offered her is sufficient, and we really don't have to go beyond that." And they really kind of dug their heels in and kept with that posture. . . . But when I talked to someone further up the line, we made much more progress. So that's basically what we found, typically, that you have to keep going up a level to get a response other than the typical, "We don't do that."

Ultimately, Ruth had to go to the top of the district ladder to get what she wanted. After initial refusals, this district administrator and Ruth finally arrived at a compromise: The district would continue to deliver almost the same on-site services to Carissa at her private preschool. This decision was groundbreaking: With her family's vision and her mother's advocacy strategies and persistence, Carissa became the first child in the county, to our knowledge, to receive on-site services provided under Part B of IDEA.

PART B SERVICES: PRESCHOOL AND KINDERGARTEN

By the time the school district agreed to continue on-site services for Carissa for one more year, it was already February of the school year. Under the "stay put" rule, Carissa's current services had to be continued until the placement decision was settled, so she had been receiving the required services. As Ruth explained, by the time the decision was made, it was time to start the battle for the next year. This, she said, proved to be "almost a carbon copy of the year before"; Carissa went on to the 4-year-old class, and the "stay put" rule once more ensured her services well into February of the school year. That year's negotiation process was somewhat more adversarial than in the previous year, and the Coates family found it necessary to be assisted and accompanied by a lawyer.

The district's recommendation this time around was for Carissa to be placed in a special education program at a center that was about to offer some integration into the Head Start program in the same building. Once more, the district offered the alternative that Carissa could go to her private program for half of the day and to the center/Head Start program in the afternoons. So there ensued a series of on-site visits, whereby school district personnel visited Carissa's private program and Ruth visited the district program. However, everyone stayed firm to his or her position, and, once more, a compromise was effected: Carissa would continue as a student at the private program, with some special services provided.

While the adults in Carissa's world strategized and negotiated, Carissa spent 2 wonderful years playing and learning with her peers without disabilities. In the 3-year-old class, she delighted everyone by mastering many of the basic academic tasks of early childhood, including learning to spell and write her name, identifying all of the letters of the alphabet, counting to 10, and identifying eight colors. Just as important were her learning of classroom routines and recognizing not only which cubbies belonged to which students but also which parents to which students! The spontaneous and accepting interactions of her classmates continued, as the following exchange illustrates: On a trip to the zoo, one classmate pointed to a cage, saying, "Carissa, say yi-on [lion]," and Carissa repeated,

"Yi-on." Her classmate clapped excitedly, exclaiming, "He said it, he said it!" Then, correcting himself, "She said it!"

Carissa's participation in all school activities and field trips was facilitated by whatever was perceived to be the least amount of support required for her success and by the use of total communication, gestures, her own imitation skills, and verbal and physical cues whenever necessary. Carissa learned that she would be held to the same behavioral expectations as her peers, with unavoidable accommodations made by the teachers in what Ruth described as a "surreptitious" manner.

In the 4-year-old class the next year, although the gap between Carissa and her peers without disabilities was noticeably wider, she continued to learn and grow at a steady pace. Again, her teachers were dedicated and creative and welcomed the input of the itinerant public providers. Tears of joy were shed in Carissa's brightly decorated classroom on the day that she spontaneously picked up the ruler and pointed to each consecutive picture on the wall, saying, "A—apple; B—bear; C—cat," and so forth.

During a site visit, one of Carissa's public providers commented, "It's really good to see how nondisabled children learn and play. So much of my exposure is to children who have disabilities that I'm not often reminded of what typically developing children are like." Indeed, it was remarkable to note how much of Carissa's behavior was really age appropriate when viewed in the context of peers without disabilities. For example, when Carissa at age 3 was undergoing a standardized assessment, one task was to stack 10 1-inch wooden blocks. Unfortunately, she could stack only five, supposedly another indication of her disability. The classroom teacher, however, decided to test all of the children, and the most that any child could stack was six.

This was the first time that Carissa had been required to undergo standardized testing, and it was clear that these tests rated her performance much lower than did the criterion-referenced tests that she had undergone in previous years. To anyone who knew Carissa well, the tests clearly underrated her abilities. Ruth insisted on having the same criterion-referenced tests from previous years administered again and on having the scores recorded in the permanent records.

Carissa's family could not praise her private preschool teachers enough. They were always eager to have more professional training in working with children with disabilities; for example, they both enrolled in the sign language class that was sponsored by the church. Ruth observed that their love, care, and knowledge of children in general far superseded any perceived deficits in their ability to teach Carissa.

After Carissa's successful inclusion in her church-based preschool, there could be no turning back for the Coates family. By the time her de facto placement in the 4-year-old class was confirmed in the family's negotiations with the school district, it was time to start planning for kindergarten placement in the upcoming year. This time, Ruth's strategy was very direct. She explained,

> I kept abreast of the time for registering kindergartners, and I walked in off the street and registered her just like any other child, although I did let them know that she already had a student ID number. And I just told them, "Her records are maintained by 'XYZ' special center." The secretary politely took my forms. Part of the strategy was that, for our family's needs, I needed Carissa to be in the morning kindergarten session. This was a popular school, and I didn't want to miss the morning slot.

As the negotiations began, the district's placement recommendation was, as expected, a special center; Ruth's was Carissa's neighborhood school, which was a magnet school for communication and academics. The decision was delayed pending the outcome of assessments, and during the summer, Ruth continued her (by then) customary practice of having private assessments of Carissa performed, one by an educational diagnostician and one by a psychologist. Strategically, she believed that it was important to have an "independent" documentation of Carissa's performance levels to minimize the potential for biases and to maximize parental input. Ruth gave an account of an incident that happened during one of the testing sessions:

> From the observation room, I saw that the evaluator had two identical sets of patterned squares, one for her and one for Carissa. She arranged her squares into a pattern and told Carissa, "Make yours like mine." Carissa looked at the evaluator's set, then proceeded to form her own pattern. She compared the two sets and immediately reached over and changed the evaluator's set to match hers! The look on the evaluator's face was priceless—sheer perplexity and amazement—and she quickly moved on to the next task. I just couldn't contain my laughter. That's my daughter!

Ruth was very happy with the positive light in which the private reports were written. The following excerpts illustrate:

. . . This also suggests that [Carissa's] score is an underestimate of her true abilities in this area. . . .

. . . This is related to her very concrete thinking and difficulty with more abstract thought processes . . . and the use of Total Communication is essential in helping Carissa improve in her understanding of abstract concepts. . . .

. . . Her performance on the cognitive test should be interpreted in light of her social skills, which are within normal limits. . . .

. . . She does not evidence any perseverative behaviors or other behaviors that would interfere significantly with her functioning in the regular classroom. . . .

The placement meeting was held in August. The school district team reviewed all of the assessments and reports and then constructed IEP goals based on the mounds of data. Ruth sensed that the air surrounding this meeting was not as tense as on previous occasions and suspected that perhaps this would not be an adversarial meeting. She was correct. The placement recommendation was for the school that she wanted!

Ruth believed strongly that a placement in an inclusive environment held more value for Carissa than an environment with atypical developmental behavior models and stereotypical expectations from the providers. The child care providers had set no predetermined expectations for Carissa, so she rose to her highest heights. Her kindergarten year, however, was by no means so effective.

CARISSA'S KINDERGARTEN YEAR

During kindergarten, Carissa was fully included in her neighborhood public school. There were advantages and disadvantages. Ruth was very much aware that some of the staff at this school (which was relatively new) had not previously had a student with Carissa's degree of developmental delays. In retrospect, Ruth noted that in-service training for the staff and more preplanning would have been beneficial. As it was, staff's expectations of Carissa's performance were mixed. Ruth attempted to help in this area by providing them with a one-page profile of Carissa and her strengths, interests, challenges, and effective strategies for working with her. No one ever made reference to this list during the entire school year.

Several meetings were held throughout the year. Early on, it was discovered that the IEP, which had been written by the team from the previous school year, needed extensive revision—for example, to include academic goals.

The Coates family had decided that during the afternoon Carissa would attend the school that their family church had recently opened. This was also to be John's first year there, as a sixth grader. Their church family had always been so close and supportive that there was little doubt that this was the best place for both children. Of greatest importance to the family is the teaching of the faith and values that they share, incorporated with academics and discipline. The pastor and his wife, school staff, and church members are one big family. Everyone chips in whatever they can to help, and everyone benefits. They often said, "When we look at Carissa, we don't see Down syndrome; we just see a child."

Both children did extremely well. Carissa amassed a considerable sight- and phonetic-based reading vocabulary and could read a number of sentences. She easily adapted to phonics and reading because she had already been exposed to the alphabet for 3 years! Perhaps one of Ruth's tenets from Carissa's infancy had merits: "If it's going to take her longer, we need to start earlier."

Carissa's public school experience contrasted sharply with this. Ruth could see that the arrangement was foreign to the school personnel and that their expectations of Carissa were not consistent. Carissa picked up on this and performed and complied more for some providers and basically ignored others. Ruth stated,

> Each provider gave a review of Carissa's performance, and I could easily see the parallel between the provider and Carissa's reported performance level. Her instructional aide said, "Carissa can do more than she lets on. I'll tell her to do something, and she'll just stare at me. Then I'll say, 'Come on, I know you can do it,' and she'll roll her eyes at me, then smile and do it. . . . She talks to me all the time, and I can understand her now much better than at first. Some things she says are very clear." Another provider said, "She seldom talks to me, and when she does, I can't understand her."

Ruth was very frustrated by the low report card rating that Carissa received for the objective "uses correct vocabulary for everyday objects." Ruth explained that she knew that Carissa does identify the objects, but the low rating was given because the staff person "couldn't understand her when she talks." As Ruth pointed out, the category was intended to address Carissa's knowledge, not her intelligibility, articulation, or the staff member's comprehension level! Nothing that Ruth said got this rating changed.

Carissa showed growth and maturity, learned new skills, and demonstrated great potential. From Ruth's perspective, it was a good year, and the afternoon schooling that Carissa received far overshadowed other difficulties. Ruth brought to the attention of the public school the successes that Carissa was achieving in her afternoon school but seemingly to no avail. Finally, at the end of the school year, the multidisciplinary team (which, as Ruth pointed out, in practice did not include her as a member) recommended that Carissa be placed in a school with a diagnostic wing, with some opportunity for mainstreaming. This would not be her neighborhood school. This came as a shock to Ruth, as the idea of such a total change had never been raised during the school year. The team expressed the opinion that Carissa's needs and goals could best be achieved at the other location. Ruth believed that they recommended what most of them professionally believed was most appropriate and best for Carissa. However, Ruth saw this as the same system's mentality that says, "We have a place that is best for people like her"—the same issue with which Ruth had been wrestling for years.

At the last meeting, Ruth admitted,

> I finally lost it and began to cry during the meeting. Up until then, I'd always managed to wait until after the meeting was over! It just seemed impossible for me to get through. My daughter's progress didn't seem to have any impact. I wish just one person would've volunteered an idea regarding supports to keep Carissa in her home school.

The Coates family decided that Carissa would attend her church's school full time, along with her brother, John. The family believed that that was the best environment overall for her. She would be fully included, and, after all, as Ruth said, "That's where she'd be if she didn't have Down syndrome anyway!"

At the end of Carissa's kindergarten year, when we asked Ruth whether she felt as though she had, ultimately, failed in the battle for inclusive public education for Carissa, she replied in her characteristic positive manner:

> The way I've reconciled any feelings of failure that might try to come upon me is by realizing that it's a path, a path that I've been able to make a little wider, a little straighter, for other families. So just as those families before me did what they could and passed the torch and the fire to me, I've done what I could and will pass it on to others. It's a process, not an event.

REFLECTIONS ON ADVOCACY

Inevitably, Ruth is full of reflections on the process in which she has been so fully immersed since Carissa's birth. Essentially, she sees the special education system in the county as resistant to change and not reflective of the spirit of the laws on disability. She described the irony of this in the following way:

> This county has been provided, well, the state has been a birth mandate state for a long time—years—even before the law that went into effect. So that certain services were provided to children. This county, of course, has a nice system, so this has been going on for years and years. Now federal law has come in and they just messed up everything! We had to change, and it's hard for systems that have become so institutionalized to change, and that's what we find ourselves in right now.

She pointed out that the interpretation of the law and the services offered differ from county to county, although the needs and strengths of the child remain the same. The services that are offered are based on what is available in a particular county or geographical area rather than on the child's needs:

> I can move from provider to provider, from state to state, from county to county, from school to school. The only thing that is consistent is Carissa because I'm going to get a lot of feedback from a lot of people with different opinions, and a lot of those different opinions are going to be based on what's available [laughter].

Ruth believed that this was reflected in the way in which annual review meetings were conducted. While she tried to focus on Carissa and her individual characteristics, she believed that people who worked for the system were keen on following the correct protocol and simply advocated for programs that were offered in that geographical area. As she said,

> I looked at Carissa's strengths. The thing about it that was very disturbing was there was a lot of talk about system and what we provide and what our program is, but there wasn't a lot of talk about Carissa and what would be appropriate for her. I would try to steer the conversation to her particular strengths or areas that needed to be strengthened . . . and why a placement would facilitate her achieving those goals. The conversation was, nevertheless, "We have this program. . . . Okay, now we want to superimpose our program on top of what we're saying." Instead of constructing the program keeping these things in mind.
> From a system's perspective, it is the resources. Funding is very, very difficult in the system environment. Legally, the funding issue is something different, the services are supposed to be provided etc., etc. But the truth of it is, I feel the brunt of the resource issue. You have to be interactive to stay at the better end of it.

Despite her frustration with the special education system, Ruth readily acknowledged the services of individual providers. She be-

lieved that they were often the victims of the system for which they
worked. Furthermore, some providers individually expressed support for Ruth's mission, saying,

> "Off the record, I really admire what you are doing. . . . " Most of
> them, I think, just go from day to day doing the absolute best that they
> can. . . . And, really, the majority have really loved Carissa. I don't
> think she gave them much choice. . . . In my dealings with establishing
> the vision we have for Carissa, I say they are very special people, too,
> because I think . . . , this is what they do for a living. So I do have a lot
> of admiration and respect for them.

Overall, Ruth's greatest concern is that the "specialist" orientation of special education has contributed to the absence of a holistic
view of children. The lack of a holistic perspective motivated Ruth
to make a deliberate attempt to educate professionals, challenge
their prejudices, and share information with them. She described
her role as similar to a service coordinator who acts as an advocate
for the child and the family. As she said,

> You know, a piece over here, a piece over there. . . . What marked those
> early days of Carissa's life and has sort of been pretty much an under-
> current throughout her life was dealing with so many specialists and
> me eventually taking the role of saying—all these people aren't talking
> to each other, this person isn't concerned with this part of her. You
> know, I'm at least going to give them information. So I had this little
> mission or game that I played: I was gonna at least do what I can to say
> things, to ask questions, get information from all these different spe-
> cialists to try and maybe get them to think outside the box—outside the
> box of their own particular specialty. So . . . it was her primary physi-
> cian, and we had to see a nutritionist because she was hyper caloric for
> a while, early on. And because of her heart . . . there was a cardiologist,
> and an endocrinologist came in after surgery, and then there was her
> early intervention team—the physical therapist, the special instructor.
> And it was just all these pieces, and I realized, when we talk about ser-
> vice coordination, I realized that the parent is pretty much the service
> coordinator in terms of bridging all of these gaps, making sure people
> talk to each other or talk through me to each other.

Ruth's own view of the school system could be described as
holistic in the sense that she is very aware of the interrelationships
among the various strands of discrimination that have been a part of
the educational history of the United States. Ruth pointed out that
Carissa is an African American girl with special needs in a society
with a history of discrimination based on race, gender, and disability. She believes that attempts to keep children with disabilities in
segregated environments indicates the system's resistance to
changes that will provide equal opportunities to all children. She

said, "You know, we talk about how we no longer discriminate in this country based on sex, race, handicap, sexual preferences. So why do we have institutions that perpetuate that type of thing?" Ruth's comment on the nature of the communication process that exists between providers and parents suggests that the process, at worst, can be a farce:

> We talked about her scores. We talked about her goals. And we talked about a program. Then we talked about the placement. The placement happened to be the only place they have [laughter]. The program happened to be the standard program they offered. It was, "Why? Why did we go through this?"

Ruth believed that these parent–provider conferences could be a meaningful exercise when the two perspectives are combined, such that providers draw from her knowledge and hopes for Carissa while also contributing their knowledge of children in general to design a learning environment for the individual child:

> When we sit down, I am looking at using the best of your skill and education and drawing from that. And you drawing from my vision and my perception. So that logistically we work together to come up with what's best for the child.

Ruth said that she sometimes felt that she was being accused of refusing to recognize that her daughter has a disability because she was seeking inclusive education for her. She described this as

> A very frustrating process. All very unnecessary. It was demeaning in some ways. You really have to be strong and know what you are doing and have confidence that you're doing the right thing. Because there are times when as a parent your competency has run into question. . . . You know. And occasionally I get accused of being in denial, that I don't realize that this girl has disabilities, that's what they say, she doesn't realize so why make a big deal. But it's . . . our focus is more . . . enabling her, you know, and supporting her, and I don't think anyone could be in denial. When I see her with 11 other children around her age, I get a real good picture of what the similarities and differences are, I mean, I can't deny when it's staring me right in the face, how could I be in denial?

By contrast, however, Ruth also met professionals who admired and supported her role as an advocate for inclusion, and she soon found herself in a chain of events that opened the way for advocacy activities way beyond the personal realm. During one of the medical procedures, Ruth met with a faculty member in the child development program at a local university hospital, who asked Ruth whether she would like to participate in a conference hosted by the university. Ruth ended up as a panelist along with other parents speaking to an audience of more than 500 people. After the presentation, an executive staff member of the disability council told her about the council. At the initial meeting with this council, one of the members turned out to be a member of the county branch of The Arc. In this way, Ruth developed an extensive network of parents, professionals, and university professors who have supported and spurred her role as an advocate.

Perhaps the most far-reaching professional relationship that Ruth developed throughout her years of learning about Carissa was with Dr. Phenius P.D. Vincent Buyck, Sr., the Governor and Founder of the National College of Complementary Medicine and Sciences, Inc., in Washington, D.C. The Coates family had been searching for a cure for Carissa's sudden onset of alopecia, as well as for preventive nutritional support for the list of common yet often serious health complications that reportedly plague people with Down syndrome. Ruth told us that Dr. Buyck (pronounced "bike") was the first medical professional whom they had met who offered a truly interrelated rather than fragmented view of all aspects of Carissa's health and well-being. "Amazing!" she exclaimed. "What a joy!" Dr. Buyck speaks of the power of "vision," which he says is

> The crux upon which the axis of inspiration, enlightenment, and deliberation spins. Carissa represents this kind of vision, inspiration, and enlightenment and will force humanity to such a deliberation. Her breaking out of the typical mold, her successes beyond her conventional science forecast will prove the manifestation of such a vision as she accomplishes and achieves far beyond the doom and gloom that has been predicted for her life and for the life of her loved ones.

Ruth concedes that many of the connections that she has made as a result of being Carissa's mother have flowered as a result of her own educational background. As a graduate in sociology, psychology, and education, Ruth had been a youthful idealist who believed that she needed to change the world in which she lived. She told us, laughing, "I was going to be one of the ones who was going to make this great change in our society. Then I got out there and couldn't find a job." Later, she completed her master's degree in business administration while in a corporate job. Her training as a young business executive helped her to develop both presentation and interpersonal skills. Acknowledging the role of her education in her growth as an advocate for her child, she said, "It has empowered me to do what I need to do."

Ruth believes that she has learned a great deal from other parents who have been through the system. She constantly acknowledges how much she has learned from their experiences and their mistakes and looks up to them as her mentors:

> I sit and read the law and interpret it and talk to different people, parents, about what their experiences have been. Some of my mentors, my very best mentors, are actually parents who have done it before, and I ask them, "If you had to do it all over again, what would you do differently?"

Ruth described herself as "150%" an advocate for her daughter. However, her advocacy activities for others have been widely spread through her role as a member of the Board of Directors for The Arc, of the local and state Interagency Coordinating Council (ICC), and of the State Disabilities Council. In addition, she has been an active member of Parents of children with Down Syndrome (PODS) and was the editor of their newsletter. She is also very active in her church.

As a result of these activities, parents frequently consulted Ruth when making important decisions about their children. For example, Alexandra and Addison, parents of another child described in this book (see Chapter 7), acknowledged Ruth's contribution when trying to negotiate services that required collaboration between two counties. Ruth and Alexandra had strategized for hours on the telephone, and their goals were achieved.

Working with other parents was a very rewarding experience for Ruth. With characteristic enthusiasm, she exclaimed,

> It's great! I love it! We cry together, we laugh together. It's wonderful. The last thing I told her was, "Just remember when you go into the meeting, they are overworked, underpaid, disillusioned bureaucrats. You are a mother with a vision, on a mission. Go for it!"

VISIONS OF THE FUTURE

In writing the final section of the Coates family's story, we went back to the family and asked each member to offer his or her personal vision for Carissa. They were as follows:

James, Jr.:   She's been a bright light to the family . . . always happy. If someone is sad or depressed, she doesn't have to try to cheer them up. Just her being herself makes them feel better. I hope we get to the place where she doesn't have to prove herself. That she'll be able to get a job and not get turned down just because she has Down syndrome.

John: It's fun when I take care of her during the day while my parents aren't here. I hope she learns to read more, and I hope she matures.

Ruth: As a little girl, I daydreamed about having a daughter one day and all the "mother–daughter" things we'd do together. For a brief instant after her birth, it seemed that those dreams would never materialize. Then I quickly realized that the most important thing was for her to breathe and live and that nothing would be more difficult to overcome and achieve if she could win that initial battle for her very life. Well, she did, and there isn't! Although in one sense I can see Carissa owning her own business and working to help others because of her displays of unconditional love and empathy. And also I know that she is fearfully and wonderfully made in the image of God. I want for her, as well as for all of us, to fulfill His plan for her life.

James, Sr.:   Originally, I wanted a third son. But Carissa came, and I haven't regretted one moment. She has added to the family, not diminished or taken away from it. She has been a blessing to us. For the future, I hope her mother and I can be here to help her to advance, but if we can't, her brothers will. I don't want to change her from who she is, but I want the perception of the general public to change. I'd rather change the public than change her.

APPLYING THE POSTURE OF CULTURAL RECIPROCITY

1. *The impact of specialized services:* To the professionals in this story, Carissa was a person with a disability. As such, it was important for them to assess her current levels of functioning to establish a baseline for their intervention and then determine which intervention and placement would be the most appropriate to achieve the goals that they set for her. Essentially, we believe that the process of professional specialization goes something like this: First, we view the individual in terms of the disability, then we view the disability in terms of its component parts, then we view the component parts in terms of deficits to be remediated.

From Ruth's point of view, the vision of the whole person becomes lost in this process. Her vision of Carissa and other children like her was based on a holistic view that included all aspects of the child's identity—gender, race, abilities, and limitations. From Ruth's perspective, Carissa could not be quantified into a disability that needed a specific number of hours of therapy per week in a special education environment. Although she might have needed special help, she needed to receive it in the context of her typically developing peers who would provide her with appropriate models for the development of all aspects of herself.

What is your view of specialization in special education? How does your training fit with Ruth's view of a holistic education for her child?

2. *Parental versus school personnel's views of inclusion:* We believe that the central values underlying Ruth's philosophy of inclusion are her beliefs in equity and individualism. These beliefs are also held by U.S. society as a whole and by the special education system, yet Ruth's goals come into conflict with those of the school system. Why is this?

Using your personal identity web (see Figure 3 on p. 9), examine the sources of your own beliefs on this issue. Then, imagine that you are one of the service providers in this story. Examine what your attitude would be in working with Ruth and how persuasive you might find her convictions. Outline how you might go through the process of cultural reciprocity in working with Ruth.

3. *Parental versus professional "visions":* Ruth emphasized that everything that she did on Carissa's behalf was guided by a vision of the kind of life that she wanted her child to have. If you were working with Carissa, do you think that you would have a long-term vision for her? Do you think that it would be very different from her family's? How can professionals respond to the fact that parental perspectives are guided by a "vision" of what they want for their child?

4. *Parents versus service providers and the assessment/placement process:* Ruth described herself as being like "an athlete in training" as she prepared for Carissa's annual review conference. How does this compare with how service providers prepare for such conferences and with their feelings about them? What could be done to bridge the gap between the way parents and providers perceive and experience the entire assessment and placement process and the conferences that mark this process?

3

Maldon

"He Can Do It!"

Maldon

In this case study, a Trinidadian American family concludes that their move to the United States was very beneficial to their son, once the family learned the ropes of advocating within the education system. Described as having mental retardation with some features of autism, this young man's strengths compete with his disabilities as he challenges service providers' and family members' views of his growing independence and cognitive potential.

During my first interview with Myrnell and Steve Chappin, they expressed the following views of their son Maldon:

Myrnell: I have my fears because I always think of the fact that the other kids will make fun of him. That's my fear, my big fear. Because there's so many unkind kids, who just don't understand. . . . It's not that I blame them. It's just that they're not educated enough to understand, although I don't think he cares if they make fun of him. I don't know if he understands that. But otherwise, I'm glad that [the school and your project are] including him because in the world he can't communicate, only with special education people. . . . You know what I mean. But I'm afraid that they would do things to him to make his spirit go out of him and I wouldn't be there to shelter him. So that's just my big fear.

Steve: I think the opposite. . . . I think that he should go out there. Go out there and take his chances.

Myrnell: It's not that I don't think he should go either, but it's just that's my fear. . . . This is how Steve is about his boys.

Beth: You're not fearful, Steve?

Steve: No, they can only make fun of you. When you're normal, they make fun of you. If you're abnormal, they make fun of you . . . anybody can make fun of you. Somebody will see you and say something to you—an unkind word, maybe—so I think he should be out there, and take it in his stride . . . and maybe he'll learn something. You learn more that way. Because, Maldon, to me, he's no fool! He's collected, he's smart, he knows his limitations. He knows danger when he sees danger . . . to an extent, that is. I mean, I wouldn't put him in a situation where someone could harm him. But I feel that, generally, he can take care of himself. . . . He can do it!

Myrnell: He thinks I shelter them a bit too much.

Steve: I think it's just her motherly instinct, actually, to shelter him. To shelter all of them.

REUNITING WITH THE
CHAPPIN FAMILY: A SMALL WORLD

The first day of field work on this project told me that there would be something special about this work. Upon visiting a high school class to identify some students for the project, I entered a classroom of about eight students and a handsome, young Black man, about 6 feet 2 inches tall, in a purple sweatshirt and black-rimmed glasses, caught my eye. Sitting at his desk and engrossed in his work, his serious demeanor did not invite interruption.

I asked the teacher who he was, and she replied that his name was Maldon and that she thought that his family might be interested in the project. On returning to the faculty office, the teacher and I went over the list of students about whom we had talked, and I was immediately struck by the name Curtis Maldon Chappin. In great excitement, I told the teacher that I had taught a student in Trinidad by the name of Curtis Chappin. At that moment, I realized that the serious young man to whom she had referred as Maldon was none other than little Curtis, whom I had taught for approximately 4 years in my small, private school in Trinidad. I had had no idea that the Chappin family were in the United States, much less that he was going to school not more than 5 miles from my office.

I hurried into the hall just as Curtis (I would soon learn to call him Maldon) was coming out of his classroom, and I immediately recognized, looking at me from his erect, 6-foot-2 frame, the grown-up face of little Curtis, whom I had not seen in 8 years. I ran up to him and exclaimed, "Curtis! It's Beth! Do you remember me?" He stared at me for a few seconds and said, "Beth! Trinidad! Immortelle Center!" We shook hands vigorously as I asked him a rapid string of questions: How long had he been here? How were his mom, dad, and older brother, Sean? Had he been back to Trinidad recently? Curtis's answers to my questions were characteristic, though much advanced of the child whom I remembered—brief and correct when required to be factual but seeming somewhat disconnected when more complex.

I sent our project's formal invitation letter home to Myrnell and Steve Chappin on university letterhead but with a handwritten note at the end. A couple of days later, Curtis's mother called in response to my letter about the project: "Beth, it's Myrnell! Is this really you? I can't believe it!" Under these unexpected circumstances, we began our work with Curtis Maldon, then almost 16, who had quite recently decided that everyone should call him by his middle name.

The family owned a small, single-family house with a huge backyard, in a suburban area approximately 10 minutes from the university. Since our time in Trinidad, they had had another son, Kwesi, who was then 8 and doing very well in school. Steve and Myrnell were particularly proud of their oldest boy, Sean, who, in the next year, received a scholarship to Yale University. They were proud, too, of Maldon, who, both his parents agreed, was "the most reliable of the bunch."

MALDON

Maldon's good looks, posture, and excellent social behavior made him a young man of whom any parent would be proud. One of the most frequent comments that his parents received about Maldon was regarding his good manners. For example, he was very particular about introductions. When we visited his school or jobsite, he stopped whatever he was doing to introduce us, saying, simply, "Miss ____, This is my friend Beth. Beth, this is Miss ____." Some features of his manners were notably Caribbean, such as using the more traditional formal greeting, "Good afternoon," whereas American youth typically say, "Hi." Maldon's insistence on correct form was not only for strangers but also within his family. For example, on returning home after school, he would call out, "Good afternoon," and would repeat this greeting until someone answered him. His younger brother, Kwesi, told his mother that he "got a break" when he arrived home from school one afternoon and Maldon was not there, so he did not have to be told, "Say, 'Good afternoon,' Kwesi."

Another great strength of Maldon's was his absolute reliability in carrying out any responsibilities assigned to him. At school, at work, and at home, this feature was evident to everyone who knew him. Steve and Myrnell explained to us that all of the children in the family had chores, and Maldon was no exception. His chief responsibility on the weekends was vacuuming the house, except for his parents' room, which he would bypass, saying to his mother, "You do that, Myrnell." He was extremely meticulous in his personal care and household responsibilities, such as keeping his room tidy and either picking up after Kwesi or insisting that Kwesi pick up after himself. His mother summarized life with Maldon as follows:

> Maldon is a joy to live with. He just—he's spontaneous in that you don't have to ask him to do anything for you. If he sees something to be done, he just does it. . . . I never have to scold him, like I do my other so-called normal kids. You know, he just never does—I mean, to have a child and say that he never does anything that deserves scolding is like—but it's true! His brothers ask, "Mummy, how come you never scold Maldon?" But he never does anything for me to scold him. And let's say, if he has a glass and it falls and breaks or something, he's so apologetic, you know, it's like, "I'm sorry. It's my fault." He would not say, "I didn't do it," or accuse someone else. He owns up to it. So he's just a joy! His whole life style. I haven't had a sad moment with him. All my moments with him have been happy!

His reliability, his strong preference for an accustomed routine, and his tendency to be a "loner" were the main features that led his father to have such faith in Maldon's ability to cope with the world. In Steve's words,

You only have to step aside from Maldon and watch how he takes care of himself. . . . See if someone asks him a question, see how he responds. . . . Because he's no fool! You know what I mean. He is not someone to just carry on a conversation with anyone. If you or someone comes to him and asks a question, he'll give you an abrupt answer and go on his way. He's not going to stop and get into a one-on-one conversation with you . . . and that's a protection for him.

Myrnell readily acknowledged that although she was the one to do all of the "school stuff" for Maldon, Steve was the one with whom Maldon identified most and wanted to do things. Their descriptions of their respective roles were amusing:

Steve: Maldon brings his homework lessons to her. If, by chance, I happen to be around, or if he asks me to sign it, I sign her name!

Myrnell: Yes! Steve signs my name. . . ! You know, since he was the one who was out and I would be looking after them. But Steve is Maldon's favorite. If I'm going somewhere and ask him if he wants to go, he'll say, "Is Steve coming?" And if not, he won't bother to go.

This couple's easy acknowledgment of each other's different approaches to their children was a frequent point of comfortable humor in our interviews and also revealed a lot about Maldon's skills and level of independence. A story about deciding when Kwesi could cross the street by himself illustrates the pattern nicely:

Steve: When we first came to this neighborhood, Kwesi had to cross the street to go for the bus. Now, Maldon could already do that. So it ended up Maldon would be the one to cross Kwesi over. . . . But really, the instructions were that *I* should do it! [Laughter.]

Myrnell: The thing was—I had to go to work at 7 A.M., and Steve had to go at night. So I left instructions at home that Steve should take Kwesi across the street. But what Steve did was to tell Maldon to take Kwesi across [laughter]. . . . Because he felt that if Maldon was here, why should he take Kwesi! So he made Maldon do it. Then afterwards, Maldon's times changed so, again, I told Steve that Maldon's bus was coming earlier so now Steve would have to take Kwesi across the street. So I told him to take him but, again, what he did was to teach Kwesi to cross by himself!

All of Maldon's strengths, plus his normal motor development, combine to mask his disability, making it very likely that strangers would be surprised when they began a conversation or activity with him. Indeed, it is in communication and in his learning style that his disability becomes apparent. As a child, at our school in Trinidad, Maldon's earliest communication pattern tended to be echolalic (echoing what was said to him), and I remember well the first time that I was convinced that he was also capable of using communication more creatively, as in anticipating an event. One day, he was standing on the edge of a group of playing children, and one boy was about to throw something at another boy named David. To our great surprise, Maldon called out urgently, "David!" and David turned in response, avoiding the hurtling object.

At 16, Maldon's early echolalia was gone and he could carry on a conversation very appropriately, although he tended to use unusual phrasing and sometimes appeared to go off on disconnected tangents. The question of how tangential his speech really was, however, was always of great interest to us, as we noted that his apparent "tangents" were usually spin-offs from some part of a conversation that he had decided to pursue but that others in the conversation had seen as peripheral to the main topic. It was truly challenging to understand to what extent Maldon's difficulties were with receptive or expressive language. Everyone who worked with him had to be prepared to assume that it could be either—in other words, that he had understood what had been said but could not produce the appropriate reply or that he really had not understood what had been said. The approach that seemed to work best was to appeal to his strong visual skills. When a task was demonstrated for Maldon, he usually could follow it very well, but following verbal instructions was very difficult for him.

Another of Maldon's abilities that masked his disability was reading, which was estimated, when we met him for this project, at about a third-grade level. From approximately the age of 6, Maldon had begun to use both sight and analytical strategies to recognize words, although his comprehension was far below his ability to decode. The difficulty in spotting Maldon's disability was dramatically evident when the Chappins first arrived in the United States. Because of his disability, Maldon was not allowed to enter the United States until he received clearance from the Centers for Disease Control and Prevention in Atlanta, Georgia. Steve had come to the United States first, then Myrnell with Sean and Kwesi, but she had had to leave Maldon behind, pending permission from Atlanta. All of the appropriate documentation had to be sent to Atlanta, through the school district's Office for International Students. But then, strangely, when Maldon did get his clearance and joined his parents a month later, the school district placed him in a general seventh-grade class, although his parents explained that he needed a special education program. As they explained,

> We submitted the documents to the International Students Office— papers showing that he was going to need a special school, and they in turn would select a school for him. . . . But they still placed him according to his age, not by his special needs. Although they had all these papers . . . they didn't act on them at all . . . even though we had had to leave him in Trinidad because of the fact that he was special and we needed special permission to bring him over. We told the teachers that he needed to go to a special school, but they really didn't take us on because they wanted to see for themselves.
>
> So when he started going, the teachers themselves realized that he was not advanced enough for his age . . . so we had a counselor who came to see us, and then they referred him to a psychologist to assess him. So she did, and she said she was sorry that he had not gotten the services from the start. She wanted to get him in a special school as soon as possible. She was the one who even suggested that if we wanted to keep him home for a while until he got into a special education school . . . but we decided that we couldn't because of nobody being available to stay home with him. Also, if we had him going to the school, they would realize that they would have to get him out. It would be better for him to keep going and to be "in their face," so to speak. If you take away the problem for them, they would not want to address it.

This strategy proved effective, and the school district soon placed Maldon in what the family agreed was a very appropriate setting for him—the least restrictive environment (LRE) program in the neighborhood middle school.

SETTING GOALS FOR MALDON

Collaborating with Myrnell and Steve in setting goals for Maldon was very easy because their clear view of his skills provided us with a lot on which to build. Increasing Maldon's employment opportunities and work skills was at the top of the list for both parents, whereas socialization was secondary. Both areas, however, required some careful thought as to what would be most appropriate, given Maldon's existing skills and personality.

Job Opportunities and Training

With regard to work, Steve and Myrnell were very clear that they wanted to maximize Maldon's strengths, particularly his abilities in fine motor skills, reading, and visual learning. Furthermore, Myrnell's fears for her son did not deter her from responding fully to the more independent thrust that we hoped to establish for Maldon, instead of the enclave type of arrangement in which he had been placed in the previous year at school.

In the first summer of the project, our initiative in this direction worked out very well: The director of the university sign shop agreed to take him on, and during that 6-week placement Maldon proved his skills well beyond our expectations. He was taught two main tasks, the first of which was to use a manual engraving machine to make signs of the sort that would be placed in a window or on someone's desk. He started by making his own "Maldon" sign and graduated, within a couple of days, to signs such as "No salesperson without prior approval." The sign-engraving machine required Maldon to work a combination of controls simultaneously, including a foot pedal, a stylus, and a cutting blade. Mike, the director, explained that this was an old-fashioned machine that soon would be obsolete, but we believed that the practice of doing that kind of manual skill was useful for Maldon anyway. Mike further explained that soon everything would be done on a computer, and we discussed the possibility of Maldon's being able to learn the computerized tasks at a later date. Maldon's second task was to finish signs by "weeding" off the background vinyl strips. He learned this quickly also, and, within 2 weeks, he was able to do both of his tasks independently, with his project job coach, Pat, acting as an occasional observer only. His boss and co-workers described him as "doing a great job—absolutely no problem!" In fact, his only difficulties arose from the same source as his reliability—his need for a routine and for perfection. For example, he was very punctual but would become flustered if he came in and found that the time clock had been moved to a different place. Also, the only problem that he really had in completing his tasks was in weeding the vinyl; he spent unnecessary time trying to fix rips in the vinyl strips that were going to be discarded anyway.

In the next summer, the project arranged a totally different type of job for Maldon—as a "counselor in training" (CIT) at the University Arts Center's summer day camp. We did not really expect Maldon to function in a "counseling" capacity, owing to his difficulties with communication, but the director was enthusiastic about teaching him to use a camera and having him do most of the photographing of camp activities for the camp's display. Maldon's visual and fine motor skills served him well in this, and he quickly learned in one lesson how to load an Instamatic camera and take pictures. The most challenging part was when he graduated to a more sophisticated camera and had to learn to focus the lens. He was also introduced to the developing of film in the darkroom, but Moni's observations of these sessions suggested that the instruction offered was too unstructured for Maldon really to benefit. She believed that with more appropriate instruction, he could have learned to do it independently.

When he was not being the cameraman, Maldon participated in a variety of the camp activities, including playing kickball, for which he knew the rules and could play quite well, and swimming, which was his favorite. He generally got along well with the children, and we noted that it was important for them to be told that he had difficulties with communication because these 6- to 10-year-olds were old enough to recognize his limitations in that area.

At the end of the summer, the camp held a closing celebration to which parents were invited, and Maldon put together a very attractive scrapbook of all of his photographs, including his own comments handwritten under each picture. This was included in the camp's displays, and, among the other closing ceremonies, Moni was invited to say a few words to the parents about our project. Moni introduced Maldon, intending to say only briefly that he was a high school student who had been learning photography at the camp. But Maldon readily joined in, speaking up for himself and explaining that he had taken many of the photographs, had worked in the darkroom, had been helped by his job coach, and had gone swimming with the kids. Moni's notes indicated that the range of Maldon's participation and learning went well beyond the specific tasks that we had planned for him. She noted,

> The kids got into a circle and did two dances with [the music director] leading the dance. It was an African dance, and then they sang two African songs. When the songs were announced, Maldon walked up and stood with the kids. . . . He sang both the songs. He knew the words and sang in tune. He tapped his foot and shook his head in rhythm with the songs. I was amazed. I had no idea that Maldon could sing. . . . His mother came later, and when I told her [about his participation], she was equally surprised and asked him if he really knew the words. He said, "Yes, I know the words." I asked for permission to show Myrnell the section of the videotape where Maldon was singing. Myrnell laughed as she watched the tape. (August 12, 1994)

Independent Travel for Maldon Perhaps more of a highlight than his actual job at the children's camp was Maldon's independent travel plan for the second summer. When I introduced the suggestion to Steve and Myrnell, Steve responded with a characteristic, "Sure!" while Myrnell interjected, "Yes, but of course we'll have to walk him through it first." We quickly assured

Myrnell that we would work out a structured plan with Meg, his job coach, who would gradually fade her support. Once this clarification was made, the rest of our conversation was spent with Steve and Myrnell making a series of rapid suggestions for the details of bus routes, the kinds of prompts that Maldon would need to learn the bus numbers and the point at which to get off, and backup plans in case of emergency. They also quickly suggested that they give Sean, then 18 and on summer vacation, the home-to-work end of the travel training because it would have been a long way for the job coach to come to their home so early in the morning. The plan was for Sean to go with Maldon on the bus, which took him directly to the university subway station, where Sean would see him onto the university shuttle, which then took him directly to the campus building where he worked. In the afternoons, Maldon would take the shuttle back to the subway, where his job coach, Meg, would meet him and see him onto the correct bus to return home. After 3 weeks, Maldon was making this entire trip independently, without either Sean or Meg.

The plan worked wonderfully, with the exception of one afternoon, when Maldon took a bus that went in the wrong direction but actually made a full circle back to the correct point. While Meg, Myrnell, and I spent a couple of hours on the telephone to the metro personnel, trying to anticipate where Maldon could be, he, with characteristic good sense, remained on the bus and just kept riding until it came to the correct stop near his house. He arrived home about 2 hours late but safe, sound, and totally unruffled.

One more person who gained confidence in Maldon's skills that summer was Sean, who, after the second day, gave up his job of escorting Maldon to the bus stop. It seemed that by the second day, Maldon was heading off on his own up the incline that led to the bus stop. According to Myrnell,

> I don't think Sean knew what to do with him. Because I think Maldon had gone previously with the job coach, so he knew the way . . . and he always likes to walk in front of people anyway. . . . And then, too, I think that Sean's sleep was being disturbed, because he would say that he was ready, but he wasn't. He wanted to sleep for a while longer. So I had to insist, but then I think the third morning, Sean said, "I'm not going anywhere. Maldon knows where he's going!"

Maldon's third summer job was at the county library, and he and his classmate Silvia (see Chapter 1) were supervised by Faustina for the 6-week period. As it turned out, it was fortunate that we had arranged for Faustina to be a full-time job coach because the library staff did not seem to have given much thought to what Maldon should do, and his first week was spent entirely on cleaning tasks, in particular, cleaning fingerprints off the glass doors. This, of course, could be a never-ending task, and Maldon kept asking why he had to do this over when he had just done it that morning! Fortunately, Faustina intervened and simply set about teaching Maldon the same tasks that Silvia was doing, which included labeling and stamping books and replacing CDs into their appropriate envelopes. Faustina believed that Maldon also could have learned other, more sophisticated tasks, such as placing books in alphabetical order, but the library staff thought this too difficult for him and did not provide much opportunity for him to learn this. The main lesson of that summer was the importance of advocacy for Maldon, a responsibility that, ever since the first year of the project, his mother had become increasingly comfortable in assuming.

Parental Participation and Advocacy   Myrnell's emergence as a powerful advocate for Maldon became a central theme in our research with this family. Very early in the project, I explained to Myrnell how important parental participation was in the planning process, and she replied that, coming from the Caribbean, where there were no special education laws ensuring children's rights or parental participation, she had not been aware of the extent of her rights under U.S. law. Prior to the first annual review conference that we observed, she shared with me some of her concerns about Maldon's current program, and I assured her of her right to present these concerns to the school team. This seemed to be all the encouragement that she needed, and, indeed, Myrnell turned out to be a very "quick study" regarding parental advocacy.

That annual review conference was attended only by the teacher, classroom assistant, Myrnell, and me. As the meeting began, Myrnell asked whether the speech-language pathologist (SLP) would be coming. The teacher explained that she might be late because she was double-booked with another annual review conference. Myrnell expressed her concern with this because she had some specific questions for her: First, she expressed her concern with the speech goals listed on Maldon's individualized education program (IEP) because more than half of the goals specified writing rather than speaking. She said that she had expected speech goals to be related mostly to oral language, such as articulation, syntax, and so forth. Second, she wanted to know more about the evaluation process that had been used by the SLP.

The teacher gave full acknowledgment to Myrnell's concern for the SLP's presence and immediately telephoned her room and asked her to come. This response was met with the SLP's promise to come as soon as she could be excused from the other meeting. The meeting continued, and, when it was about to end and the SLP still had not arrived, the teacher advised Myrnell that she could consider signing the IEP, with a written proviso that her agreement was dependent on her meeting with the SLP. The alternative, the teacher pointed out, was that Myrnell could simply request that the meeting be held again, with the SLP and the worksite coordinator present because transition planning was becoming important for Maldon. Myrnell had just agreed to do the former when the SLP appeared.

As Myrnell explained her concern about oral language, the SLP replied that the intent of the goals was oral but that she also liked to have Maldon write down his sentences, to reinforce them. Myrnell questioned her carefully on this, and then said, "Oh, well, if you're working on speech, then we're really not in disagreement. You're saying what I'm saying, but, by looking at the goals written here, I could never know that, since all that's written here is about writing!" The teacher then suggested that the SLP write in the oral aspects of the goals, which she did. Myrnell was satisfied with this outcome because she believed that having oral goals on the IEP would ensure their actually being addressed.

After that meeting, Myrnell moved more and more confidently into an advocacy role. Maldon's success in the first summer job at the university sign shop marked the beginning of this process. The skills that he revealed that summer made Myrnell determined not to accept a group or enclave type of placement for Maldon ever again! That school year started off with his being placed with a group of students at a department store, but Myrnell wrote a letter to the school telling them that she wanted him to be placed in a situation in which he could learn a skill—not necessarily sign painting—because, as she said, "I wanted him to be exposed to things that he can choose from." Myrnell was advised by the school that the independent jobs were usually reserved for the students who were about to graduate because they were paying jobs and would get the students in line for a job upon graduation. Nevertheless, that fall, Myrnell's letter resulted in Maldon's being given an independent placement in a sign shop run by the county. That job worked very well for Maldon, as he improved on many of the same tasks that he had started to learn in his campus summer job. Unfortunately, the job was terminated before the end of the school year because the sign shop was moved to a distant area of the county to which the school bus would not provide Maldon with transportation. When it was decided that Maldon had to get another placement, Myrnell was disappointed but did not worry too much because, as she told the school personnel, "I don't want him only to do the signs, but a million other things, too!"

Subsequent to this, Maldon was placed in a private printing and engraving store, which did not prove very successful, partly because of the store's unpredictable pace of orders and, Myrnell believed, mainly because private enterprise works on such a profit motive that it is very unlikely that an entrepreneur would take the time to teach someone with Maldon's limitations. Myrnell believed strongly that a less competitive atmosphere, such as the county office or the university job, would always prove more appropriate for Maldon. These perspectives showed Myrnell's understanding of the constraints of a small, private jobsite for Maldon; nevertheless, she also pointed out the importance of adequate monitoring of jobsites by school personnel. For example, as Maldon wrote his homework one night, filling in his answers to questions about what he did at his jobsite, Myrnell noticed that he was consistently writing that he vacuumed or emptied the dumpster. She told me,

> So I was very disturbed, because, I mean . . . there's nothing wrong in emptying trash or doing vacuuming, but he can do that already! He does that at home! And that's not what he went there to do. So I was upset and called the teacher the next day. And I said there's nothing wrong with doing trash, but Maldon went in there to learn a trade, and I was very much disturbed that he's not being given the opportunity to learn a trade. So she was very apologetic and said she didn't know that's what was happening. Maldon is the only child from [his school] that's there, and the teacher is supposed to go there and . . . be a kind of overseer for him, but it seems there wasn't adequate supervision, so the people who were on the job put Maldon to do anything simple. So when the teacher realized that Maldon was coming home and telling me exactly what went on, since then nearly every day, I'm getting notes.

Another aspect of Maldon's program that was problematic to Myrnell was the difficulty of achieving the appropriate balance between academics and job training. She believed that everything should be done to maximize Maldon's potential in both areas. One year, in the annual review meeting, she asked the school team whether, in the next year, they could modify his program to allow him more time in the classroom to work on more academics, in particular his math and comprehension skills. The teacher replied that she was not the one to make that decision and that the only alternative available was for him to go to the shorter day vocational program provided for the class below him, which meant that he would be with younger students.

As the discussion seemed to come to a dead end, Myrnell said, in an even tone of voice, "Well, you said that you don't make that decision on your own, so is there someone else I could talk to? I'd be most willing to do that." The teacher then commented that perhaps a solution was to look at his schedule and see if maybe they could adjust his work hours; for example, if his upcoming summer travel training proved successful, then it might be possible to arrange for him to go to classes in the mornings, then to the job at lunch time, and then straight home after his job, which would save the time taken by one of the bus trips back to school. In the long run, Maldon did continue as before in the vocational program, but it was interesting to note how the insistence of a parent could result in creative thinking about a variety of options.

Over the years, Myrnell often referred to her efforts on Maldon's behalf as a "fight" to get the best for him. Although she believed that he had had good teachers and a good school experience, she concluded that much of what went best for him may not have occurred if she had not been consistently vocal about every concern that arose. As she said,

> The teachers are the ones who really know the system. They're the ones who can guide you. . . . But even with the best teachers, I had to fight for certain things or write to them, actually keep on top of them. But now once they know, I don't think they want me to call so they try to be one step ahead of me.

The only great disappointment of Maldon's school career was a very unfortunate episode at his job placement in his junior year. He had been placed at a grocery store in a large chain and was mostly carrying bags to customers' cars. The first difficulty that he had was in the unpredictability of the social interactions that could occur in doing this apparently simple task; Maldon relied precisely on predetermined types of interactions and routines. So, for example, he would become ruffled when some customers wanted the bags in the trunk, others wanted bags on the car seat, and others even wanted to place some of the bags themselves. He tended to argue with customers who wanted to do other than what he had been taught. Another aspect was some co-workers' concern with Maldon's tendency to talk to himself whenever there was down time. It seems that once these concerns had been raised, Maldon's behavior became a point of focus for certain co-workers, and the person in charge, who had no previous experience with people with special needs, did not address his needs in a proactive way. The crucial concern that arose, however, was one that anyone who knew Maldon would recognize as entirely innocent but that was taken as threatening by a co-worker. A young woman was wearing a very short skirt, and Maldon expressed his curiosity by bending down in an effort to peek under her skirt. This unfortunate episode resulted in the administration's asking Maldon to resign. Everyone who knew Maldon, including his teachers and therapists, knew that there was no ill intent in Maldon's action. Myrnell believed that it would not be appropriate for her to intervene on Maldon's behalf because the school had an arrangement with the store to employ several students and she did not want to endanger the school's relationship with the store. Both Maldon's parents and the school personnel discussed the episode with Maldon, and he has never had another problem of this nature. However, Myrnell believed that the whole episode was particularly sad because it was evident that Maldon did not understand what all the fuss had been about. Myrnell concluded that, in the future, it would be important to be very explicit with Maldon regarding various do's and don'ts in the workplace.

Social Activities

Socialization was our second main goal for Maldon, but, as with all of our students in the project, we soon learned that this goal would have to be defined in a very individualized way and tailored to the particular personality of the child as well as to the cultural style of the family. The main observation made by his parents regarding Maldon's social interests was that he was generally "a loner," who often chose to be on his own rather than to go with the group. On family outings, for example, it was only when his father was going that Maldon would be interested. Similarly, although Maldon always greeted visitors with appropriate good manners, he usually retired to his room quite quickly rather than stay in the group. This tendency was also evident on his jobsites, where Maldon was polite to everyone but always preferred to have his lunch alone, sitting comfortably at a table by himself. He often initiated conversations with his co-workers, however, or spontaneously joined in their conversations.

I asked Steve and Myrnell whether they believed that Maldon's "loner" tendency was natural to him or he actually felt left out or even lonely. They consistently replied that he seemed to prefer this lifestyle and showed no signs of feeling lonely. For example, they explained that one year, there was a classmate who always called him on the telephone; Maldon responded pleasantly to him but showed no interest in returning his calls even when his parents prompted him to. I suggested to them that it might be important for them to watch for any signs of interest in a particular friend because if he did start to develop such an interest, Maldon's general reluctance to initiate conversations might mean that he would never let his parents know. Because of Maldon's limited communication skills, his parents' support would be needed in pursuing personal relationships. We agreed that the most appropriate approach for our project to take would be just to expose him to group activities that he could choose to pursue or not.

School-Based Integration for Maldon

Because Maldon's school placement essentially was a self-contained program, it was up to his teacher to find opportunities for inclusion with general education peers. In the first year of the project, Maldon's teacher had been very proactive in advocating for him to try out for the school's track team. He was accepted on the team, and we were able to observe some of these activities. Maldon ran mostly in relays and at one point competed, quite ably, in the shot put. He turned out to be an able member of the team—as the coach described, "an asset." The only accommodation needed for him in this situation was some extra attention in teaching him the routines of team practices; and once he had learned them, he was fine.

Another inclusive activity was the class's home economics project, in which students from general education were teamed with Maldon's class to be "buddies" in the home economics class. Our observations showed that Maldon was a very sociable young man who did better when his buddies were males because he was always comfortable joining in or even initiating conversations about sports. Maldon knew about all of the key teams and players and would accurately recall the scores of recent games.

Community-Based Activities

In the fall of the second year, we set about trying to find opportunities for social activities for Maldon in the community. Moni, Steve, and Maldon made the initial visit to the closest community center to find out about their activities. Moni's notes indicated an unenthusiastic director, who seemed to condescend to Maldon. They returned that evening, but it turned out that the kids present were watching a movie in a rather small room that did not seem to offer many options for activities.

Also, although Moni could not hear all of the comments that passed between Maldon and the small group of kids, it appeared from the facial expression of one boy that there was some discomfort in the communication as he noticed Maldon's disability. We concluded that it would be challenging deciding how much adult intervention and/or support Maldon would need to allow him to be comfortable in these situations.

One of the staff people at the center told Moni and Steve about a new drop-in program that would soon begin in a nearby mall and said that she would be the director of that program. She was very encouraging about Maldon's participation because it would be a new program and he could join before the kids had already started to form their cliques. A few weeks later, Moni and I met Maldon, his mother, and Kwesi at the new drop-in center, which opened to teenagers in the mall between 6 P.M. and 9 P.M. every evening. The room had a sitting area with magazines and was equipped with a Ping-Pong table, a basket for shooting, a football table game, a television, a VCR, and an organ.

Moni observed Maldon's first evening at the center, and the director agreed to keep an unobtrusive but watchful eye for any assistance that he might need in participating in the group's activities. As was typical for someone meeting Maldon for the first time, however, the director tended to underestimate the amount of assistance that he would need, and Moni recorded the initial tension of the evening as Maldon attempted to join in a game of table football. The director took Maldon over to the group and introduced him, but Moni could not hear what she said. As he joined in, the other boys welcomed him but quickly noticed his lack of understanding of how to play:

> The boy next to him, who was his team member, put his hand on Maldon's hand and showed him in which direction to turn the bar and said, "Turn it like this." But, not understanding the general rules, Maldon continued to make the wrong moves. After a while, his teammates told him, "Come over here," and they changed his place so that his teammate was now defending the goal and Maldon was playing with the forward team members. It seemed to me that the other boys were getting a little frustrated and some tension was building up because the game couldn't go very smoothly as Maldon was not understanding the rules. . . . I felt that at this time I needed to intervene because I could tell the tension was building up because the boys now weren't saying anything. There was a kind of unusual silence. They weren't cheering and arguing like they had been before. So I went to the director and asked her, "Can you please explain the game to Maldon?" I suggested

that she explain to him which goal post he needs to aim the ball at. She said, "Oh, I thought he was doing fine." (December 3, 1993)

After the director gave Maldon some specific instructions, the game went much better and Moni's impression was that the other kids became more comfortable with him. They went on to shoot baskets and then to watch a basketball game on television. Moni's closing comments were as follows:

> From my observation of Maldon in this group, I felt he fit in better here [than at the previous center]. All the boys and girls over here were African American, and they're probably a bit younger than Maldon. For whatever reason, they appear to be more accepting [than at the other community center]. I was wondering if that might be because of the director's introduction, but I'm not sure what it was she said. I also felt it would be a good idea to teach him the games so that he can actually play with his peer group and they don't have to teach it to him, since that kind of adds an extra burden to them. In general, my overall impression was that Maldon enjoyed being there and the other boys were very accepting of him.

However, we did not have time to intervene by teaching Maldon the games, as Moni had planned. The next Friday, Maldon's parents came home to find that Maldon was not at home. Myrnell, characteristically, was ready to dial 911. Steve, however, immediately assumed that Maldon had gone to the community center because they had discussed in front of Maldon the possibility of his walking over to this center, as it was near their home, but never imagined that he would think of going on his own. Myrnell rushed over to the center:

> There was Maldon with a couple of other guys playing the football table game. The director told me he had been there for about half an hour. So I go up to Maldon, and I say, "Maldon, did you come down here by yourself?" He says, "Yes, Myrnell. You go home." But the lady is watching us and I'm feeling stupid, and here it was raining. He had an umbrella and he had his coat, and I said, "Maldon, it's raining." He said, "That's my umbrella over there." So I just left him and that night we had to pick up Sean, so, although I really wanted to stick around, I forced myself to go for Sean and then come back. When I came back, it was about 8:45 P.M., and when I went, he was playing the game "Uno" with about five other kids. (I knew he could play that because I bought this game about two Christmases ago and Maldon actually taught me how to play because he had learned to play at school.) So anyway, I called to him to come. And he was standing with his back to me, and he said, "Okay guys, I'm leaving." And he put down his cards, and he left. So I said to him, "Maldon, you went down there by yourself." And he replied, "Yes, I was supposed to go on a Friday."

We decided that the next goal would be for Maldon to learn to leave a note on the refrigerator, telling his parents that he had gone to the drop-in center. Unfortunately, however, there were not many more opportunities for Maldon to visit the center as Christmas came and Maldon was busy with family events, and early in the new year, we heard that the program had been dropped by the county because of poor attendance. Myrnell believed that the sporadic attendance of the teens reflected the very limited facilities at the center.

We were disappointed in the short-lived nature of this first really independent social opportunity for Maldon. However, we had certainly learned a lot about his ability to make appropriate decisions for himself, which, of course, was totally in line with his father's view of him! Furthermore, we had learned the importance of facilitating his participation by adequate explanation to his peers and adequate instruction to him in the rules or routines of new activities.

Girlfriends   Another aspect of our observations of Maldon's social life was his growing but mildly expressed interest in girls. In one of our earliest conversations with him, Helena asked him whether he had a girlfriend. Maldon replied, "Yes." She asked him her name, and he replied, in a rather mumbling tone, "TJ." As he repeated this, I somehow guessed that TJ referred to the initials of his previous school, and I asked him whether that was correct. He replied, "Yes," and then specified the name of the school. So I said, "Oh, so your girlfriend went to school there, too?" to which he replied, "Yes." When I pressed him further for the girl's name, he gave us a name that Myrnell later confirmed was the name of a former classmate at that school. We were intrigued by Maldon's manner of communicating on this matter. At first, we believed that it was an example of his tendency to respond with a statement about a related matter, just a bit off target of his real meaning. However, another possibility was suggested in a conversation with a friend about this event: He said that, as a young man, if someone asked him the name of his girlfriend, he very likely would avoid being put on the spot and would just mumble something vaguely related to her, such as, "Oh, just someone I go to school with!" We were intrigued with the possibility of this interpretation.

Maldon's parents did not think that he had begun to experience any specific sexual interests but were advised by the family doctor, when Maldon was about 17 and a very healthy 6 feet 4 inches, to start explaining these matters to him. In our first interview, when Maldon was just turning 16, I received typically divergent responses from Steve and Myrnell regarding their expectations for him in this area.

Myrnell:	Well, I don't think that he ever will. But Steve doesn't think that way. . . .
Steve:	I think I look at this more positively. When I say positive, I mean that maybe something will work out for him. This is the way I look at it. . . . It will work out for him in time, and in years to come he's going to develop more. He may not approach some girl, but some girl will approach him.
Myrnell:	What I worry about is that they will take advantage of him.
Steve:	I don't feel so.
Myrnell:	I think somebody is going to take advantage of him.
Steve:	I feel, then, that his abilities will develop or show up. I don't think that people can fool him.
Myrnell:	Well, yes, because he is maturing slowly.
Steve:	People tend to think that because he's special you can tell him something and he's going to run and do it. No, I don't think so.
Myrnell:	That's true, because he knows right from wrong. . . .
Steve:	Yes, and I'm thinking that he is developing. And your mind develops with your body also. So in time to come, he's going to get girlfriends or whatever. . . .
Beth:	So it sounds like, as far as you're concerned, you don't really have any limits in this regard.
Steve:	Right. I think it's a matter of letting him go as far as possible.
Myrnell:	Even here, of course, Steve has always been open.
Beth:	So, Myrnell, what about in a few years if he wants to go on a date or to a prom?
Myrnell:	Oh, that's no problem.

Much of this conversation would resonate in our discussions over the next few years. Steve's expectation that "some girl would approach him" came true only 1 year later, when Myrnell reported that she saw Maldon with a Valentine card, which he was holding behind his back. Asking to see the card, Myrnell noted the name of the girl and learned from Maldon's teacher that this girl frequently dropped by the classroom to say hi to Maldon. Myrnell found this quite disturbing because she believed that someone without a disability who would make advances toward Maldon would probably have some ulterior motive, in some way intending to take advantage of him. To Myrnell's relief, however, this particular relationship did not go any further.

Two years later, upon Maldon's graduation from high school, the same issue arose in the decision about Maldon's date for his senior prom. By this time, the Chappin family had bought a new home in a different area, and Maldon had moved to the LRE program for that neighborhood. The teacher and Myrnell had become very friendly and had shared ideas about many prospects for Maldon, including his plans for the prom. As it turned out, everyone had his or her own ideas about who should be Maldon's date. Maldon told his mother that he had been invited to the prom by a girl who, the teacher reported, was in general education. Myrnell simply ignored this suggestion and thought for a while about a Trinidadian girl whose family she knew well. The teacher, however, suggested a student who was then in her junior year and who also had a disability. She believed that this student, Annie, and her family would be delighted at the invitation. After much discussion, Myrnell and the teacher told Maldon that they would arrange for Annie to be his date. Maldon did not protest, and the adults went ahead with their plans. The occasion turned out quite beautifully; Annie's family arranged an elaborate reception at their home, and Steve and Myrnell provided the couple with transportation to and from the prom. According to Myrnell, it was obvious that Maldon had a great time because, when his parents arrived to take them home, "Everyone was all slumped, and Maldon was on the floor with a burst of energy, still dancing, while his date was sitting at the table, too worn out to move. He didn't stop until the last song had played!"

I asked Steve how he had felt about Myrnell's and the teacher's intervention in the prom plans, and he replied that he did not really object but thought it rather humorous that they had taken the matters totally into their own hands. He believed that this approach was acceptable at this point in Maldon's life but that there soon would come a point when his mother would have to let go of the controls!

VISIONS OF THE FUTURE

Maldon graduated 2 years after the end of our project, and when I visited the Chappins for an update, I learned about the graduation and about Maldon's activities since then. Maldon's teacher had given the family a list of agencies that provide services to young adults with disabilities, and Steve and Myrnell had studied the range of services carefully, looking for the agency that was most likely to treat Maldon as an individual and to build on his skills. They were extremely pleased with the agency that they had chosen, which provided job placement, training, monitoring, and coordination of any other services that he might need. The funding for these services, they said, was guaranteed to Maldon for life. After evaluating Maldon, the agency expressed surprise upon hearing of the problems that he had had with the local grocery chain some years before and decided to approach the same chain again but at a different store. The manager at the store was totally accepting of Maldon and started him off with a part-time placement for 3 hours per day, with the promise of a full-time placement in a few months. We were very gratified to learn that our early efforts at travel training for Maldon had paid off; he had almost immediately mastered the travel plan for his new job and was now traveling independently to work by public transportation.

Myrnell was fully satisfied with the agency's efforts but did express some disappointment with the future outlook for Maldon. As she explained,

> You know that I had really hoped that he would be able to learn a skill of some sort. Something specific that he could get a job with anywhere he goes to live, rather than just a general worker in like a grocery store or that kind of thing. . . . But, I guess there are some good points to this, since it means he would stay with this company and move up gradually and become entitled to benefits and everything. So, I still think he could have done something more in the line of a specific skill, but maybe this is better.

This was not the only vision of Myrnell's that had been altered somewhat. Many years before, we had spoken about the couple's vision of Maldon's future, and it was clear that they both saw different levels of independence for him. Steve had had no trouble envisioning Maldon's living on his own or with a friend and could readily specify most of the areas of self-care in which he expected Maldon to be fully capable. His only area of doubt had been with regard to taking care of money, but he had expressed the belief that arrangements could be made for Maldon's job to pay his salary directly into a bank account and that Maldon could learn to handle money for simple transactions such as routine shopping, transportation expenses, and so forth. Supervision of more complex transactions could, ultimately, be done by a guardian or by the bank.

Myrnell, typically, had been much more cautious. Her vision had been for Maldon to be partially independent but essentially reliant on his parents' support. Her dream, at that time, had been to build an apartment for Maldon in the large backyard of the house in which they then lived. However, in a later interview, her perspective had shifted slightly:

> We won't be around forever. . . . That's why, even with the idea of a group home—although I don't like it—I've been asking questions about it. . . . Because every day he does something new . . . but I actually

don't really like the idea. If I have to, I'll put him in a group home. I don't really like it because to me it's too institutionalized.

When I asked about how they saw the role of Maldon's brothers, Myrnell referred only to Sean, saying,

> Well, he has an older brother, but one never knows where he would go, and I don't want to burden him with Maldon. I ask him, I speak to him about it. I say, "You know, Maldon is special." And he says that he will look after him. He says . . . but one never knows what the future holds.

In our update interview, Myrnell's vision had, once more, shifted somewhat. Their new house, beautifully appointed, in an upper-income neighborhood, had a huge basement that was, as yet, unfinished. According to Steve, Myrnell already had plans for *him* to finish the basement into an apartment for Maldon! Myrnell spoke of the new plan as a compromise: It would be a comfortable and semi-independent situation for Maldon whenever he was ready for it, but she willingly saw it as "possibly, a transitional situation that he could do for a while and then move on to his own thing, if he wants."

One final aspect of Maldon's activities that must be mentioned is his "second job." Over the past 3 years, Steve had started a small janitorial business that he did after his regular job in the evenings to supplement the family's income. The business, they told me, was the chief reason that the family had been able to afford a new home. Maldon played no small part in this: He was a nightly and full-time assistant to his father, with specific cleaning tasks. Steve said, "I never have to tell Maldon what to do or check his work. I know that it's going to be done to perfection. And, you know, of all my helpers [laughing and waving his hand to indicate whoever else might be in the household], he's the only really reliable one!"

Overall, the Chappins were pleased with Maldon's progress and current situation as a young adult. All of the "fighting," the learning of the ropes, and the getting accustomed to a new life had been worth it. In Steve's words, "There would've been no opportunity for him at home [in Trinidad] once he left school. His progress has made it worthwhile coming here!"

Most important, however, is Maldon's own satisfaction with what he has accomplished. He never was a child to tell his parents much of what he was thinking, so Myrnell had long been accustomed to getting information from Maldon's loud self-talk in the evenings, when he often talked to himself about events of the day.

In our update interview, however, his mother's source of information was much more poignant. She told me,

> I think Maldon realizes that he's reached another point in his life. I hear him praying at night, thanking God and telling Him what happened during the day. His grandmother was visiting recently and she heard him, too, and she said, "I didn't know Maldon could pray!"

APPLYING THE POSTURE OF CULTURAL RECIPROCITY

1. *Becoming aware of ethnic and gender-based stereotypes:* Studies of families' use of residential placement for their children with disabilities show that ethnic minority groups tend to retain their children at home more than do Caucasian families. The differences in Steve's and Myrnell's visions of Maldon's future place of residence, however, illustrate that we cannot assume that ethnicity or culture is necessarily the dominant influence in parents' views. We also cannot be sure that the gender of the parent determines the parent's perspective, although Steve and Myrnell tended to see it that way. What would be your own view of an appropriate adult residence for Maldon? Would your view pose a problem for you when developing transition planning with Maldon's family?

2. *Advocacy in work and social situations:* The case study relates a couple of occasions on which intervention by our researcher/advocates proved helpful to Maldon: When Faustina, noticing that Maldon's library job was not challenging enough, stepped in and taught him some other tasks, Maldon became less frustrated about the lack of challenge. Again, when Moni stepped in and asked the director of the drop-in program for teens at the mall to teach Maldon the rules of the game, a potentially unpleasant situation was averted, resulting in the boys' accepting Maldon and everybody's enjoying the game. Do you think that these situations were handled appropriately? Can you suggest some more effective ways of approaching these situations for Maldon?

3. *Independence, work, and socialization:* The value of independence clearly underlies many of the decisions that Steve and Myrnell made for Maldon. Although they both held this value, they had different interpretations of his readiness for various levels of independence. They tended to agree with each other regarding appropriate independence levels for Maldon at work,

but they had some differences regarding his social independence, both at present and in the future.

a. *Independence and work:* As Maldon's success at his first
summer job became evident, Myrnell became convinced of
the importance of Maldon's being given individualized job
placements, as opposed to being placed at jobsites with a
group or an enclave of students or workers with disabilities.
Even though individualized placements were not the norm
in Maldon's high school vocational program, Myrnell insisted and succeeded in getting him individually placed.
What is your response to this? Use your personal identity
web (see Figure 3 on p. 9) to figure out the source of your
agreements or disagreements with her actions.

b. *Independence and freedom of choice:* Myrnell described
herself as a bit overprotective of her children. Steve emphatically agreed, although he seemed to respect this quality as a
part of her natural "motherly instinct." As Maldon matured,
the possibility of sexual interests began to become a reality,
and Myrnell's protectiveness guided her responses to her
son's social development. This became most evident in her
engineering of Maldon's date for his graduation prom. What
is your response to this? Do you believe that freedom of
choice ought to be a guiding principle for Maldon in such a
situation? Use your personal identity web (see Figure 3 on
p. 9) to trace the source of your belief, then imagine that you
are Maldon's teacher and figure out how you would have responded to the situation. If your point of view proved different from Myrnell's, then work out a process of cultural reciprocity with her.

4. *Researcher–participant relationship (researcher role):* My previous relationship with Myrnell and Steve Chappin in Trinidad
provided us with a common core of shared experiences, perceptions, values, and expectations. Culturally, I was very much "in
sync" with the family. Myrnell told us that her emergence as an
advocate with Maldon's teachers was facilitated by our explicit
efforts to increase her awareness of her rights as a parent and,
implicitly, by having someone she trusted with whom to discuss these matters. Through this process, Myrnell was developing the "cultural capital" to work effectively with special education service providers. Consider the following questions:

a. Do you think that the relationship between me and the
Chappins shows up in this case study? Do you think that

there are any ethical concerns about doing research of this nature with a family with whom you already share so much?

b. Do you agree that encouraging and supporting parental advocacy is an appropriate role for a researcher? In which ways does this approach change the nature of traditional research?

4

Maher

"He Is My Heart"

Maher

This Palestinian American family responds with a mixture of faith and practicality to the changing needs of their charming, lovable, frustrating, growing-up son, who has mental retardation. Service providers will be challenged by the family's blend of a strong Moslem tradition with American ways, as they assist the family with decisions that revolve around independence, individualism, and advocacy.

117

The prophet Moses was on a journey. Allah [God] sent him a righteous man whose name was Alkhidhr, mentioned in the Qur'an, who had two special gifts from Allah: mercy and knowledge. Moses, not understanding the full import of what he was asking, wanted to learn something of the knowledge Allah had bestowed on Alkhidhr and asked if he could follow and learn from Alkhidhr. Alkhidhr answered, "Lo, you cannot bear with me. How can you bear with that whereof you cannot compass any knowledge?" Moses said, "Allah willing, you will find me patient and I shall not in anything gainsay you." Alkhidhr replied, "Well, if you go with me, ask me not concerning anything till I myself mention of it to you."

So the two set out until they came to a ship, and Alkhidhr made a hole therein, and Moses said, "Have you made a hole in the ship to drown the folk thereof? You surely have done a dreadful thing." Alkhidhr reprimanded Moses for challenging him, and Moses, repentant, apologized and asked forgiveness. So the two journeyed on until they met a lad, whom Alkhidhr slew. Once more, Moses challenged the wise man regarding his reason for this horrid act, and, once more, Alkhidhr reprimanded Moses, who apologized and asked forgiveness. So the two journeyed on until they came to a certain township, where they asked the folk for food, but they refused.

Then the two travelers found a wall upon the point of falling into ruin, and Alkhidhr repaired it. Moses said, "If you had wished, you could have taken payment for it." Alkhidhr said, "This is the parting between you and me. But I will announce unto you the interpretations of that which you could not bear with patience: As for the ship, it belonged to some poor people working on the sea, and I wished to mar it, for there was a king behind them who was taking every ship by force. And as for the lad, his parents were believers, but he was not, and we feared lest he should oppress them by rebellion and disbelief. So we intended that their lord should change him for one better in purity and nearer to mercy. And as for the wall, it belonged to two orphan boys in the city and there was beneath it a treasure belonging to them, and their father had been righteous. And your lord intended that they should come to their full strength and should bring forth their treasure as a mercy from your lord. I did all this not upon my own command. Such is the interpretation of that with which you could not bear."

The foregoing story was told to me by Salah Zaghal, Maher's father. He and his wife, Laila, and I were sitting in the Zaghal family's comfortable living room, bringing our update interview to an end. Laila and I had jokingly been exchanging stories about superstitious practices in which we engaged for good luck. She had pointed to an anklet that she had worn since Maher's birth, in the hopes that it would bring him better luck. I had told her of a silver turtle ring I had worn throughout my own son's illness as a reminder of my need to be strong. The turtle symbolized the memory of a deceased friend whose personal strength had been a source of inspiration to me. Salah listened to us and, inclining his head slightly to one side, commented, "But, you see, we cannot under-stand the reasons that things happen to us. We cannot know the future, and we cannot comprehend God's plan. It's not for us to say." Then he told us the story of Moses and Alkhidhr.

MAHER: "THE BIG GUY"

When we met Maher, he was 17. At approximately 5 feet 10 inches, with handsome Middle Eastern features and a teasing sense of hu-mor, Maher was a charmer. As his father said, "Maher has such a likable personality. He could fit in with anyone!" It seemed that, more than anything, Maher wanted to fit in with his teenage peers. At school, he was happiest walking down the hall among the throngs of teenagers, greeting the "guys" with a hand slap and a, "Wha's up, man?" When meeting someone for the first time, he of-ten introduced himself by saying, "I'm the big guy, man, I'm the big guy!" When we first went to observe him at his job, I said, "Oh, so this is where you work, Maher." He replied, "No way! I'm the boss here!" In his teacher's words, "Maher? You can't not like him!"

However, Maher could also drive anyone up the wall when he was not comfortable with a situation! It soon became evident that he was really very shy, and it was his self-consciousness that made him "act up" when he felt uncomfortable socially. He would try to make himself more comfortable by his joking manner and would be very friendly to other males but rather uncomfortable around females until he got to know them. His shyness resulted in a habit of initially saying "no" to just about any invitation; as his father explained, "Don't worry about that, his 'no' really means 'yes'!"

Maher would become intensely embarrassed when he felt "put on the spot" or even when he unexpectedly saw someone he knew and liked. At those times, he would often hide his face, turn his back, or appear to begin insulting the person with phrases such as, "You a turkey!" or, "Don't mess with me, man!" At these times, he could become extremely stubborn, absolutely refusing to cooperate with whatever was being requested of him.

Boredom or simply not knowing how to fill "down time" was another problem for Maher. On a jobsite, for example, where we saw that he did not have enough to do and had no apparent motivation to do as he was told, he would engage in a stream of self-talk, often quite loud, usually using phrases such as those quoted previously. Or at lunchtime on the job, after eating, if there were no one who initiated appropriate verbal interaction with him, he would often start pacing and carrying on a loud monologue.

When we met him at first, we wondered whether his use of language was really meaningful or more of a "filler"—using stock phrases to fill uncomfortable moments. We soon concluded that although this sometimes was the case, Maher most often used his stock phrases very meaningfully and with appropriate humor. For example, when we went to observe an annual review meeting for Maher, Miss M., the classroom aide, reported that as Maher was coming down the hall to join his teachers and his father for the conference, he said to a group of kids, "My father's here. No bullshit, man!" His friendly teasing of classmates was also often evident, as in a counseling session, when the counselor was talking to a group of five students about relationships and asked Maher's classmate Silvia whether she had a boyfriend. Silvia replied, blushing and emphatic, "No!" Maher quickly interjected, "Aw, c'mon Sil! C'mon!" and later, "Aw, Sil! Why not?"

Maher's father, mother, and teachers all saw his sense of humor as a key indicator of his intelligence. For example, his mother reported that he would stay up late to watch Arsenio Hall's and Johnny Carson's late-night television talk shows, and his ability to absorb the humor in these shows was surprising. According to his teacher,

> Some days he's so funny, it's hysterical. . . . And this Arsenio thing. . . . He has to be pretty bright to be into all of this Arsenio stuff and keeping himself up late at night to watch it. . . . He mimics Arsenio. . . . He doesn't really care for the guests on the show, he just cares for Arsenio's style. He loves that polished look and all his mannerisms. . . . I mean he just incorporates them into his own Maherisms, and he's *so* funny!

Another feature of Maher's social relationships was that he was very aware of people's feelings and often expressed regret after acting inappropriately. On one occasion, Maher got fired from his job. His teacher was absent, and the substitute teacher had difficulty keeping him in line. We were not sure exactly what Maher had said, but the result was that he came home very worried about his co-workers and kept saying, "Poor Dave! Poor [names of other co-workers]." His father took Maher to the store so that he could apologize and was gratified to find that the co-workers greeted him fondly, and the boss told Salah that Maher should not have been fired and that he would telephone the school and tell them that he could have the job back. As it turned out, however, the teacher had already started him at a new job, and his parents agreed that they should stay with that plan. Over the years that we worked with

Maher, his attitude toward his co-workers became a key feature of our observations and concerns, as we came to realize that positive relationships with these peers were supremely important to him and could be a powerful source of motivation for him. We detail these factors in our discussion of employment efforts with Maher.

MAHER'S FAMILY

When I first contacted Maher's family, I was greeted very cordially by Salah, who explained that the best time for me to visit would be at 8:30 on a Monday morning, before he went to work. He and Laila were involved in both insurance and furniture businesses. Laila was away at the time, so my first interactions with this family were with Salah. I arrived on time at their house at the end of a circular cul-de-sac in an upper-income suburban neighborhood. I was welcomed at the door by Salah, who invited me into the hallway. To my immediate right was his study, where we would talk, but the living room to my left caught my eye, with its very attractive furnishings, plush champagne-colored carpet, Middle Eastern–style rugs, and glass tables with shining brass and crystal ornaments. Diane, an elderly woman who had provided assistance to Maher for 7 years, also appeared in the hallway and, after being introduced by Salah, offered me a cup of coffee, which I gladly accepted.

We stepped into his study, and he sat behind the desk after offering me a chair facing the desk. I sat and began to say how glad I was that he could make the time; he interrupted me quickly, saying that he and his wife were happy to participate in the project because Maher's welfare was very important to them. The small study, as attractive as the surrounding rooms, had several photographs of the family, and Salah pointed to each one in turn, telling me briefly about his two daughters—one married with a child, one recently graduated as a teacher—and his other son, a young man of about 22, who at that time was living at home and working. Salah's manner in our interview was formal but personal, and he spoke with a compelling intensity as he described his feelings for his youngest son. After telling me about his three other children, Salah said,

> And Maher—he's with me all the time. I won't leave this one. I love them all, but this one is my heart. I don't care what happens, I want this boy to be with me always. . . . I love this boy—you cannot imagine. I will do anything for him.

Salah explained that Maher had developed behavior problems very early. As a child, his temper was very volatile and he would have extreme temper tantrums. Salah explained that he and Laila had sought professional help and had learned some behavioral strategies that did help to some extent. He explained that

> It was hard [to learn to discipline him]. We were afraid that he might think, this father and mother who love me very much—how could they be so strict with me. . . . I mean that's what we thought. But we had to learn how to calm or how to control our emotions. But really, we've come a long way, in terms of his behavior.

One aspect of Salah's view of Maher that came through very forcefully was his strong faith in Islam. When I asked how Maher would be viewed by the Moslem community, he said,

> Actually, we do take this as, "This is what God gave us," and we have to accept it. And of course this could happen to any one of them. So they really do take it, from a religious point of view, very nicely.

Salah frequently referred to the Qur'an to make a point about his view of a situation. For example, on my first visit to their home, I told Salah about my own experience as a parent of a child with a disability and that I had started a small school in Trinidad for children with disabilities. His reply was very comforting to me:

> In Islam, we have a saying from one of the prophets: There are three contributions that do not die when a person dies. These are *gelm nafiegh,* which means science, from which people benefit, so that even after you die, you will still be giving rewards. Then, there's *sadquah jarieah,* which means that if you build a school or a mosque or anything that people will benefit from, this is a reward that people benefit from after you die. And then there is *wald saleh,* which means a child that you raised, and you raised him good, you raised him in a way that he will always pray for you after you die. So all those things, they never die. So you see, you fit in one of those categories.

As the project progressed, we came to know Laila also and learned from her a great deal about Maher's childhood and the many efforts in which the family had engaged to learn more about Maher's condition and the challenges that he faced. Laila described her approach as "not as religious" and "more practical" than Salah's, and her efforts to understand Maher's condition had involved her extensive interaction with therapists and other professionals over the years. As Maher moved toward adulthood, Laila and Salah agreed that Salah would take more responsibility for Maher's personal care and for some of his social activities.

One of the things about which we spoke with all of the parents was their views of the future for their children. For all families, this was an emotional topic, and Salah and Laila were no different. The first time that I asked Salah whether he had given any thought to any kind of out-of-home placement for Maher, he replied slowly and intently, pausing at some points to collect himself as his voice choked with emotion,

> Of course, we want him to be like his brother and sisters as much as he can. We want him to have a life of his own. We want him to be as independent as he can. Of course, Maher's going to be Maher. He's going to be limited in where he can work. His knowledge is going to be limited. . . .
>
> You see, it's hard to trust anybody as far as taking care of him. His brother and sisters, fine, they love him and such, but not to care for him, to put up with his handicap. . . . And sometimes I get very sad and I hope that—if anything—I hope he will die before me, because I don't want anything bad to happen to this boy. I love him a great deal. . . . We were thinking about sometime going home [to Palestine], but for Maher we will stay. Besides, at this point . . . he has to finish his school. It is very difficult, but as far as homes and such, I think that I have to be realistic and maybe I have to think about it. Life is not guaranteed and we might die tomorrow, and we have to face reality. I really do have to think about that.

Laila described herself as sharing Salah's fears for Maher's future safety. However, Salah's comment about needing to be realistic pointed to some aspects on which Laila's and his views differed. One aspect was acculturation to the United States. Laila described herself as "more adapted" to the United States than her husband because she had come to live in the United States at the age of 15 and had graduated from high school here. She did share some of the same concerns as Salah on issues of acculturation, however, such as expectations of the rate of children's independence from the family, and she said that these differences had been quite challenging because their children were definitely "American." Salah agreed with this and said that the rapid independence from the family and much more democratic view of authority were very different from the Islamic tradition, in which children were raised to have absolute respect for their parents and to see parental authority as unquestionable.

Regarding the idea of plans for Maher to move out of the family home at some point, Laila's more "adapted" and "practical" perspective contrasted with Salah's. Laila was more inclined to see a group home as a reasonable option, whereas Salah continued to have great difficulty with the idea of Maher's living with anyone but the family. When Maher was 19, his parents were beginning to think about the possibility of returning to Palestine when Salah retired. That year, Laila took Maher on a visit to Palestine. Although their family there were very welcoming of Maher, it was evident that services for him would be very limited. Laila explained that, in Palestine, "there wouldn't be opportunities for him like there are here. I mean the cousins and the uncles would love him and talk to him and all that, but that's about as far as it would go." Because of this, Laila wondered whether they could possibly leave Maher in the United States in a group home or whether perhaps she might be able to get financial assistance to start such a program in Palestine, if they really did return there.

When I spoke with the family 2 years later, which was the year after Maher's graduation from high school, Salah had retired but they had, at least for the time being, given up the idea of returning to their native country, partly because of the unstable political situation there and largely because there would be no services for Maher. Meanwhile, Laila had sought, without much success, to have Maher considered by The Arc (formerly the Association for Retarded Citizens [ARC]) for residential placement. Until that time, however, his father still saw that idea as an option only for some undetermined time in the future. As Laila spoke of her disappointment with the unavailability of residential services, Salah shook his head and said, "That's all right. There's no need for that now, anyway."

GOALS FOR MAHER: SOCIALIZATION AND EMPLOYMENT

As we observed Maher at school and discussed our plans with his family during the first year, we concluded that there were two very important goals for him: socialization and employment skills. Maher's family involved him in a variety of social activities for young people with disabilities, such as the Special Olympics, special camps, and basketball and volleyball for students with disabilities at the local community center. His father accompanied him to these activities and said that Maher needed a lot of encouragement to participate. Salah described his family as belonging to the Moslem community, and, when the children were small, he attended the mosque regularly with the family but less so as they grew older. Whenever he went, he would not take Maher because Maher did not enjoy it. He explained that that community was not a potential source of activity for Maher because, although they were accepting of disabilities, they did not provide recreational activities. He made it clear from the start that he would be interested in any help that we could offer Maher in finding some social activity that would help him to have "a life of his own."

We realized that socialization and employment were very closely interrelated because Maher's difficulties with social interactions were one source of his problems on the job. Another was his difficulty with staying on task. At school, Maher was engaged in a vocational program that placed him in a range of jobs, each lasting for a semester or sometimes for a year. In the year prior to our project, Maher's job had been in a sheltered workshop program, where he had been engaged in simple office tasks.

In the year that we began observing him, he was working in a department store, with responsibility for tasks such as stacking items on shelves and stamping price labels onto items. In our observations of him at work, we noted that Maher was certainly able to do these tasks with regard to being able to understand and remember what to do. The chief challenge was keeping him on task and keeping his behavior appropriate. With regard to the first aspect, it seemed that the main problem was Maher's level of interest in the task, which overlapped with his being very distractible socially. Thus, if there were not enough structure to the task, such as a clear time frame in which it should be accomplished, then Maher would lose focus quickly. This meant that he was perceived as needing one-to-one attention from his job coach almost all of the time, a demand that was impossible for the school personnel supervising three or four students at the same jobsite. For example, at the department store, the teacher gave Maher a box of bathroom scales to unwrap, unpack, and place on a shelf. My field notes read as follows:

> Maher managed to take about 10 minutes to half way get the tape off the box, partly because Miss M. was busy talking to me and partly because he didn't pay attention to what needed to be done to get the tape off. He was clearly bored, and after they had put the four scales on the shelf (he putting and she making sure it was secure and wouldn't fall), there was nothing left to do. Miss M. told me how well he used to do in the "workshop" last year, stapling, collating, stuffing envelopes. She said that the problem with "real work" jobsites is that it's hard to get the appropriate level of work for the kids and to get it adjusted if a site wasn't right. Maher, she felt, needed much more structure; on the other hand, the dilemma was that excessive structure would be unrealistic because real jobs aren't all that structured. . . . She went on to say that he needs one to one and would never be able to work independently

without one to one. I replied that he certainly does need that now but didn't think she should assume he always would, considering he's just started this kind of thing. She kept shaking her head and didn't really agree with me. As we talked, Maher got more and more restless and started kicking a box down the aisle, and after she stopped him he did a few constructive things, such as try to open another box of dishwashing liquid and try to put two plastic packets that were sitting on the shelf onto their rightful hooks with the other packets. He had to give up since they were broken. I commented to her that he was trying to find something to do, and she agreed, saying this was really a problem on a day like this and that Tuesdays were better when someone was there that planned more carefully for the kids. (February 22, 1993)

Besides too much down time and the difficulty of staying on task, another problem that Maher had on the job was being able to discern with whom he could joke and with whom he could not. For example, our observations revealed very pleasant and appropriate interactions between him and some co-workers, and the teacher told me that there were certain co-workers who always joked pleasantly with him. Maher ran into real trouble with this job, however, when he called out to an African American customer who passed him in the aisle, greeting him with, "Hey, bro! Wha's up?" The customer's complaint to the manager almost cost Maher the job.

Summer Jobs

In the first summer of the project, we discussed with Maher's parents the possibility of our finding Maher a summer job for which we would provide a job coach and ongoing evaluation. They had planned to enroll Maher in a "traveling teens" program for youth with disabilities, arranged by the county's Parks and Recreation Department. They responded immediately to our suggestion, however, saying that they thought that the job would be better for Maher. They emphasized that Maher would do best working in the company of men and would probably respond best to co-workers who were a bit older than he.

In keeping with our principle of "in your own backyard," which had quickly become a motto regarding the best place to start a search for occupation or assistance, we approached the university's grounds services, seeking summer employment for Maher. Although our initial meeting with these personnel started off with a very positive and upbeat approach, the process of coming up with feasible jobs for Maher and two other students in the project took about 2 weeks; the university personnel made numerous suggestions that at first seemed very likely but turned out not to be feasible for one reason or another. For example, an initial plan that Maher would work on washing cars proved inconvenient when it was discovered that all of the car washing was done at night. A suggestion that he work with a campuswide trash pickup crew was soon abandoned when it turned out that the pickup schedule began too early for our students, meaning that they would have to go to different points every day to catch the crew in transit. Then, a suggestion that Maher work in the warehouse was turned down when the supervisor explained that she really did not have enough work for Maher to do and that they already were having trouble finding enough work for another employee with disabilities who had been working there for many years.

At one point, we became so discouraged that I was about to call Maher's family and tell them to go ahead with the traveling teens program, whose deadline for registration was pending. Just in time, however, the physical plant director suggested that we try the grounds crew, who provided a range of cleanup services on the campus. This situation provided some of the key features that Maher's teacher and his parents had identified as appropriate for him: first, work that relied on gross motor rather than fine motor skills and, second, work that would be done mostly in the company of men. His parents did, however, warn us that Maher would be sure to object to working outside in the heat. Also, his job coach was to be a woman, Pat, who was one of our graduate students, and we wondered how he would respond to that.

On the Grounds Crew   Maher began work on a steaming hot day at the end of June. He was placed on a work team that had a range of tasks, including collecting trash, cutting and blowing grass, and tending flower beds. He would work a 4-hour day, and his job coach's goal was to assist Maher in learning the ropes of the job but to fade out her support gradually. The first couple of days were very challenging for Pat, who reported that Maher spent most of the day complaining about the heat. Her notes recorded a very frustrating first day:

> Maher spent a lot of time sitting today. He didn't want to work. He said he couldn't work outside—"It's too hot. I can't do that. I'm tired. It's hot, I need to sit down. A bug bit me." He spoke about not coming to work tomorrow. The first reason was that it was Saturday, he would get to sleep late, and then it was because he was going to camp. . . . He did a lot of mimicking—when the guys were spitting, he would spit. He didn't want to be outside. He didn't like getting the gloves dirty. Every time he picked up something, he'd wipe his gloves off and make sure that all the dirt was off them. (June 28, 1993)

By the third, day, however, Pat's notes indicated the beginnings of what would become Maher's steady improvement on the job. As his comments about the heat, the work, and being tired decreased, Pat noted that the most important factor in this improvement seemed to be the spontaneous mentoring by two co-workers, Dwayne and Jim. Dwayne was an African American man who consistently emphasized that Maher "has feelings just like anyone else," and Jim was a Caucasian man who told us that he had a stepson with autism and so was accustomed to adapting to a person with a disability. Both Maher's work skills and his social behavior improved in response to their support and guidance. The greatest evidence of Maher's success at this job was that at the end of the 6 weeks allotted for the job, Maher's co-workers requested that he be allowed to continue for 2 more weeks, without the job coach (who, by then, had faded much of her support). This would have to be voluntary because the county agency that was paying Maher's salary would not agree to an extension. Maher's parents agreed readily, and Maher himself was very enthusiastic.

In the fall, we interviewed four of the men who had been on Maher's crew. In describing his progress over the 8-week period, the men detailed for us the kinds of improvement that they had noticed. Dwayne remarked,

> This may seem like a low opinion, but to me it's a high one because of where he started from. When he first started he couldn't even put leaves in a bag—he *wouldn't* put leaves in a bag! He wouldn't rake, he wouldn't do anything for more than 5 seconds without saying, "I'm tired," or sitting down. But after those 2 months—in the last 2 weeks he could actually fill up a whole trash bag, in fact, 1½ bags.
>
> Now, the only thing he really didn't respond to was change. Like at first, when he got accustomed to Pat coming every day, when she stopped coming, he kind of got upset a bit. But after a while, he gradually fit in. When I or John wasn't there and he had to go with another crew, he just wouldn't accept that. . . . He wouldn't work. He would refuse to do things. But as long as he stayed with a person he knew . . . he was okay.

Jim joined in:

> A lot of the things that we did, he didn't want to do. But I think that the proper motivation, with me anyway, with us, was getting him involved with the group and getting across the idea that it was a group effort. . . . Like one time when we changed locations and I told him to clean up the area, he just sat there and smiled, and I had reached a point where I said, "Alright, you can stay there." And I went and

picked up the trash and about 5 minutes later he said to me, "How's it going, big guy?" And I just told him, "Don't talk to me." He said, "What's wrong? What's wrong?" And I told him, I said, "Look, we're a group here, and you're making me do all the work." And that got him motivated immediately, and the rest of the day he was willing and glad to work.

Dwayne added,

Then, too, you've got to realize that . . . no man, I don't care how old or young, wants to be the lowest on the totem pole. If you have six guys operating machinery and you keep asking me to pick up trash, then eventually I'm not going to want to pick up trash. Now, a couple of times, we got permission from the supervisor to give him a blower. So one day, he was blowing grass and the next day, he would work fine again. . . . If you keep just giving him trash, trash, trash, he'll lose perspective and he don't want to do it any more. Now that could've been Maher, could've been me, could've been any one of us losing perspective.

This comment was typical of Dwayne, who consistently referred to the normal aspects of Maher's responses. Another such occasion was when he emphasized the importance of Maher's receiving a paycheck, while we had assumed that the paycheck did not really mean anything to Maher.

We learned three key points from Maher's co-workers on this job: First, a personal relationship with a mentor or mentors was the key to his attitude. They described the way this worked as follows:

You had to build that relationship with him, or he wouldn't perform. He needed a lot of positive reinforcement. . . . We also had several incidents where he was put with a person who had no patience, and the worst-case scenario was that we put him with one employee and they wound up mad and yelling at each other and cursing . . . and we resolved not to put them together again. If you have a negative attitude towards him, he's not going to try.

The men explained that Maher had begun by paying attention only to the job coach but had spontaneously transferred his attachment to the two men who showed the most interest in him. They thought this was good for him and that a male coach would be better because he could also be "his buddy."

Second, Maher needed time to learn. They said that the reason that they had requested an extension of his job was that by the fifth week he was really showing consistent progress, not only in the work but also in his ability to hold a sustained conversation. One of his mentors said, "I think that if he would have had 2 more weeks, you might have seen something unbelievable. He probably just needs more time."

Third, Maher's presence was like a "morale boost" for the crew, and they became increasingly supportive of him:

> Another thing that happened in the last 2 weeks—we all got together and talked about it, and everybody pitched in money and we gave him a good party the last day. And that was outstanding. People that I didn't think even knew him said, "Yeah, I'll pay." We had a good time. . . . We told him not to bring lunch that day, since we were having a party for him, and he kept saying, "Party now? Party now?"

This interview with the grounds crew ended with an indication from the boss that they might be willing to consider Maher for a job the next summer. However, when I approached the boss the next spring, he said that Dwayne, the man who had been Maher's mentor, had left the job and that it would be possible only if someone would be willing to be responsible for him. He soon called back to say that he had checked with the men:

> I'm so sorry, but Jim's the only person who'd be willing to really offer him some support, and that would just put Jim out of commission for too much of the time. There's really no one else who'd be willing to take on the responsibility of supervising him. If it were a student who's more independent, we'd certainly be willing to do it again.

In the Dining Hall   We had only just begun to understand the importance of individual mentors in Maher's life. The second summer underscored this lesson but also added another dimension: Maher's increasing sexual awareness would further complicate his dependence on personal relationships for his motivation.

In the second summer of the project, after being turned down by the campus grounds department, we were able to arrange for Maher to work in one of the campus cafeterias. This proved very appropriate because in the previous semester, his school vocational program had placed him in the dining hall of a local community college. His goals had included a range of dining hall and kitchen tasks, such as cleaning tables and counters, emptying trash, taking dishes from the conveyor belt, rinsing and stacking dishes, washing and drying pots, and so forth. These were exactly the tasks required on the summer job. Even more fortunate, we were able to engage as a job coach a young man who had been a classroom aide in Maher's program, which fit his need for both a male mentor and someone with whom he already had a relationship.

Once more, our goal was for Maher to make natural alliances on the job, allowing Keith, the job coach, to provide initial training and then fade out his support. The dining hall supervisor assigned Maher a work mentor, Marvin, an African American man of about 40, to whom Maher responded very well. Marvin later told us that he had a "handicapped sister" whom he had to teach when she was young. Within a week, it was obvious that Maher tended to work better when Marvin was around. He learned to perform the tasks quite well, and one of the main goals after the first couple of weeks was to increase his work speed and concentration because he tended to be distracted easily.

As the dining hall manager described Maher, "When he's in a good mood and he's got a good attitude, he does an excellent job. He's very precise." Both this manager and Marvin believed that Maher could handle a job like this very well as long as the environment is structured and his routine is consistent. The manager also expressed the opinion that Maher would need to have a job coach on most jobs because he does need a lot of individual attention. Marvin's summary of his view of Maher was as follows: "I know he can do the work. I know he might be a little slow, but he's pretty smart!"

There were two main challenges on this job. First, because of the relatively low work load in the summer, the dining hall was not consistently busy and there was a lot of down time. This was difficult for Maher because he tended to engage in a lot of self-talk and to become restless when there was not enough to do. The other difficulty was that he went through several periods of irritability resulting from his attachment to various co-workers. At those times, he resisted doing his work.

We came to see that Maher's dependence on personal relationships was both a blessing and a limitation. As he became attached to certain co-workers, he also tended to become frustrated when they were absent. This reaction occurred first in regard to Marvin, but after a couple of weeks he seemed to develop a "crush" on one female supervisor and later on another. He became very distressed when these co-workers were absent, and he showed his feelings by refusing to work or by becoming verbally abusive to others. One day this behavior became so extreme that Keith had to terminate the day's work and call Maher's parents to come for him. A serious talk from his parents that evening and from Keith and Marvin the next day seemed to settle Maher down. On another day, when the absence of another co-worker caused him to become upset, Maher spoke very disrespectfully to Marvin. After a quiet reprimand from Keith, Maher went back to Marvin and said, "Marvin, Marvin, I'm sorry, man!"

Conversely, when Maher was feeling happy, he was a charming companion, teasing and joking with his co-workers and getting a very positive response from them. Interviews with several co-workers indicated that he was well liked, and several people "took him under their wing," had lunch with him, chatted with him during down time, and occasionally telephoned him at home in the evenings. The problem that arose from this, however, was that Maher quickly came to expect these telephone calls and to become very disappointed and upset when he did not receive them.

At the end of this summer job, as in the previous year, Maher's co-workers all agreed that he would be capable of holding a job like this, provided that he had a job coach to do the initial training and provide ongoing support and provided that the environment was supportive of and friendly to Maher.

There was also a social aspect to our second summer with Maher. Keith involved him in activities such as going to the student union to play video games and going swimming at the community center. He also teamed with the job coaches for our three other high school students, and together they took the students on outings to the zoo and to a movie. Although these activities provided Maher with some enjoyment, they did not begin to approach our project's goal of increasing his social network or his range of social activities.

A Social Life for Maher

Besides employment, our second goal, in accordance with what we had learned from Maher's family and teachers, was to try to help him develop a social life. Unfortunately, our efforts in this direction had nothing of the success of the employment efforts.

Once more, the explicit inclusion thrust of our research project was a factor in our decisions about socialization opportunities for Maher. In my early interviews with Salah and in observations of the annual review conference in the first year, Salah commented that it would be very good for Maher to engage in more activities with "other children like himself." In planning the first summer's activities, therefore, I explained to Salah that our project was very focused on activities in which the students would participate with peers who do not have disabilities and asked him how he felt about that. He said that that would be fine, too, but he assumed that it would be easier to arrange activities with people with disabilities. Salah was genuinely open to our ideas and agreed readily to replace his original plan for the traveling teens program with our proposal for a summer job, as well as to our suggestions about activities with youth without disabilities.

In the first summer, we initiated a plan of pairing Maher with a school peer, Jerry, whom we had learned about from Maher's teacher because he had a sister with Down syndrome who had been in Maher's class. Jerry had been a volunteer at the Special Olympics in the previous year and had shown a particular interest in Maher. He had indicated to Maher's teacher that he was interested in doing some social activities with him. Maher's parents were very pleased with the suggestion because they remembered Jerry from the Special Olympics and believed that he would be good with Maher. Consequently, Helena, the research assistant, made arrangements to meet with Jerry at Maher's home to plan how to go about this idea.

Both Jerry and his mother came to the Zaghal family's home to plan the approach to social activities for Maher. Maher's reaction to this visit was great excitement, prefaced by his total disbelief that Jerry was really coming to his house. As Helena explained to him that Jerry was coming, Maher kept saying, "No! Get outta here!" and he refused to answer the door when Jerry and his mother arrived. During the discussion, Maher initially spent much of the time covering his face with a pillow while showing great excitement. Jerry seemed very comfortable with Maher, drawing him into the conversation with reminders about schoolmates whom they both knew and telling Maher the kinds of activities that they would do together. Everyone participated pleasantly in this meeting and clarified many details, such as the fact that Jerry did not have a driver's license and needed Maher's parents' permission for Maher to ride with Jerry's friend. They had "no problem with that." One stipulation was that Jerry stick to an agreed-on time frame so that Maher's parents would not be worried about their arriving home late. Jerry was very enthusiastic and made several suggestions about activities, including going to the movies, going to the swimming pool, and even just coming over to visit.

These plans did result in two outings for Maher and Jerry— once to the movies and once to the swimming pool. In a telephone conversation with Helena, Jerry reported that they had enjoyed their outings. However, after those two outings, Jerry did not follow up, and he did not fulfill an appointment to talk with us about how it had gone. Finally, after two broken appointments, I called Jerry's home and spoke with his mother. Jerry was out, and I asked whether she knew anything about how the efforts with Maher had gone and why Jerry had not kept his appointments with us. She did not know anything about his appointments with us but told me that she believed that Jerry had started off "very enthusiastic" but "kind of ran out of steam." Then she added, "But that's the story of his life! We're working on it." She said that Jerry was very good with his sister and really did enjoy being with Maher. Jerry found Maher very funny—"a scream!" They had gone to the movies along with some other friends of Jerry's and had seen a scary movie, and Maher had confided to Jerry, "Jerry, I'm scared!" Jerry's mother promised to have him call me, but none of us ever heard from him.

We decided to try a more structured approach to social activities for Maher, and that fall we began discussions with the community center in his neighborhood. The one in Maher's area was newly renovated and had very up-to-date facilities. Moni's appointment with the special needs coordinator at that center, however, was not encouraging. She explained to Moni that she had asked the center's "Teen Advisory Club" whether there was anyone who would be interested in being a "buddy" with Maher. No one had responded, she said. Moni's notes read,

> She seemed to be in a hurry. . . . She shrugged her shoulders and asked if I had any other questions. I asked if Maher could join the club anyway, even if the buddy system didn't work. She said that it was possible but mentioned that they would not be making any special allowances for him and that he would have to obey the rules of the group. If he could fit within the rules, it would be fine. At this point, she introduced me to the coordinator of the Teen Club, and he said that they were having a hard time with the teen group. For some reason, it wasn't picking up, and the response was very poor. He mentioned that the group of teenagers was not constant, so it would be difficult to find a buddy. Also, he said, it's difficult to get a commitment from teenagers in general. (October 25, 1993)

The last comment was very much in line with the view that we got from Maher's teacher, who said that most of the high school–age kids are "just like Jerry—they're very willing until something else comes along."

That fall, we also discussed with Maher's teacher the possibility of identifying a small core of school peers without disabilities who would act as an in-school support for Maher, with the hope that out-of-school activities might also occur. The teacher thought that this was a good idea and even spoke of trying to work this idea into the recently mandated state requirement for community service credits for high school graduation. These ideas, however, never materialized, and we felt that it was beyond the scope of our abilities to influence directly Maher's school-based social experience.

Overall, we had much more success in helping Maher with job skills than with social activities and relationships. He certainly enjoyed the activities that we did with his schoolmates who were in the project, but we were never able to link him with young people without disabilities who might have helped him to have more of an independent social life. In terms of jobs, his summer jobs definitely showed that he was capable of learning appropriate job skills and carrying out his tasks reliably, as long as he had support and could control any feelings of frustration.

When we asked Maher which of the two jobs he preferred, he said that he preferred working at the physical plant. We asked why, but he said that he did not know. We did believe that this was the more successful job, mainly because of the presence of two men who were patient and supportive but also quite firm and demanding of Maher. We believed, too, that the close company of women on the job was more of a distraction than a help to Maher and that he found his relationships with them too confusing and disturbing. Keith, Maher's job coach at the dining hall, reported conversations with Maher in which he said things such as, "I'm lonely," "I need a friend," and, "I need somebody." We could not be sure whether these comments reflected sexual or simply friendship needs. Indeed, issues of sexuality were of concern to Maher's parents as he grew older and was a topic on which they sought professional advice regarding how to counsel Maher as his sexual awareness developed.

Parental Participation in Education Planning

Maher's parents were very appreciative of the school's efforts and fully supported their initiatives, such as allowing Maher to go to camp, the Special Olympics, and any other activities. Salah sometimes went as a parent chaperone to these outings. As Maher's teacher put it, "Any activity that we have sent home or that's on a weekend, his father brings him, he makes sure that he's there. He's always handsomely dressed and ready to go." Laila chuckled at this comment, observing that she was the shopper for Maher's fine wardrobe.

Salah's view of his role in Maher's special education program was quite traditional, in the sense of being deferential to professionals and quite accepting of their proposals for Maher. As he put it,

Well, you know, when you go to school for just one meeting, you cannot really tell what's going on. Of course when I go there, they are always very cooperative. They will answer any question you ask and so forth. But . . . my knowledge is limited as far as what they should or should not do. When I go to the meetings, they tell about the activities. They tell you what their goals are, what they are striving to reach as far as Maher's abilities and such. Well, of course, whatever they teach him, it is beneficial to him, and probably at the school they have the knowledge, the education. They're professionals and they know how to work with him probably better than me. They know what certain things they should emphasize, this is their business, their profession.

Sometimes they used to really ask us what we want to do here at home. We should set certain goals for what we want him to do. We followed those things, but still, as far as the schooling, they have all the tools and the techniques and we don't.

In the summer of 1998, in sharing these case studies with the students' parents and in updating information on them, I learned of Maher's graduation from high school and his subsequent placement at The Arc in a day program. Upon his graduation, Maher's teacher had informed the Zaghal family of the various agencies that they could contact for services for Maher. The first one that they had approached assessed Maher and concluded that the kinds of job placements that they provided would not be appropriate for Maher, so the family went to The Arc, knowing that they served a broader range of skill levels. Also, Laila was interested in The Arc's residential services.

The Arc placement turned out not to be as satisfactory as Maher's parents wanted. Salah expressed his feelings about it in reserved tones. He was grateful that Maher did have somewhere to go and something to do each day but was disappointed that the activities provided at The Arc did not seem to include any training for Maher but rather were mostly make-work, with a lot of down time. At one point, Maher had been engaged in packing apples into a crate and now did some packing of eggs. For these simple tasks, Maher was paid a miniscule sum, which, Salah explained, was calculated according to the weight that he had packed. The egg-packing tasks brought him approximately $5 every 2 weeks; the apples paid a bit more.

Salah and Laila had somewhat differing opinions on this situation. Salah's concern was the absence of any training; Laila agreed, but she also believed that Maher should be paid more, no matter how simple the task. She believed that Maher did know that money was valuable and could be taught more about its value and how to use it. She also believed that real pay would provide him with some incentive to do the work and contribute to his developing a sense of independence for the future. When I asked the family whether Maher was enrolled in The Arc's day program or in their supported employment program, they were aware of the difference but were not sure of Maher's status. They explained that their understanding had been that Maher would be in the supported employment program, but it seemed to them that he was actually in the day program, possibly in a mobile crew structure in which a group of young people were taken out to do tasks such as distributing fliers.

Salah and Laila told me that there was an Arc meeting soon, and they hoped to raise these issues then. As we talked about the need for parents to be assertive when necessary to get the most appropriate services for their children, we all agreed that Salah's approach was much more inclined to be accepting of what was offered, whereas Laila was more inclined to be assertive. For the most part, however, Salah was not very hopeful about being able to influence Maher's program. As he said,

> As a parent, you have your opinions. But, really, what can you do to change it? How can you force them to do what you want? I mean, you can go and say what you would like, but you don't really have any power, so to speak.

Although our official work with Maher has ended, we promised to do the best that we could to assist the Zaghal family in pursuing more effective and appropriate services for Maher. We emphasized the need to meet other parents with whom they could share their concerns and, possibly, as a group have more of an impact on their children's services.

On my last visit to the Zaghal family, I took Maher a T-shirt of the University of Miami Hurricanes. Because he had not seen me in 2 years, he was pretty reluctant to come downstairs to greet me, even though he had been looking through the window for my arrival. When he was finally coaxed into the living room and realized that the T-shirt was for him, he held it up, scrutinizing the logo. As he quickly changed shirts, he gave me that characteristic turn of the head and exclaimed, "A T-shirt for me? Aw, get outta here!"

APPLYING THE POSTURE OF CULTURAL RECIPROCITY

1. *Researcher effectiveness:* When we began working with Maher's family, we hoped that through the efforts of our research team

we would be able to develop his employment options and build his social relationships. We wanted to provide opportunities for him to maximize his potential to become motivated to keep a job because of the opportunities that it provided for acquiring financial independence and making friends. We were somewhat disappointed in the outcomes of our efforts. Consider both of the following:

a. *Summer jobs:* Maher's first summer job, with the university grounds crew, seemed to hold great promise, and we had hoped to secure that job again in the second summer, building on the relationships that Maher had already formed on the job. What could we have done differently to ensure greater success in job preparation for Maher?

b. *Social relationships with peers without disabilities:* Our first idea about helping Maher to build a social network of peers without disabilities was to build on expressed interest of Jerry, a young man who had assisted Maher at the Special Olympics and who had a sister with a developmental disability. Jerry started off well but did not follow through, for reasons unknown to us. Later, we discussed with Maher's teacher the possibility of trying to find a buddy or buddies among the general education students who were friendly to Maher. The teacher thought that the idea had some potential, but nothing came of it. One summer, we appealed to our university campus volunteer offices for students who might like to do some social activities with Maher and another of our students. We got no replies. In the long run, we believed that we had accomplished very little for Maher in the realm of social relationships. What could we have done differently?

2. *Parental participation:* Maher's parents were always receptive to our ideas. His welfare was very important to them, and they saw the opportunities that our project might offer as another piece of good fortune that Allah had provided for Maher. They wanted Maher "to be as independent as he can." They involved him in a variety of social activities with other young people with disabilities, and they hoped that our project would also help him to "have a life of his own." When it came to working with the service providers, Salah did not see it as his job to "tell the professionals what to do." He would do his job as a parent, and the professionals would do theirs.

Consider your reaction to Salah's style of parental participation with service providers. What do you think your own style might have been in helping this family to plan for Maher?

3. *The meaning of acceptance:* We were intrigued by Salah's combination of acceptance and challenge in relation to setting goals for Maher. For our part, in keeping with the belief that success is upward mobility through work, and in the best American tradition, we were in pursuit of Maher's happiness. Through Salah's eyes, we saw that acceptance also was important. This did not mean a lowering of expectations for Maher. It did not imply a fatalistic resignation. We could still hope for and work toward a better quality of life for Maher, as his parents did, but it was just as important to appreciate what Maher had done and would continue to try to do, to see each event, each summer job, each effort to build a new friendship in terms of the larger scheme of things. We learned that to strive for the best with what you have can be as powerful a vision as striving for better than what you have and that what you have is always good and to be appreciated. Other good things would happen, God willing, and one could not necessarily make them happen.

    We suggest that this approach to life differs in important ways from the typical American approach. Using your personal identity web (see Figure 3 on p. 9), consider where you stand on this philosophy and how your position might influence the way you would work with this family.

4. *Planning for the future:* Maher's mother and father had contrasting opinions on future living arrangements for Maher. Laila saw an out-of-home residential placement as a possibility, whereas Salah preferred that Maher continue to live with them for as long as they could maintain the arrangement.

    a. Use your personal identity web (see Figure 3 on p. 9) to examine what your responses might be to Salah's and Laila's differing points of view. Would their differences make you uncomfortable? What might be some of your biases if you worked with Maher's family on this issue?

    b. What might be some alternative living arrangements that you could develop and that you think would be compatible with both parents' points of view?

5

Brianna

God's Challenge

Brianna

A single African American mother responds to God's call to adopt an infant with a disability. Full inclusion for this mother means including whatever educational approaches will support her goal of raising her daughter to be a Christian young woman, Down syndrome notwithstanding. Some service providers will be challenged by this mother's strong pro-life stand and by her preparedness to advocate for her daughter.

Sometimes God asks you to do something—you can't understand why. Why He would want me, you know, a Christian who has worked hard, in management in the government, active in the church and trying to help mothers and babies stay alive—why call on me to adopt a baby? Especially, knowing I was just recovering from those teen years with my oldest! You see, the more I ignore God, the more He puts things in my way to remind me of what He wanted me to do. He was gently pulling at me to adopt. Like, one day, I looked up and there was all the information I needed to adopt at the county's adoption services. I was going, "No, no! I'm not going to do this!" But, finally, I called. And there wasn't any reason not to go . . . so I went to the orientation thinking, "I really don't want to do this!" But I know God is in charge, that He is Sovereign and His plans can only be for my good. I was worrying, though, maybe God had made a mistake, maybe he'd had a bad day and was talking to the wrong child! So I sat there, listening to the social workers explain the two programs: one for the "healthy" babies and one for the "hard to place." That's where the handicapped and those in foster care more than 3 years old were. Surely He didn't want me to stop my exciting "good government job" or my church activities. Surely He didn't want me to get all burdened down with a baby, one that would take a lot of work. Okay, now I know I speak out about how babies are killed by abortions, I put in hard hours working with the mothers. Did that mean I was to juggle a baby along with everything else I was doing? You see, that's how I was thinking then. I felt it was wrong to kill them, but I wasn't willing to bring one home. But you know, God has a way of spiritually pushing a person. And with me, I was being obedient, but it sure wasn't with a grateful heart. Boy oh boy, I fussed all the way to the meeting! I just kept saying, "No. Now, God, I came here, but I'm not going to get myself involved with a handicapped child." But I went over there—to the side of the conference room to talk about adopting a handicapped child. You know, it was like I knew my life was about to change. But I was determined to control that change . . . at that time I didn't care anything about the Almightiness of God. . . . This was going to be on my terms. But, you know, I had no idea what God's change really would be like. I think about "the Hulk"! It's called metamorphosis! Well, that's what happened to me: My spiritual life went from the fugitive, David (I think that's what his name was on that TV show), to a spiritual life that's still growing into the Hulk! You know, it's from one centered on me—asking God to bless me and what I want—to a life centered on God, just wanting to be a broken vessel for use by Him in His plan. (Paulette Roseboro)

Brianna (Bri) was adopted by Paulette Roseboro and came to live with her at the age of 5 months. When we met Bri, she was 2½ years of age and lived with her mother and her 22-year-old sister, Ranetta (Netta). The Roseboros lived in an attractive suburban neighborhood in a single-family home surrounded by a neat lawn and numerous flower beds.

Paulette always welcomed us with a smile, cheerful Christian greetings, and an offer of something to drink. Passing through a comfortably furnished living room full of plants, we would go downstairs to the basement family room, off of which was a small playroom where Bri would play with her toys and would check in with her mother from time to time. Before starting our interviews, Paulette would always ask Bri to show us what she was learning. The last time we visited the family, Bri, by then age 5, showed off her ability to identify all of the letters of the alphabet.

Our first observations of Bri were at home and in the family child care center that she attended. She was a very active child who explored her environment with great enthusiasm, interacted well with children of different ages, and clearly enjoyed the rough-and-tumble play initiated by the child care provider's sons, who were 8 and 10 years of age. Commenting on Bri's extroverted personality, Paulette explained that this child was totally different from the stereotype of the "docile Down syndrome child," which had been described to her by the social worker who had been involved in Bri's adoption process.

> Bri has always been full of energy, outgoing. She likes the stimulation of hard play activities. She would fool her uncles and cousins. At first, she had a heart problem and then surgery, and everybody was so dainty with her, she could sort of get away with looking real dainty and catch them off guard, then suddenly giving them a sock or something, or jumping on their back or something like that. She's really a hard player. I don't worry about other children picking on her. To the contrary, I warn older kids to be careful, she's not as harmless as she pretends. But, she learned that children smaller than herself always get lots of hugs and sharing.

ADVOCACY FOR LIFE

Paulette's decision to adopt a child was prompted by her religious beliefs. As well as being very active in her church, she is a strong activist in the pro-life movement. The quote at the beginning of the chapter was her report of the experience that prompted her to the momentous decision to adopt not just any child but one with a disability.

Her initiation into the world of disabilities began with the "classes" required for parents who want to adopt one of those "hard to adopt" children. The information and perspectives that she gained there strengthened her already powerful commitment to the pro-life movement. She came away with a conviction that

Every single child that has been aborted—there is a home for that child. It might not be in the same racial mix, but all of the 35 million that have been aborted in the last 20 years, there is a home for that child. Even these with handicaps. Society is so quick to abort these children because to them they have no human potential or social value; they only bring disappointment and drain family and societal resources. Instead, I say, give them a chance and some consideration and an investment of a little resources, and these children will grow to be viable members of mankind.

Paulette was very open on her views on abortion and used every opportunity to share them. For example, the message on her answering machine ended with, "Every life is precious in God's eye." After she adopted Bri, she frequently included her in local pro-life activities.

In the last interview for the adoption process, Paulette was accompanied by Netta. After the social worker read to them Bri's history, Paulette said, "We feel in love with Bri before we've even seen or met her." However, Paulette believed that, other than the placement social worker, the agency staff did not expect that a single, African American career woman would volunteer to adopt a child with a disability. Bri was 3 months old at the time and had been in foster care from birth. The foster mother sent a picture of Bri, but the picture was very unattractive. Paulette said that because they were already committed to Bri, the picture served as a kind of endearment. She believed that the foster mother was concerned about the type of people who would be interested in adopting Bri and, at first, misguidedly wanted to discourage any halfhearted prospects. She would have been interested in adopting Bri herself if no African American family could be located for adoption. However, any disappointment that Paulette felt with the photograph disappeared the minute that she saw Bri. She bonded with Bri immediately. She recalled with fondness,

> Netta and I, we looked at this picture, and as we walked out of the agency to meet Bri for the first time, I said, "Boy! I'm glad we liked this kid before we saw the picture!" But when we met her, that was it. Any concerns about looks went out the window. This bundle with the little wrinkled face was my baby. I couldn't believe it. Every inch of me knew that this was my child—through sickness, surgery, homework, and teen years. This child—God conceived this child for me to be her mother. I was amazed by what God knew and what I didn't. And I completely just let go. I just surrendered to His will. I was already looking forward to raising my little Bri.

The placement process took 2 months, during which time Paulette was a bit anxious because she believed that it was important to bond with the child early. Bri was scheduled to have corrective heart surgery, and Paulette wanted to build a relationship with her prior to this procedure. However, the adoption agency expressed concern because Paulette was single and working. They did not want Paulette to send her to child care, and, according to Paulette, "they talked about old germs and new germs." The meaning of this phrase was never clearly explained to Paulette, but because she realized that they were concerned, she arranged for someone to take care of Bri at home. She quickly realized that she would have to advocate for herself as a parent, so she sent a letter to the county explaining how she was going to care for Bri:

> Because the children have their own attorney and . . . this attorney had her own biases that she had to overcome. So what I ended up doing was I wrote out an entire plan. This is what I will be doing. This is how I will find in-home care, and these are the qualifications. This is what we're doing about sanitation. I have plenty of leave from work. You know, the whole thing. Then I ended it with, if you still have a problem, I can talk to my county representative to see if he could explain reasons for your concern.

The agency responded quickly to this letter and asked when she would like to pick up Bri. She used this opportunity to practice her skills as an advocate because she anticipated that she would require these skills later. As she said,

> When you have a special-needs child, I think, no matter what, you're going to always be addressing the system. And if you're going to be an advocate for your child, you're going to be stressed out. So I started right away, right away, right away.

Paulette's advocacy activities regarding Bri had only just begun. In addition to advocating for herself at the adoption agency, she had to negotiate at her workplace to work out of her home. So she decided to take 3 weeks of leave spread over 6 weeks, while working from home. This was a new situation for this federal agency; only one other person had done this before her. However, Paulette believed that her proven abilities in her work convinced her superiors to agree. Unfortunately, after she had made all of the arrangements, the administration changed and she had to fight for her leave once again.

During this process, Paulette told us, the infant/toddler program did an excellent job of collaborating with the different agencies. Bri was receiving early intervention services in a neighboring county when she was with her foster mother. When Bri came to live with Paulette, the local infant/toddler program started providing on-site services at home and collaborated with the hospital as they followed Bri's development over the years. Later, when Bri went to child care, they provided services in the child care centers, although this effort proved quite challenging, as the next section illustrates.

FINDING APPROPRIATE CHILD CARE

According to Paulette, "When parents work, everything doesn't center around the home, everything really centers around the day care." Paulette quickly found that finding good child care for her daughter with special needs was quite a challenge. Legally, child care providers cannot refuse admission to children with disabilities. However, she found that they discriminate in more subtle ways by frustrating the efforts of the parents. According to Paulette,

> It was very difficult to find day care. Okay, even though day care providers, through their license, are not supposed to discriminate because the child is handicapped, they would send you through some changes. They'll tell you to come in, and you will come in and all of a sudden it is full. Or I would tell them on the phone, "My child has Down syndrome, but let me come in for the interview because you will see that you don't have to do anything unique or special." But they just seemed to be afraid. One even mentioned concerns about insurance coverage being available to care for such a child.

Paulette told us how the child care providers set different obstacles for her to frustrate her efforts. A director of one center required Bri to prove that she could sleep on a cot. Even though Bri was not used to this, she was able to sleep on the cot and passed the criterion set for her admission into this center. Then the director asked Paulette to come back after 2 weeks because she was about to hire new staff and did not have adequate staff at that time. Two weeks later, the director told Paulette that the new person had not shown up. This process continued for 2 months before Paulette gave up.

For the first 6 months, Paulette hired someone to take care of Bri at home. This was as she had agreed with the adoption agency. At 11 months, she did find a family child care provider who seemed appropriate, but the provider turned out to be "superstructured" and was not very accommodating to the early intervention staff who came to work with Bri. Paulette had especially chosen a family child care provider because she believed that a private provider would be more flexible and would work collaboratively with the special education professionals. Soon, Paulette arranged for Bri to be picked up at the child care center and taken to the county's special education center for the therapy. However, it was apparent that the provider (who took good care of Bri) did not want to be responsible for taking Bri to the curb for the school bus to pick her up and drop off. Finally, Paulette concluded that if a provider or child care center did not want her child, it did not matter that the law required them to accept her; she did not want Bri in that kind of environment. After much prayer, she responded to an advertisement in the Yellow Pages and finally found the kind of child care for which she was looking.

When we first met Bri, she was 2½ years of age and was enrolled in the second child care center. There were two other children in child care there, a 4-year-old and a small infant. The child care provider, Mrs. B, also had her own two sons, ages 8 and 10, as well as a few other kids who joined the group after school or during the summer vacation. Paulette's religious values matched nicely with those of Mrs. B, who provided religious education and a fixed routine for the children in her care. According to Paulette,

> The day care provider is very much into giving her children a very solid religious introduction as well as educational activities. So they have a very structured day in what the children do. However, she's flexible in the individual care each child requires. On Thursdays, they go to the library. The library has different experiences for children. Like I said, they learn the days of the week, the months of the year, the colors and all that. . . . But it's very, very structured, so the children have a variety of repetitive educational activities. Mrs. B cooperates with the early intervention staff. She feels she can learn something useful that she'll be able to apply in the future.

Child Care–Early Intervention Collaboration

Although Paulette had chosen a center that was congruent with her value system, there were a couple of issues on which the values of the early intervention therapists who worked with Bri were different from hers and Mrs. B's. For example, Paulette believed that the early childhood specialists were trained to follow the child's lead, which could conflict with the philosophy of a structured learning environment. The infant/toddler program had agreed to send their staff to Mrs. B's to provide services on site, and Paulette believed

that it was up to the therapists to learn to adapt to the situation because she saw the role of a professional as supporting or teaching a
child in the environment in which he or she is functioning. She believed that therapists should not walk in with their own agenda and
expect the child care provider to oblige and follow their style.

Another issue that concerned Paulette was that the various
adults who worked with Bri assessed her differently, based on how
she reacted to that individual, the amount of time that the individual spent with her, the adult's expectations of what is "normal" for
a child of her age, and the adult's own approach or teaching style.
Bri's personality and performance varied, depending on who was
interacting with her. The following quote from Paulette illustrates
how the relationship between various providers was strained as a
result of these differences:

> Sometimes kids do things for different people, and she does more in
> the day care environment than she does anywhere else. This is proba-
> bly because she wants to keep up and outdo the other children.
> Bri loves competition. Then, she does the least amount for the thera-
> pist . . . so the PT [physical therapist] would come in and say, "Well,
> she's not doing this, this, and this." Then Mrs. B would get upset be-
> cause Bri *does* do this, this, and this, and she took pride in what Bri
> was able to accomplish. So, anyway, it was a struggle between the ther-
> apist's evaluations and the day care provider's.

Paulette believed that people working in the special education
system come in with biases because of their training and lack of exposure to typical children with different abilities. She also believed
that what is viewed as atypical by a professional may be viewed as
typical behavior by a parent or a child care provider and that the
child care provider or parent, who spends more time with the child,
is able to see the child's performance in a variety of situations and
have a better sense of the child's developmental level on the whole.
As a result, the therapist's expectations of Bri seemed unrealistic to
Paulette:

> What the therapist was looking for is more of "you sit down, you do an
> activity geared towards you. Then you finish that activity, and then
> you go to another activity." And I'm going, "Okay, but she's still 2½." I
> felt it was best to introduce Bri to the desired activity but don't mark
> her down when she acts in the age-appropriate manner.

Because the services were both on-site and in-facility, Paulette
finally resolved this situation by requesting that the infant/toddler
program provide services at home. This way she was able to ob-

serve Bri's interaction with the therapist and develop strategies to assist Bri. From her observations, Paulette believed that the approach of the therapist was not compatible with her daughter's learning style. She also differed from the therapist in her view of how children make the transition from one activity to the other:

> The first time the therapist came in, it was very, very rushed and hurried. It was like—we did the puppet, and we said, "Hello Bri, hello Bri," with the puppet very excitedly. "Okay, Bri, now we are going to choose! Okay choose which toy." Bri chooses her toy, and then we play and then, "Bri all finished! Oh, okay, now choose! Bri all finished. Okay, which one do you want to choose." I went, "Wait a minute," and I could see that Bri was so hyper. I had never seen Bri so hyper. I mean she was, I could feel the hyperactivity in her. I just said, "Hold it, hold it. Let's just concentrate on a couple of toys here, okay. I can understand why you want her to choose, I understand that you want her to finish an activity, but let's only have a couple for her to choose from and that's it."

Talking about children in general, Paulette continued:

> If you notice, they only flutter between a couple of different toys. I have several available for Bri's selection, and I change the toys around because I like her to have different experiences. But when she's fluttering, she's fluttering between a couple of things, back and forth, not 10 or 12 as the therapist encouraged. You know, I am not a specialist, but I know what Bri does.

Paulette also was concerned about appropriate coordination of Bri's services. Although she did not have specific complaints about the service coordinator, who was from the school system, she felt uneasy with the arrangement because she believed that there was a potential conflict of interest in the service provider and service coordinator being one and the same. Paulette was a member of Parents of Children with Down Syndrome (PODS) and had learned from other parents that they had requested that their service coordinator be from The Arc (formerly the Association for Retarded Citizens [ARC]) in the county. Paulette explained the issue as follows:

> So Bri's service coordinator was through the school. And that was one change that I definitely made because there was a conflict of interest. You had the school providing the services and the school doing the coordination; it's just a conflict of interest. So Bri's service coordination is now through The Arc. Because the service coordinator really acts as your family advocate; and the school system—they have money crunches, I mean, they have their agenda. So no matter what, when they start recommending services, they're going to be doing things

based on what they want to do and the program they want. . . . The Arc is paid by the system, but The Arc is separate. So I did change my service coordinator."

Paulette initiated the change, and her decision was supported by the staff of the infant/toddler program without any resistance.

Another area in which she believed that there was a conflict of interest was in choosing goals for Bri. Because of the family-centered focus of Part H services of the Individuals with Disabilities Education Act (IDEA) of 1990 (PL 101-476; now Part C of the IDEA Amendments of 1997 [PL 105-17]), the staff asked her what she wanted and asked her to choose goals. Initially, Paulette had trouble with this approach because she believed that the staff were trained to do this, but soon she realized that she wanted Bri to be in a general first-grade class, so it would be important for her to start identifying goals accordingly. However, it seemed to Paulette that the teachers at the special education center were resistant to pursuing individually derived goals and were recommending goals that were common to the group of children with whom Bri would be placed.

The professionals who were working with Bri were picking goals based on her current level of performance, goals that could be met safely in the next year and for which the teacher could allocate adequate time. Paulette saw these goals as too short term. When we asked what she meant when she said that the staff were recommending common goals, Paulette said,

> Because in talking with the staff that were involved in it, they said, or they almost said, and I read between the lines, it was—the teacher can't focus on too many different goals. All these goals are listed, and she sits down and she decides on what activities the class as a whole will have—grouping the similar individual goals of the kids in the class. So if you have a class of 10, and 10 of them are working on eating and on potty and on paying attention but you have one person working on jumping—that's something different. That's something outside of what the whole class is doing that requires a different time with the teacher. Because what happens, from what I understand, is that the teacher has to come up with some explanation as to why a child does not meet a goal. So the teachers don't want to have too many children with diverse needs and goals to be put in the classroom and pulling the teacher in more than one direction. When parents were setting goals within what was envisioned by the teachers—all is well. But when you get to more challenging work, that's when I feel the friction.

MEANINGS OF INCLUSION

The child care program that Bri attended from about 1 year of age until age 4 served as a rather unique inclusive placement. The fact that it was family child care meant that it was more like home than a classroom situation. Despite Mrs. B's structured routine, the atmosphere was very homelike. Before lunch, she allowed the children to play in the backyard and kept an eye on them while preparing lunch. In the summer, she put out a small plastic pool, a sandbox, a plastic cooking range, and a small plastic jungle gym.

The interaction between Bri and the other children was similar to that of siblings. Moni's notes from an observation illustrate this well:

> Bri is in a light blue bathing suit, and she's sliding down the small slide attached to the pool. One of Mrs. B's boys comes and watches her for a minute or so and then goes away to play by himself. Y, the 4-year-old girl, comes and gets in the pool, then she loses her balance and falls gently on the side of the pool. She says, "I wet my butt," and walks off to the plastic cooking range. Bri follows her and takes a fork and spoon, which Y had put on the table. Y screams, "Stop!" Bri pushes her a little bit and then sits with her in an adult beach chair in front of the cooking range. Y takes out a yellow plate and a spoon. Then she walks off casually towards the plastic pool, and Bri follows her. Y returns to the kitchen, and they both sit down in the chair. Y takes a plate and spoon, pretends to feed Bri with the spoon, and says, "Bri, you don't want this?" Bri leans forward and pretends to eat from the spoon. Then she gives the spoon to Bri, and Bri pretends to feed herself with the spoon. Y gives her a light hug, singing, "Bri aa nna, Bri aa nna." Brianna gets up and the spoon falls, and Y says, "Bri!" reprimanding her. Y takes out a few more plates and tells Bri, "Look carefully, look this way." Bri walks closer to the cooking range. Then Y wanders off and joins A, an 8-year-old boy lying on a towel. Bri follows her and sits next to them. (August 11, 1995)

The 8-year-old boy, A, was also very fond of Bri and would hug her from time to time and ask her for a hug or a kiss. At times he would sing a song, slowly moving closer to Bri: "Bri, Bri, hi! How are you?" He would step in rhythm with his songs, and she would usually respond by giving him a hug. Sometimes Bri hugged the kids on her own initiative. The boys in the child care were very affectionate to Bri and actively encouraged her to learn. They not only facilitated her learning but also took pride in her achievements. Moni's observation notes from a cookout in the backyard reflect their role as teachers for Bri:

> Bri is standing in front of a plastic equipment similar to a basketball hoop. C runs up to her and demonstrates to her how to put the ball in the opening. Then he gives Bri the ball, holds her hand, and makes a hand-over-hand demonstration. Bri does not resist, and next time she is able to perform the action successfully on her own. C is all excited.

He calls out to the other boys, "Look! Yeh, yeh! Look, Bri can do it." Bri keeps repeating the action, and C is all excited, "Oh, she got it again. Look, B!" B and D run up to the equipment, and Bri repeats it a few times and they clap for her, then Bri walks off and the boys walk away. Bri looks really little next to these boys, who are around 10 years of age. Then she bumps into B, who gently rubs her head, and Bri protests, "Aaah," and moves away. Bri goes to a wooden table and climbs on the bench next to the table. B brings the equipment to her and encourages her to throw the ball again. Bri does it once or twice and then walks away. (August 23, 1998)

Paulette valued these interactions highly, and, when the time came for Bri's transition to Part B services, she believed that Bri could benefit most if she attended this general child care program and a special program simultaneously. As she said,

I mean, that's my goal for her—to be inclusive. But I don't—maybe because she is adopted and such—I don't carry the guilt that sometimes birth parents carry. I want Brianna to realize she has a special need, she is a special person, but you can overcome, especially with the Lord on your side. You can overcome anything, but first you have to identify and understand and cope with what you have and not necessarily be ashamed of it but to recognize and accept it. So I think that this is good that she goes into the special care, the special education program where she is with other children that have special needs. That's for half the day, then she comes to the day care where it's regular old world and you have to be inclusive and interact. She'll get both. That's what I'm looking for, and so that's inclusive. *Inclusive* doesn't mean that you disregard something else, it means that you include it. That's how I look at the word *inclusive*.

Paulette viewed the preschool years as preparation for school, and, initially, her plan was that Bri would participate in general education, with whatever backup she would need from special education. In her words,

Typical class. Now she may have to go to some special services, okay. But I expect Bri to be sitting right there with everybody else. Well, with the early intervention, she has gotten what she wouldn't have if she had not had Down syndrome. So this is like an extra. Yes, that's how I see it. But when she goes to school, you know, when everybody else goes to school, I expect her to be in a classroom with everybody else. I mean that's why I'm going through all of this.

VISIONS OF THE FUTURE

Two years later, in Bri's prekindergarten year, we conducted a follow-up interview with Paulette. She had changed her position about

Bri's education in elementary school because she had become very concerned about the kind of negative exposure that children receive in the public school environment. Paulette expected Bri to function like any other child, considering her special needs, but believed that Bri, with her strong imitation skills but delayed judgment development, needed a more sheltered environment until she could determine what is appropriate and safe to imitate. She acknowledged that even in the special education environment Bri would be exposed to some negative models. At the same time, however, she saw that environment as being more controlled and more protected. She said, "There's a difference between keeping your child sheltered as they learn the proper coping techniques and keeping your child ignorant of how to cope in her environment."

Thus, Paulette's plan was that after the preschool years, Bri would continue her schooling in the special education center as long as possible and as long as her needs were being met. She had also given thought to home schooling, although she laughingly commented that she was not sure that she herself was cut out for that. (Paulette took an early retirement from the federal government and is now a stay-at-home mom.) She was not concerned about Bri's social interaction because she would have ample opportunity to socialize with her peers at the child care center and at the church. This way Paulette could ensure that Bri was socializing with children whose families shared Paulette's religious views and philosophy of life. Bri will also continue in the separate speech center that she has attended since age 4 years. This 1-hour weekly session is very valuable for Bri, and she has always loved the individualized attention provided by this type of environment.

Paulette's vision of her daughter's growing up continued to emphasize normalcy. She anticipated that Bri, far from the "docile" image given her by the social worker so many years before, would grow into a pretty typical teenager when the time came, and decisions would have to be made about all of the usual challenges, including dating. By age 5, Bri was a very attractive child, in both her physical appearance and her personality. Paulette even commented that she was considering trying her out for modeling because she had all of the attractiveness needed, and Paulette believed that it was time that advertisers included children with disabilities in more everyday environments. Besides, Bri loves attention.

Paulette fully expects that Bri will be married as an adult. She exclaimed, "I'm beginning to be one of those people who want to choose their daughter's husband. Yes, I am, I really like that." When we asked whether she was expecting that Bri would marry a person who has a disability, however, she allowed for considerable choice by Bri, saying, "Not really. I don't know. It's up to her. She *may* fall in love with someone with a mental disability or a physical disability." From Paulette's perspective, disability was really not the issue. Her main concern was that Bri find someone with a strong religious foundation. Her wishes for Bri were no different from what she wished for her older daughter. She summed up her vision of Bri's future as follows:

> I'm looking for her to be around families who are grooming their sons to be Christian men. Our children need to be taught how to be good husbands and wives. You see, Bri will always be special and need a very, very special kind of man. So that the special responsibilities he will have for her, he will be able to accept them, accept the responsibilities. Scripture tells husbands to love your wife as Christ loved the church, and Christ died for His church. Can you imagine the satisfaction, the happiness of a woman, the joy my child would have, being a part of a family headed by a Christ-centered husband! Looking for that material in a Christian household doesn't guarantee such a husband, but it sure does increase the odds of finding one. I'm bringing her up to be a wife and mother. Yes, I am bringing her up to be a wife! I don't have a problem with that—and to be a mother. Committing herself to the home to care for her family is the hallmark of a virtuous woman. She will be quality wife material, a pearl of rarest find! Whatever limitations she has, I don't see that as something to prevent her from achieving this goal.
>
> I think Bri will have so many choices. I want her to fully develop all her skills, potential, and talents. She can pursue a career if she wants. But, you see, she is being raised to understand that her first responsibility will be to her husband and children. Most of us find out too late. Careers, yes, they are great, but the time for rearing a family is so short—they're babies and then they're grown. God gives us plenty of time to have our careers, but real fulfillment is in the success of your family. Few women trying to be supermoms get that the odds are against you and the stress will kill you. It's in finding a loving and faithful husband, okay, being committed to caring for him and your children and your home. That's the meat and potatoes, you know, *and* the cake! The rest is the sweet icing God gives from his abundance.

APPLYING THE POSTURE OF CULTURAL RECIPROCITY

1. *Perspectives on inclusion:* We were intrigued by Paulette's perspective on inclusion. She pointed out that there was a differ-

ence between being sheltered and being ignorant of how to cope in society. In her view, inclusion does not mean that you disregard special education, it means that you include it wherever appropriate. This point of view was a new one for us because we saw inclusion as participating in the mainstream. Paulette's approach, however, was to "mix and match" Bri's environments to create an individualized education: a child care center that provided both religious education and interactions with typical children and a special education environment that responded to her needs and provided opportunities for her to meet other children with disabilities. What is your reaction to Paulette's view of appropriate education for Bri?

2. *Parental knowledge versus professional knowledge:* Paulette found that the process of having therapy services delivered on site ran into several difficulties. One point that she made was that the therapists should be prepared to fit into the environment in which they offer their services. She also believed that sustained contact with Bri enabled her and the child care provider to see Bri function in many contexts and to develop a more holistic view of her than the therapist who saw her only briefly. By Paulette's assessment, one of the therapists did not seem to notice that her professional style was not compatible with Bri's learning style or that her approach was making Bri increasingly "hyper."
   a. What was your reaction to this anecdote? Use your personal identity web (see Figure 3 on p. 9) to identify the source of your reaction.
   b. Imagine that you are the therapist trying to come to some agreement with Paulette about how to approach the on-site delivery of services to Bri's child care program and also about her perceptions of the inappropriateness of your style of working with Bri. Work through a process of cultural reciprocity with Paulette on these issues.

3. *Pro-life advocacy and adoption:* Paulette is a mother who chose to be the parent of a child with a disability. This choice was a charge from God, which she could not ignore. Her goals for her daughter reflect this deep belief and conviction as well as her pro-life philosophy. What is your personal reaction to her position? Using your personal identity web (see Figure 3 on p. 9), identify the source of your reaction.

4. *Visions of the future:* Paulette expects no less than marriage and motherhood for her daughter. What would be your reaction to

this view as an early interventionist or as a transition specialist assisting Paulette in developing a transition plan for Bri as she graduates from high school? Work through a hypothetical process of cultural reciprocity as you work with her on this issue.

6

Kyle

"A Fun Person to Be with"

Kyle's art

This case study describes the increasing cognitive and social development of a boy with mental retardation as he moves from elementary to middle school. Kyle's family reflects a blend of Chinese and American traditions and a winning combination of acceptance and advocacy. Service providers will be challenged to respond to the very individualistic approach of this family, who emphasizes that no one philosophy can fit all children.

He's a wonderful little boy. He's like a big, warm teddy bear! He's just a joy to me. You come in, and he's just there waiting for you. (Martha Lee, speaking of her son Kyle)

I can't tell you what joy I get from my children. Sure, if by some miracle, they could be cured of their disabilities tomorrow, I'd be ecstatic. But they are just wonderful children. I wouldn't trade them! (Ryan Lee, speaking of his sons Kyle and Jimmy)

We arrived at the Lee family's home for the first time on a Sunday morning in January. The American flag at the doorway of their attractive suburban home provided an easy marker for recognizing their house. We were met at the door by a polite and handsome youth of high school age, who called out to his parents and invited us in. As we stepped into the foyer, another young Lee peered through the doorway of the basement stairs and, with a mischievous expression, reached for my hand, pointing to the stairs. Ryan Lee, his father, stepped into the foyer from the living room, greeted me with a smile and a handshake, and admonished his youngest son: "No, Jimmy, Dr. Harry can't go downstairs with you to see your video games right now."

Within minutes, we had been introduced to the entire family, which consisted of Ryan and Martha Lee and their three boys, Lennie, age 15; Kyle, age 10; and Jimmy, age 7. Kyle was the child who had been referred to our study by his teacher. Kyle's father, whose ethnic heritage is Chinese American, is an architect, and his mother, who is Caucasian, is a stockbroker. The mischievous youngster who had invited me to the basement turned out to be Jimmy, the Lees' youngest son, whom his mother described as "the troublemaker" in the family. Jimmy has a disability similar to Kyle's. At that time, Lennie attended a prestigious private high school and has since graduated and moved on to an equally prestigious university.

Ryan and Martha lead very busy professional lives and, for years, have had a consistent child care provider who stays with the children every day after school and another regular provider who cares for the children occasionally in the evenings or on weekends. The couple described themselves as having been "blessed with people who have helped us with our children." They saw this as an important blessing because of the extreme vulnerability of the two younger children.

Upon the recommendation of Kyle's teacher, Ryan and Martha had joined the study readily because they were "interested in anything that would be good for Kyle." In our first interview with this couple, we recognized that their interaction style was somewhat different from the style that characterized most of the other families: We felt that the Lees preferred to come quickly to the point rather than spend time chatting about personal or casual issues before beginning the official agenda of our meeting. Our interviews with them were always informative and friendly, and it was interesting to note that our conversations usually proceeded like an "interview," as compared with the more casual, even tangential discussions into which our interviews with other families often evolved. Ryan and Martha made it clear that they are a "very private" family and did not want their lives or their children's to be made public. Accordingly, for them, we use pseudonyms in this chapter to comply with their requirement of privacy.

After preliminary explanations of the purpose of our study, we began our first interview by asking Ryan and Martha to describe Kyle. The following exchange introduced us to the loving relationship that characterized this family's view of their son:

Ryan:	He's a very loving child.
Martha:	He's a sweetie.
Ryan:	Very good disposition, easy to laugh. He gets temperamental, too, but I'd say that he's pretty easygoing, by and large.
Martha:	Very loving.
Ryan:	He's very affectionate and gentle. That's his personality.
Martha:	That's just his personality. He's a sweetie! He's a fun person to be with.

We also found Kyle to be a very friendly and gentle child, whose physical features do not suggest disability. It is not until one notices that Kyle communicates only by gestures and that his motor coordination is weak that his disability becomes evident. His parents reported that he had certain definite interests, including favorite television shows, airplanes, bowling, and, perhaps most of all, food! He also loved going to school and was very disappointed when he could not. His interest in specific television shows was a new feature of his development in that year, and his mother described the delight that she experienced when she realized that Kyle was intentionally choosing to watch *Barney, Carmen San Diego*, and *Thomas the Tank Engine* and paid attention all the way through the shows. They also explained that routine was very important to Kyle and that he became upset when his routine was disturbed.

Most of the parents' social activities included the younger children, and they described themselves as not having a lot of friends but being very close as a family. They enjoyed playing tennis and often took the children along with them. They described themselves as being particularly close with Ryan's family, who had been "solid as a rock" in their support for their grandchildren; indeed, "they never blinked an eye" when they learned of the children's developmental difficulties. During a period when Ryan had to travel a lot for his job and Martha was going to night school, Ryan's parents were "always there to babysit at night." Kyle also had a favorite uncle, whose occasional visits were a source of great delight to him.

PARENTAL ADVOCACY: "WE TRY TO BE PART OF THE TEAM"

Kyle's parents proved to be very active participants in their children's education. During the first 3 years of the study, they took turns going to annual review or other school meetings. Throughout that period, Ryan and Martha expressed continuing satisfaction with Kyle's special education program, but this did not mean that they never disagreed with the school's recommendation. Rather, they seemed to develop considerable skill in advocating from a position of being "members of the team." This section details what this style of advocacy looked like to our research team.

Like all of the other children in our study, Kyle had started his schooling in one of the school district's "special centers" for children with moderate to severe disabilities. Prior to this, he had been served by the county's home-based infant/toddler program, a program that his mother described as "unbelievably good." Quite satisfied with Kyle's experience in the special center, his parents reacted with cautious concern when the school district proposed to move Kyle to their least restrictive environment (LRE) program—a self-contained classroom in a general school building. Martha told us that she was worried about the move:

> I had a terrible feeling that Kyle was being pushed around . . . downsized, in that special services would be reduced. . . . I went to those meetings, and I really thought the children were going to suffer. But I was wrong.

As it turned out, Martha and Ryan agreed that the curriculum of the LRE program "worked perfectly" for Kyle, with its functional emphasis in the self-contained classroom and a buddy system that supported partial mainstreaming into activities such as music, school trips, lunch, and recess. At first, Kyle had some difficulty with making the transition to the new school, seeming a bit "agitated and unfriendly to the teachers," but this settled down within the first year. Furthermore, Kyle's teacher had been wonderful—

with qualities of caring and commitment that Ryan wished "could be bottled and taught to all teachers because it worked so well."

After 3 years of participation in the LRE program, Kyle's parents concluded that more is demanded of students when they are around typically developing children. Furthermore, as Ryan put it, he was gratified to hear that Kyle's peers without disabilities would call out to him and that he was known and accepted.

During that 3-year placement, the only aspect of Kyle's individualized education program (IEP) that was of concern was the provision of occupational therapy, for which the school team had recommended decreased services for 2 years in a row. In the second year, the occupational therapist consulted in the classroom once per week. She observed Kyle's use of materials, such as cutting with a knife, stapling, or stacking paper, and made recommendations to the teacher. At the annual review conference, the occupational therapist recommended a "slight decrease" in service, to 5 hours per year instead of 6–8 hours. She went on to say that she was concerned about Kyle's distractibility and short attention span.

Ryan's style of parental advocacy in this exchange was remarkably effective. With no change of facial expression and in a very controlled tone, Ryan asked her to explain how they would decrease service from once per week. The therapist explained that the IEP states hours per year, which could be delivered weekly or monthly, so that although she now does it once per week, it could be done in 15-minute rather than 30-minute blocks, which would be up to the next year's therapist to decide. Ryan responded, "I'd like to go on record that I request there be no change. I don't see any reason to decrease." Once more, Ryan's tone and facial expression were very controlled, almost matter-of-fact. The message was that he was not interested in any further discussion. He was simply stating what he wanted. At that point, the teacher said that they needed to consult with someone, apparently an administrator in the special education program. While the therapist left the room with a sheaf of papers, the meeting continued with a very upbeat speech-language therapy report on Kyle's communication. Toward the end of this discussion, the occupational therapist returned with a man who introduced himself by his name and administrative role in the program. The following dialogue and signing of papers took no more than 5 minutes:

| **Administrator:** | Mr. Lee, I understand that you have some concerns over the level of occupational therapy. |
| **Ryan:** | The therapist is recommending a reduction in Kyle's hours, but I would like the same level of service. |

Administrator:	[To the therapist] What are our alternatives?
Ryan:	I don't see any reason to reduce it. It's not very much anyway.
Therapist:	The hours were reduced last year to 1–3 hours, but I really see him for 6–8 hours.
Ryan:	I would like it to remain the same. It's not like I'm asking for an extra week.
Administrator:	That will be no problem.

The papers were promptly passed around for the appropriate signatures, the occupational therapist and the administrator left the room, and the conference resumed, with the teacher immediately beginning her very lengthy, detailed report on Kyle's progress and goals. Throughout the entire discussion, Ryan's tone and affect remained unruffled.

As the teacher offered some positive comments on Kyle's progress in communication and fine motor skills, Ryan asked her whether the occupational therapist worked along with Kyle. The teacher replied that she did not, and Ryan commented, "I've heard the 'attention span' complaint for years now, but if you're familiar with him and you get him focused, you don't have a problem with him." The teacher agreed: "When he's on task, you can't distract him from it." Indeed, the teacher then gave the example that Kyle could work up to 40 minutes on a work task (e.g., rubber banding packets) and would forget to go to the bathroom until prompted. Overall, her view of his progress was captured by her statement that "he's made more progress than we could ever write down!" Toward the end of the conference, Ryan commented to the teacher, "I'm such a pushy person! I hope [the occupational therapist] wasn't offended."

In Kyle's final year at the elementary school, there was one other concern that arose. Parents of children in Kyle's class became aware that there were too many children in the class. Kyle's parents told us that "another parent took the lead" in getting together signatures from the parents and sent a letter of complaint to the school district, which resulted in the hiring of an additional teacher within a month. Ryan and Martha participated fully in this process and were pleased with the outcome. When we asked how they felt about taking on these advocacy roles, Martha replied, "Well, it wasn't a problem getting involved. . . . This is for our kids, and we don't mind being a bit aggressive if we have to be. We used to be a bit reticent, but not anymore. . . ." When I commented that Ryan, in particular, had struck me as a very confident advocate and asked whether it came naturally to him, he responded,

No, it doesn't come naturally to me. But if you go to enough of those meetings, you develop a pretty thick skin and you go in prepared to say no if you have to. . . . We've both learned to do it. We're both older now, too!

In the final year of the study, the Lees were faced with an apparent dilemma regarding Kyle's upcoming middle school placement. Kyle was to graduate to middle school, and his parents were comfortable with his moving on to a "continuation of a similar program that's appropriate for him." In the annual review conference, they reported that they had visited the LRE program that was being recommended but believed that the class that they were shown was much too verbal and advanced for Kyle; for example, students were counting by twos to 100. They had also visited a special center (segregated program) and did not think that he would fit in there either because one class had students with much more severe disabilities than Kyle's, whereas the other was a group of 20-year-olds. They had been told that a new class would be coming in but that those students would be of high school age. At one point, the teacher commented that if Kyle went to the special center, "He would be a star there!" His father responded, "Then I don't want him to be a star!" In a later conversation with me, Ryan expanded on this comment, explaining that he would not want Kyle to be "a star" in an environment that has low expectations for him because that would be of no benefit to him.

Throughout this project, one of our dilemmas as researchers was how to balance our research goals with the advocacy needs of the students in the project. Also, because our school-based observations were at the sufferance of the school district, we could not afford to be too intrusive. In Kyle's transition-planning conference, the discussion about an appropriate middle school program for Kyle was particularly frustrating for me as an observer because the school team seemed to be taking the approach that the parents must choose between alternatives already available in the schools, thus fitting the child to the program rather than the program to the child. Furthermore, I was suspicious of the limited placements being offered the Lees because I had heard that the school district was trying to become more restrictive and trying to place only the highest functioning students in the LRE programs, returning many others to the special centers. Consequently, I tried to move the discussion forward by asking whether the school district had to provide an appropriate program. The teacher replied that the IEP determines placement so that goals could be written to specify what is to happen and where. At that point, Ryan asked whether the teacher could sit down with the parents and write the IEP and whether that would mean that the district would have to find the appropriate placement for those goals to be implemented. The teacher nodded, and Ryan stated, "Well, I formally request [that they have such a meeting]."

This discussion was particularly difficult for Martha, who was fearing the thought of Kyle's being placed in an uncomfortable situation. She commented that if the school district did not come up with a good fit for Kyle in an LRE program, then perhaps "we can look back at the special center," at which point her husband interjected, "Or somewhere else." Ryan went on to say that having heard about kids waving to Kyle in the hall and that he had become so much more sociable, it would be wrong to move him backward. The meeting concluded with the agreement that the teacher would contact the LRE program and set up with them a date for an IEP meeting, at which the parents should decide what they wanted to ask for.

We were not able to observe that final meeting, but Ryan and Martha reported that it went well, and it turned out that there was another class available at the same school, with another teacher, who seemed to be excellent. They observed the class and concluded that it was appropriate for Kyle. We were not sure whether that class had been available all along and the parents had not been made aware of it or the class had been added recently. Martha told me that she was very relieved at how it had turned out because she was so fearful for Kyle that she was tempted to choose the special center, where he would be safe and protected. She said that she was glad that her husband had felt strongly about Kyle's need to be in an integrated program and had stuck to his conviction. She knew this was the best for Kyle.

Two years after the end of our study, Kyle was about to make the transition to high school. Once more, his parents showed their determination to exercise their right to select the most appropriate program. They wanted to be certain that the program in the zoned school, with transportation provided, was indeed the most appropriate, because Kyle's teacher had suggested another school that she believed had a better vocational program. Ryan and Martha visited both programs and explained to us simply that they would not settle for a school just because that was the one that provided transportation. Kyle's right to an appropriate education is, after all, a centerpiece of the law. After discussion with the teacher at the assigned school, who assured them that the programs were equivalent, Martha and Ryan agreed to go along with the placement on the understanding that they could request a change later if they were not satisfied with the program.

Ryan and Martha's view of their child's education was very clear: It should be tailored to his level of need at any given point in time. They did not see inclusion as a must for Kyle, except to the extent that it was clearly going to be of benefit to him; that is, they did not hold a philosophical position that inclusion was preferable on principle. It all depended on what Kyle needed. Consistent with this view, they dismissed the principle of "full inclusion" because they believed that this was a kind of one-size-fits-all approach that did not take into account the variations in children's needs. As Ryan consistently said, "It all depends on the child."

KYLE AND HIS PEERS

One of the main goals of our project was to offer opportunities for the inclusion of children with disabilities in the social activities of their peers. At the beginning of the project, Kyle's parents reported that they had not yet thought about helping him to develop particular peer friendships. For the most part, they reported, Kyle was more interested in adults with whom he had formed relationships, such as family members and teachers.

In the first year of the project, our efforts were focused on observing Kyle at school and talking with his parents and teachers to gain information about his social skills and interests. Kyle was in the same class as Rafael, another child in the project (see Chapter 8), and was included with peers without disabilities at lunch, recess, and school assemblies. He also participated in activities with third and fourth graders without disabilities who signed up in a buddy system to visit Kyle's classroom. Our observations confirmed his parents' report that Kyle was more interested in relationships with adults than with children. At school, he became very attached to the teacher and was just beginning to pay attention to his peers. The teacher reported that he would sometimes suddenly go up and hug another child, but most times he tended to hang back and observe from the periphery of the activity. Once at recess, however, Kyle stood for a while looking at a group of kids playing ball, then suddenly ran out into the middle of the playground and spent the rest of the recess turning round and round with a smile, watching the activities of the crowd. When we described this to the teacher, she said that this was new behavior for Kyle. In the second year of the project, our school observations noted that Kyle was becoming more sociable with and interested in his peers and would now go closer or even join in a group physically, to watch what they were doing.

Our attempts to increase Kyle's opportunities for social interaction really began in the second summer of the project. First, we arranged for him to participate in a summer day camp that was run by the county. As a trial run, he participated for only half-days during the final week of the camp, accompanied by Faustina, our graduate assistant. We did not formally prepare campers or counselors, but Faustina casually explained to the other children that Kyle could not talk and asked them to encourage him to participate in the activities. She found that some kids took a definite interest in Kyle and invited him, encouraged him, or reprimanded him if his behavior was inappropriate. Kyle consistently responded appropriately to these overtures and followed his peers' suggestions. By then, his friendliness was evident, and at times Faustina had to remind him that kissing or hugging "is for family members." In physical activities, such as group games, he tended to hold back unless Faustina also participated but expressed enjoyment whenever he did join in. Overall, we believed that he did enjoy the week at camp and that, with better preparation for the counselors and more opportunities for the children to understand Kyle's disability, this could be a very rewarding experience for him.

In the week after the camp, Faustina arranged daily outings for Kyle, along with his schoolmates Rafael and Dorothy, as well as Rafael's brother and Moni's niece, both of whom do not have disabilities. Their trips to a nearby playground, the bowling alley, and Rafael's house all went very well, and Faustina observed that Kyle responded particularly well to Rafael, who is quite verbal and who frequently encouraged Kyle to participate more actively.

Overall, during those 2 years, Kyle's interest in social activities increased considerably. Although he often did not participate directly or spontaneously, he showed his interest by positioning himself close to an activity or a group of children and watching them with a smile. If, however, the activity was one that was easily at his level of motor skill, he sometimes joined in spontaneously, as in playing on the seesaw at the playground or sitting on the swing. At the bowling alley, Kyle pushed rather than carried the ball, which was too heavy for him to lift. At one point, he sat down at the table and, picking up a pencil, began to imitate the actions of a person recording scores. He did this very appropriately, watching the players with a smile and scribbling on the paper with his pencil. At Rafael's house, Kyle followed his host's lead in looking around the house and seemed to enjoy being there. Kyle's level of physical energy in an activity was often lower than the other children's, and he had to be encouraged to continue to participate rather than find a place to sit or lie down and watch the activity. However, it was hard to tell how much of this was related to his feeling of competence in the activity. We wondered whether increased skill in certain kinds of play might lead to increased energy and interest on Kyle's part.

In the third summer of our project, we supported Kyle for 1 week at an all-day camp. We had wanted him to go for a longer period, but, unfortunately, by the time we got to the Lees with the suggestion, they had already signed him up for summer camp at the special center that he had been attending in the previous summers. Between that plan and the family's vacation plan, there was only 1 week available. I would say that Ryan and Martha generally viewed the integrated summer camp activity as experimental and were more comfortable with the center-based summer program to which Kyle was accustomed.

In that year, we decided that it was imperative to do some preparation with the counselors and campers prior to Kyle's inclusion. Faustina, consequently, with the support of a colleague, Dr. Sherril Moon, devised an "orientation" program for personnel and children at the summer camp. Faustina conducted two sessions at the camp—1 hour with the counselors and 30 minutes with the youth. Both groups showed great interest in the information that she shared and the discussion that it generated.

As we did with Rafael, for whom we also made summer day camp arrangements (see Chapter 8), we found that the best plan was to have Kyle grouped with the 10-year-olds because he was much more out of place with the children of his age (then 12). The main conclusion of our observations in that week was that the orientation that Faustina had conducted with the campers was very successful. In the previous year, some children had shown an interest in Kyle but had been hesitant about approaching him, seeming unsure of what would be appropriate. This time, from the first day, there were certain children who explicitly expressed a wish to associate with Kyle.

A common type of interaction that we noted was essentially that Kyle's peers instructed him, but in a friendly manner that we believed was very appropriate and that Kyle responded to happily. This type of interaction was very helpful in Kyle's learning the routines of the camp. The following excerpt from Faustina's field notes give an idea of the tone of these interactions:

> A boy came up to me and said he wanted to be Kyle's buddy. He said his name was John. He held Kyle's hand, and they climbed onto the

stage. A second guy, named Don, once in a while would try to involve Kyle by pulling or touching him in a friendly way. Their game continued until lunchtime, when they all sat in a group. John guided Kyle to sit with the group, but while they were waiting for lunch, Kyle became restless and started to get up. John told him to sit down. Then when it was time to get up and go for their lunchboxes, John pulled Kyle's hand and said, "Let's go." So they went together to another room where they usually have lunch. John then told Kyle, "You don't eat yet, until you're told to eat." So even though Kyle kept pointing towards his mouth and saying, "Ah, ah," John said, "No, you have to wait 'til you're told to eat." When John gave Kyle the go-ahead to eat, he took out his sandwiches and ate along with the others. (July 31, 1995)

We also noted that children tried to teach Kyle to talk. One girl, in particular, made several efforts in this direction, usually by showing Kyle an object, saying its name, and asking him to repeat it. Although Kyle has not been noted to say these words since that time, on that occasion Faustina's notes recorded the following:

Beverly came by and asked Kyle what he thought she had in her hand. She had a little, very tiny ball. She said, "Kyle, say, 'Ball.'" Kyle said, "Ball." . . . Then she brought the rollerskating shoes and said, "Kyle, say, 'Skating shoes.'" But Kyle said, "Yah." . . . Then she brought back the ball, and Kyle said, "Ball." Beverly jumped up and ran to her friends to tell them that Kyle had said "ball." (August 2, 1995)

Later, Beverly came back to Kyle, and, as she used the same strategies, another girl commented, "My little sister says nothing when I ask her and my mother says things for her, just like you're doing."

Perhaps our greatest encouragement came on occasions when we noted play interactions that were just for fun rather than for teaching or helping. Both the campers and the counselors quickly got the hang of making simple accommodations to include Kyle in their games. For example, they allowed Kyle to be the nonblindfolded member of a partnership in which a blindfolded camper had to tie the shoelaces of his partner. Kyle laughed happily throughout this game. Also, in a kind of tag game in which each camper had to touch a person in the other group, no one got upset—rather, they laughed good-naturedly—when Kyle ran from one place to another, laughing and touching everyone whom he could.

On the last day of camp, we noted the only occasion of negative interactions with Kyle, and we were gratified to see that these attempts were not tolerated by Kyle's friends. Faustina's notes read,

The campers were all at a game, and I encouraged Kyle to join them. Now this particular group that were playing this game were not Kyle's group. The groups were all mixed up. I could see that some of this group did not want to accommodate Kyle. You could see from some of their reactions. As Kyle sat behind one guy, like all the campers had done at that point, the guy in front of him decided to be very mean, moving away and making faces at Kyle. The guy's friends immediately screamed at him and said, "Stop doing that to Kyle. Sit right there in front of him! What has he done to you that you don't want to sit near him? He hasn't done anything!" The boy was very embarrassed at his friends screaming at him, so he decided to just sit in front of Kyle to keep his friends quiet. (August 4, 1995)

Kyle's spoken language tended to remain much the same over the years that we have known him, being restricted to "yah" (yes) and "okay," which Moni and Faustina heard him say a couple of times. His pronouncing of "ball" at the request of a camp peer makes us wonder whether he could talk more when he felt it necessary. One day, in the second summer, Faustina heard him say, "I like that!" three different times. His parents, however, have not heard him say this.

Kyle's use of a communication symbol book, however, distinctly increased over those 2 years. During the second summer at day camp, he used his book spontaneously with Faustina and, on occasion, approached a peer and used the book to communicate a wish, such as wanting to eat or to go to the bathroom. His parents acknowledge that they do not reinforce the use of the book at home as much as they should because they already understand his meanings so well. This was evident in their ability to describe subtle differences in the meanings of his gestures, which he used consistently—for example, that he would touch his eyes to indicate feeling sad but would touch them in a slightly different way to indicate being tired. When angry, he would hit a table or tap gently on his leg. Sometimes, Kyle could demonstrate his intention very explicitly. For example, after the family had returned home from a trip to Florida, which Kyle had enjoyed tremendously, Kyle brought down the suitcase, emptied his dad's drawer, and laid the clothes out on the bed!

Overall, we believed that our efforts to provide Kyle with new social opportunities were rather limited, but we were gratified to see that he did enjoy the efforts that we made. We believe that his continuing integration with children without disabilities will contribute to his growing social skills and enjoyment.

"A LEAP OF FAITH": KYLE'S CONFIRMATION

Ryan and Martha are Catholics who include their children fully in the practice of their religion. In the first year of the project, we attempted to follow the parents' interest in having Kyle enroll in confirmation classes offered by their church. An interview with the director of the confirmation programs indicated that it would be appropriate to enroll Kyle in the church's special program for young people with mental retardation. She explained that although the general classes did sometimes include students with disabilities, this depended entirely on the willingness and the skills of the teacher. Both the program director and Kyle's family believed that the general class would not be appropriate for him because of its cognitive focus. This, his parents emphasized, would be meaningless to Kyle. The class for people with mental retardation typically focused on somewhat older individuals, so we did not pursue the idea further at that time.

Our explorations on this topic prompted us to reflect on one aspect of our role as researchers: our perception that there was a potential conflict between the explicit inclusion goals of our project and the idea of our supporting a church effort that served only individuals with disabilities. As it turned out, the deciding factor was Kyle's age, but the process brought to our attention the importance of professionals' being prepared to honor the preferences of families and not trying to impose their own philosophies.

Five years later, we received the wonderful news from the Lees that their wish had finally been fulfilled: Kyle was to be confirmed and take his first communion in the spring of 1997. Faustina and her two daughters attended the confirmation and the Lees' home reception afterward. She reported that it was a very touching experience, with grandparents, uncles, and aunts from both sides of Kyle's family present. Ryan and Martha echoed her description of the event and explained how Kyle had been prepared for it. He had not, after all, participated in classes; rather, it was "home based." The Sister from the church brought materials, such as videos, pictures, and symbols, that she and Kyle's parents then went through with Kyle. In his father's words,

> It was a leap of faith that the message and meaning would be/subliminal, which made it, in a way, better than approaching it in a cognitive way—just learning the catechism and so on. It was a wonderful day. . . . Very touching. Father called him an angel from God, and that's what we've always said—that he is our gift. We believe that on that day he was infused with the Lord's spirit.

VISIONS OF THE FUTURE

We were concerned about how all of the parents in the project saw their children's futures. To some extent, the views expressed

seemed to reflect certain cultural traditions, such as whether extended families were part of the expectation or the families sub-
scribed to a more "nuclear model" family. Their views also reflected the financial circumstances of the families, as well as the
family configuration—in particular, whether there were available
siblings.

In the case of Kyle's family, we were particularly interested in
how their mixed cultural heritages affected their views of their children and their plans for the future. As always, we discovered that
cultural influences are very complex, often not falling into any clear
stereotype of a cultural group's beliefs and usually revealing the
powerful influences of a mixture of different heritages and personal
experiences.

When I asked Ryan and Martha whether they thought that
culture played a role in the way that they have experienced their
sons' disabilities, Ryan replied, "To a point, I think," whereas
Martha exclaimed, "Definitely!" As we talked, these parents
shared with me their perspectives on these very personal questions. The Lees had often described Ryan's parents' unconditional
acceptance of their grandsons, and Martha, in particular, had interpreted this very much in terms of a cultural tradition. It
seemed to her, she said, that traditional Chinese values held the
family as "almost sacrosanct." This tradition, combined with her
parents-in-law's strong Christian values, produced an attitude of
absolute acceptance of their grandchildren. Along with this, she
believed, was a kind of traditional Asian "fatalism," which she
saw as a positive philosophy that accepts rather than fights the
facts that a person faces. Martha's family, by contrast, were "very
American, where you just fight everything"; her parents had had a
very hard time accepting the children's disabilities. Martha herself, also "very American," had experienced a very difficult ad-
justment to the reality of her sons' disabilities. When Jimmy was
born, Martha was "devastated" and experienced intense embar-
rassment and discomfort at her children's conditions. But now,
she explained,

> I'm so different now; I've adopted the Asian way. Now I feel so far be-
> yond social norms. I come from a very materialistic family, where hav-
> ing two handicapped kids just isn't part of the picture. . . . Sure, I still
> like nice things, but you get to realize that there's a cap on the pleasure
> you can get from them. There are so many positive aspects to the expe-
> rience. . . . You get a clear perspective on life, values, what's important
> and what's not.
> But I don't mean to say that [being materialistic] is totally American.
> In fact, I really think we're moving towards a much better world, in

spite of all the problems. So many people have been so very kind. So *many* people! And God knows whose heart [Kyle] has touched.

Ryan spoke of his Chinese heritage in somewhat more modified terms. His father having been born in China and his mother being first-generation Chinese American, Ryan explained the gradual process of acculturation that he believed had occurred in his family. Whereas his grandparents were a traditional Chinese family, his parents were more acculturated to American ways and were deeply influenced by Christian values. Ryan saw himself, culturally, as more American than Chinese. He explained,

> Although I also have those Asian traits of being rather calm, not getting excited over things. . . . I'm really an American. And I think I've taken on some of Martha's traits, too. I don't always accept things. I've become more of a fighter.
> I believe my parents' attitude does have something to do with their culture—a tranquility, or acceptance of nature, accepting people as they are. I think their attitudes are rooted in that tradition, but then, my parents are also very Christian people. So I don't know if it's really a Chinese tradition as such. Really, I think that they're about the most nonjudgmental people I know. Their reactions have certainly made it livable for us.

Ryan and Martha spoke of their sons' disabilities as an experience that had drawn them closer together and also closer to Ryan's family. Also very important, they described their oldest son, Lennie, as "wonderful" in his relationship with his younger brothers, taking a great interest in their training and, sometimes, doing a better job than his parents.

With regard to Kyle's and Jimmy's futures, Ryan and Martha had already made financial arrangements for their sons' lifetime support. They anticipated that the brothers would be able to hold simple jobs and would, eventually, reside in "some kind of protected setting" with the stipulation that they be placed together. The details of their living circumstances would be worked out later. In Martha's words, "There are lots of programs out there. It's just a matter of sorting through them and finding the right one." The Lees' view of Lennie's role in Kyle's and Jimmy's lives was very clear. They knew that they could count on his love and concern for his brothers, and they envisioned his role primarily as overseeing his brothers' welfare:

> It's going to come down to [him] ultimately, but we don't want it to come down to him too much. We want him to have his own life. So, to

a certain extent—we believe he'll be willing to help. Yes, we will need his help.

APPLYING THE POSTURE OF CULTURAL RECIPROCITY

1. *Creating inclusive opportunities:* The Lees had a very clear perspective on the issue of inclusive versus separate educational placements for Kyle: "It depends on what's appropriate for him." Just as they were able to utilize an individualized home-based program to prepare Kyle for confirmation, so did they hold out until they were offered a middle school placement that ensured some inclusion but offered a curriculum suited to Kyle's level. Their overt rejection of a one-size-fits-all approach on decisions about Kyle's life made us aware of the significance of this philosophy in their own lives. Martha tried to adopt the strong Asian tradition of acceptance that she saw in Ryan's parents' response to the disability, whereas Ryan liked and had acquired the fighting spirit that he saw in Martha's European American tradition. Together they had created a unique family culture that demanded, just as Kyle's needs demanded, an individualized response.

   Imagine that you are one of the professionals, perhaps a teacher or a summer camp counselor, working with Kyle's family. What might be some of your biases as you begin to work with this family on the issue of Kyle's educational placement and summer activities?

2. *Becoming aware of ethnic stereotypes:* There were several factors that would have made it easy to stereotype the Lees as a "typical" Chinese American family: the physical appearance of father and sons, Martha's reference to a close-knit extended family of paternal grandparents who were always supportive and willing to help, the fact that Ryan was an architect and their oldest son, Lennie, was in a prestigious private school—all of this bringing to mind the stereotype of "the model minority." However, many features of this family's functioning reflected mainstream rather than "ethnic group" traditions. These included that they paid non–family members to provide child care after school and on occasional evenings and weekends and that, unlike many ethnic minority families, they envisioned Lennie's role in the future as primarily overseeing his brothers' welfare but not as providing a primary home for his brothers.

Use your personal identity web (see Figure 3 on p. 9) to identify the stereotypes or ethnic biases that you might have held as you approached this family. What would have helped you to break down that stereotype, and what lessons would you have learned about ethnic identity?

3. *Researchers' inclusion bias:* One of the dilemmas that we faced as researchers working with this family was what appeared to be a potential conflict between the explicit inclusion goal of our research project and the preference of the Lees for services or activities that were carefully tailored to Kyle's needs and developmental level. They were not advocates of inclusion for inclusion's sake. When we began to seek an opportunity to fulfill the parents' goal of having Kyle confirmed, there was a point at which we thought that we might have to agree to support his participation in a segregated program of religious preparation that catered to people with mental retardation only. We perceived this as a potential conflict for us and actually were relieved when it turned out that the program was for older individuals and that Kyle was too young to participate. What do you think of this "conflict"?

4. *Developing a communication system for Kyle:* Although Kyle used a communication board, he was able to communicate with his family through a personalized system of signs. If you were a speech-language pathologist or a special education teacher working with Kyle, how would you have targeted his communication needs? Identify the professional and personal values that would have affected your decisions.

5. *Parent–professional interaction styles:* We mentioned in the story that the Lees' interaction style was somewhat more structured than was common among many of the other families. In many families, there was a great deal of coming and going of visitors or extended family members, less predictability regarding planning interviews or other activities, and a more tangential style of conversation. Think about any interviews or home visits that you have paid to families. How would you describe the organizational and interaction styles of those families? With which kind of style were you more comfortable? Use your personal identity web (see Figure 3 on p. 9) to explore the source of your preferred interaction style, and consider how you might have reacted to what we have said about the styles of the various families in these stories.

7

Theresa Marie

"An Absolute Miracle"

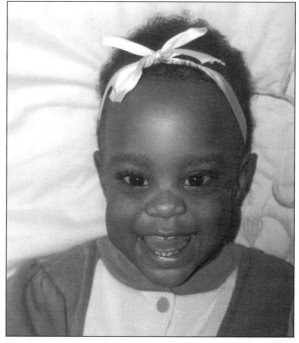

Theresa Marie

This case study documents the transformation of an African American preschooler from the status of a "preemie" with developmental delays to that of a kindergartner in general education. Her parents' struggle to obtain all to which their daughter is entitled while keeping her from being relegated to a disability track will challenge service providers to review their assumptions about segregated services. Issues of equity and rights are central to the study.

You think education is expensive? Try ignorance. Being educated doesn't mean the person will have a lot of degrees, but someone who is aware and knowledgeable can make so much better choices. And education is power, you have much more negotiating power. . . . To me, children and their education is so important. To me that's the core of our country. (Alexandra, Theresa Marie's mother)

When we first met Theresa Marie's family in May 1995, we were struck by the parents' clear-cut vision of providing education and social opportunities for their family. Their new house in a suburban neighborhood was surrounded by a well-tended garden with seasonal flowers. As we entered the house, Alexandra greeted us warmly and led us to the family room, which was furnished with comfortable, modest sofas and a large-screen television, whereas the living room, which was opposite the family room, was unfurnished. Alexandra emphasized that the children's education was the family's first priority. A native of the Caribbean island of St. Lucia, Alexandra is a nurse and was working in an intensive care unit in the cardiology department of a major urban hospital; her husband, Addison, who is American, was a respiratory therapist in the same hospital.

Alexandra and Addison were on a strict schedule as a pair of working parents who were determined to accomplish their goals. After a busy day at the hospital, Alexandra sometimes returned our calls at 10:00 at night while watering her flower garden in the summer months. The couple tried to stagger their work schedules so as to have one parent in the home at most times, but they were also assisted by Alexandra's cousin, who had come to the United States from St. Lucia to live with them. This young lady provided child care for Theresa Marie, then age 2½, and her brother, Patrick, then age 1.

We conducted four interviews with Alexandra and Addison, observed their participation in annual review conferences, and made several observations of Theresa Marie at home and in her child care program.

"KNOWLEDGE IS POWER": BECOMING ADVOCATES

When Alexandra and Addison decided to have children, they made a conscious decision that their children would be "our first business." They planned to empower their children with the best education that they could afford, while participating and staying involved in the education process. They did not anticipate, however, how intense that process would be for their first child, Theresa Marie.

When Theresa Marie was born prematurely, her parents were not prepared for her birth and it was a difficult time for them. At only 26 weeks of gestation, Theresa Marie was totally unexpected. Her mother had not experienced any major problems during the pregnancy and had just returned from a trip to St. Lucia: "All of a sudden one day I just went into labor. I went into the hospital and they couldn't stop it!" This was a traumatic experience for both parents even though they both worked in medical environments. Theresa Marie weighed 1½ pounds at birth, and she was taken to the neonatal intensive care unit (NICU). After 3 months, several infections, and numerous setbacks, she came home weighing approximately 5 pounds.

After overcoming the initial shock, Alexandra and Addison began by trusting the medical and educational systems, respecting the authority and skills of the professionals. However, they realized early that they would have to become watchful advocates for Theresa Marie to ensure that she was, in fact, getting the services that she needed. Their advocacy as parents was spurred by their interaction with two other parent advocates, who advised them of several strategies to use in advocating for Theresa Marie in various circumstances. In their effort to get the best services for their daughter, they realized that formal degrees were not enough. "Knowledge is power" became their motto, and they decided to become as knowledgeable as possible about their daughter's rights and services.

Alexandra's and Addison's medical training proved to be a tremendous asset in this process. At one point during her hospital stay, Theresa Marie experienced a temporary setback that prompted Alexandra to call every morning to ask for Theresa Marie's vital signs. One morning, the nurse in charge of her care was not able to report the vital signs; when Alexandra called later in the day, she was still unable to get any information. Becoming very uneasy, Addison quickly paid a visit to the NICU, only to find that Theresa Marie had a heavy mucus discharge around her mouth and, instead of suctioning and cleaning the air passage, the nurse was turning up the oxygen. Addison's own knowledge of these issues led him to realize that Theresa Marie's air passage was blocked, which resulted in low levels of oxygen in her blood. However, he was concerned about long-term effects of exposure to oxygen, which sometimes damages the tissues of the eye. Their impression that the nurse was not performing her duties competently was confirmed by a family friend who was working at the hospital and who, upon visiting Theresa Marie, also believed that the nurse was not taking good care of the child. Alexandra and Addison expressed their concern to the head nurse and requested that the nurse be changed. The head nurse responded promptly to the parents' request and took care of Theresa Marie herself until she found someone reliable to replace the previous nurse.

Despite setbacks like this, however, both parents believed that, on the whole, Theresa Marie benefited from the medical intervention and the services of the Infants and Toddlers program that began serving her soon after her discharge from the hospital. They believed that these services were essential for Theresa Marie and allowed her to develop her potential. As Alexandra said,

> So we've felt that all the help that she has gotten really helped. We enrolled her very early in the Infants and Toddlers program, and they used to come to the house. She had a teacher, a physical therapist at first, and I think that was it—PT and the special teacher.

As crucial as these services were, Theresa Marie's parents soon concluded that they could not sit back and assume that agencies would automatically deliver the most appropriate services. They became convinced that the county's drive to guard the limited resources of the special education system was not working in Theresa Marie's best interest, especially in relation to the fact that Theresa Marie's special education teacher also acted as her service coordinator. After being refused certain services, Addison and Alexandra realized that this service coordination arrangement resulted in a conflict of interest for the service providers. Only after Theresa Marie's parents expressed concern with their current coordinator were they told that they were entitled to get a coordinator from The Arc (formerly the Association for Retarded Citizens [ARC]). The parents' realization that they had not been given this choice at the onset led them to see that they were not getting all of the information that they needed to make informed decisions. They made it clear that their initial trust in the system was soon replaced by a certainty that some of the service providers were taking advantage of the fact that they did not know the rules and the laws of the special education system. Addison explained:

> Whatever they would tell us, we would believe, because we felt that they were the authority when it came to the child. So they used this against us, so the person who was Theresa Marie's teacher was also Theresa Marie's coordinator. So, in essence, she was part of the school

system, she made all the decisions for the child. . . . [But] there were certain things that we looked at in Theresa Marie, where we felt she needed services. So in order to kind of fight the system, we went outside, because we could see that the child needed certain things, like occupational therapy [OT]. What was happening was we were being given the runaround by the school, and she instantly came back and made the decision that Theresa Marie couldn't have this. So Theresa Marie went maybe a good 6 or 7 months without the occupational therapist.

The private evaluation that the parents sought concluded that Theresa Marie's fine motor skills needed attention and that she could benefit from OT. The service coordinator from the school, however, discounted the report and said that Theresa Marie was not eligible for OT, and she did not recommend an evaluation of Theresa Marie by the occupational therapists within the system. So Alexandra and Addison paid for private OT services. They thought that services were denied because the providers believed that the family could afford to pay for the services privately, and used this as a strategy to handle the resource crunch that the system was experiencing. In speaking of Theresa Marie's initial service coordinator, Addison said,

She found ways to get by us, by the lack of us having any knowledge. Even when we did intervene—because sometimes we'd sit down and we'd watch and go over with her, but the lack of us having any knowledge of the situation, and the more we gave her the authority, [the more] she took advantage of it.

Alexandra added,

We never knew anything about due process. So we never knew that we could say, "Well, listen, I don't agree with that, let's call a meeting." And we were so thankful when we found out the program was there. And we were like, "Oh, please, thank you for doing this! If you do anything, we will agree with it!" And that was what it was: We were so concerned about Theresa Marie being educated and developing naturally that we would do anything. If the school said jump, we would jump. But after a while, we began noticing, well, something isn't right here. And when we asked questions, we were cut off immediately. So we started having more questions and more questions. After a while, we became upset. We said, "Something is wrong here."

Charlene, the service coordinator from The Arc, was also a parent of a child with a disability, and she confirmed Alexandra and Addison's hunch that "something is wrong here." As a person who was very familiar with the laws of the special education system and the bureaucracy of the service provision organizations, she was a great help to these new parents. In addition, she introduced the parents to Ruth Coates, another parent advocate who was also very helpful (see Chapter 2). Theresa Marie's parents viewed Charlene as an advocate for the child and the family and made good use of her knowledge of the special education system. They summarized the experience as follows:

Addison:	Basically, at first, we were blind. As parents, we were blind.
Alexandra:	Because we didn't know, we didn't know what was going on.
Addison:	We didn't know anything, and we were blind to the situation. In fact, it was when . . .
Alexandra:	Our new coordinator . . .
Addison:	And Ruth Coates came along. That was when we started to learn exactly what needed to be done. What had basically been done to us—what one would have said is that we were being "ripped off" by the system.

As they became more knowledgeable, Theresa Marie's parents noticed a difference in the attitudes of the service providers. In addition to just gaining information about their rights, Alexandra and Addison were learning how to use language that would be effective in getting the services that Theresa Marie needed. The following conversation indicates how their learning process progressed:

Addison:	That's when they really started going in the right direction with everything because at that point they realized that we were becoming more knowledgeable, and we had someone who was just as knowledgeable. So the paperwork that before we weren't doing actually began to be done. And so they could only go in one direction. Basically, we were being taught by Charlene, when we approached [the service providers], how to open or close an announcement or remark. So they had no way of saying anything else.
Alexandra:	Well, an example is when Theresa Marie needed an occupational therapist and they were saying things like, "Well, we don't have," because they have their own staff or pool of people from wherever, and after they have exhausted their occupational therapist with children, or her schedule is completely full, then they will tell you, "We don't have someone." Which means that the child kind of goes on a waiting list until somebody shows up. So we learned to say, "Well, this is administrative. This is an

administrative issue, and I don't want to hear that." Or, "We're here to discuss the needs of my child." And also we were able to tell them, "Well, if you don't have anybody in the school, then you have to hire somebody from the private sector." Which is what they are supposed to do.

Another example of learning the language of the system was Alexandra's comment, "You know, if I tell them, 'My child does it again and again and again,' they don't understand. If I say, 'My child perseverates,' they go, 'Aah!'"

When the family moved to a new neighborhood to provide a better environment for their children, they were confronted with another bureaucratic problem. Their community was divided by the county line; as a result, even though Theresa Marie's child care center was two blocks down the road and her parents walked her to the child care program, that program came under the jurisdiction of a different county. The county that was providing services continued to do so while the parents began the process of negotiating with the county of their residence to pick up the services. Alexandra and Addison were determined to have Theresa Marie continue in this child care program, which they had chosen after screening 20 or more programs. They believed that Theresa Marie was "blossoming" in this environment, where she participated with typically developing peers while also receiving on-site services from the Infants and Toddlers program.

The parents wrote a letter to the county to which they had moved, explaining why Theresa Marie needed to remain in that center and receive services there. Alexandra took great care in composing the letter in an effective manner, and she also requested a letter from Theresa Marie's special education teacher to validate the parents' claim that this was an appropriate learning environment for Theresa Marie. These strategies paid off, and the county of their residence started providing services to Theresa Marie in the neighboring county. This was a unique situation: It was the first time that county services had agreed to cross county lines, and it required considerable coordination between the two counties.

Theresa Marie's enrollment in that child care program was one of the most important decisions that Alexandra and Addison made in response to the suggestions from the service providers in the early intervention program, who had advised the parents that interaction with other children would motivate Theresa Marie to talk and improve her social skills. The learning environment was structured more like a preschool than a child care center, and they believed that this would be good for Theresa Marie. The decision worked well, and

Theresa Marie was, very soon, showing a great increase in sociability and language.

"THERESA MARIE JUST BLOSSOMED"

Through their advocacy, Alexandra and Addison ensured that Theresa Marie was in an environment in which she was able to come "a long way from the NICU." Her mother described her as "energetic, full of life, and has a purpose. She knows what she wants." Her father's description was, "She's very popular with the children. Because Theresa Marie stands on her own. She is neither a leader nor a follower." This sounded like the characteristics that we had noted in Theresa Marie from our earliest observations. The following excerpt from Moni's notes on an observation at the child care center gives a vivid picture of Theresa Marie's ability at age 3 both to sustain an activity and to pursue her own agenda:

> The playground is enclosed in a wire fence. There are two swings, a plastic tunnel, a plastic jungle gym, and a sand pit. Theresa Marie was watching two girls on a swing and a third girl, Y, was pushing one of the swings. . . . A teacher said it was Theresa Marie's turn to swing. Theresa Marie got on the swing, and Y came to push Theresa Marie's swing. Theresa Marie turned and said something, and Y went away. Theresa Marie held the chains on either side of the swing and stood. She turned and watched some of the other kids. She walked back and forth holding the two chains of the swing. . . . Then she called out to Y, and Y came to her and tried to sit on the swing that Theresa Marie was holding onto. Theresa Marie let out a loud, acute sound of distress, and Y went away. Theresa Marie kept on holding the two chains on the side and walking back and forth or moving sideways but didn't sit on the swing. . . . After about 5 minutes, she sat down on the swing. . . . Y came to the swing next to Theresa Marie and yelled out to the teacher, "Miss! Look at Theresa Marie!" The teacher came and stood behind Theresa Marie and said, "Ready?" and Theresa Marie smiled. The teacher helped Theresa Marie sit firmly on the swing, adjusted her position, and then pushed her. . . .
> Theresa Marie was on the swing for about 20 minutes while most of the other kids were moving from equipment to equipment. Y was still swinging next to Theresa Marie, then she looked at Theresa Marie and said something. Theresa Marie looked at her and nodded but didn't say anything. Theresa Marie was watching the other kids. She was sitting on the swing and playing with the pebbles with her foot. Y was going away, and Theresa Marie pointed to the swing and said something. Y came back and sat on the swing. They talked to each other sporadically. Y went to chase a bird. Theresa Marie called her, and Y came back to the swing. . . . Theresa Marie watched some other kids and pointed them out to Y and said something. The teacher came back and pushed Theresa Marie on the swing. (May 23, 1995)

This observation indicated that Theresa Marie had a very distinct style of her own, and it supported her father's comment that she would neither follow nor lead a group. She preferred to interact with children individually or in small groups. She was never physically aggressive, but she never allowed anyone to take her toys, take away her turn, or push her around. She had a loud voice, and she would protest with a firm "NO" or a sharp, loud cry, which was enough to warn the child who was trying to encroach on her territory. The following field notes clearly illustrate this style:

> I entered the classroom, and the teacher pointed to Theresa Marie and mentioned that they were not having any structured activity. I noticed Theresa Marie in a corner of the classroom along with some other kids. She had a toy banana in her hand. When her name was mentioned, she looked in the teacher's direction and then at me. She put down the toy banana and slowly walked toward me. I walked toward her, kneeled down, and gave her a hug. I told her I was here to watch her play with the other kids. Theresa Marie did not hug me or say anything, but she did not protest to my hug and had a slight smile on her face. Then she went back to the corner where she and some of the other kids were playing. She picked up the toy banana, looked at me, and smiled.
>
> A boy was sitting at a circular table and looking at a book. Theresa Marie pulled a chair and sat next to him. Another girl pulled a big cushion and sat next to Theresa Marie. The first boy left, and another boy came and sat next to her and started looking at the book. The book was near Theresa Marie's side of the table, encroaching on her space. Theresa Marie pushed the book towards the boy and said, "No." The boy said, "Yes," and pushed it back towards her. They repeated this exchange 14 times. Then the boy decided to give up and kept the book near his end of the table. Theresa Marie did not express any special feelings after having the argument. It seems she very clearly knows what she wants, she fights for it, but when she wins she simply takes it in her stride. (July 17, 1995)

When we first met Theresa Marie at age 2 years 8 months, she was using two- to three-word phrases, such as, "Don't do that," "Sit down, Patrick," "Stop," "Move," and so forth. At that time, her articulation was not very clear, as Alexandra explained: "She may say something to somebody on the outside and they don't know what it is, but we know." She enjoyed nursery rhymes and was able to imitate the tunes correctly. Four years later, at age 6 in her kindergarten class, Theresa Marie was able to speak fluently and no longer required anyone to interpret for her. How she arrived at that point also reflects her parents' continuing advocacy efforts.

ADVOCACY FOR INCLUSION

By the time Theresa Marie was to make the transition from Part C to Part B services, her parents were well acquainted with federal laws and county policies. They took a proactive stance and found out that the county did not offer inclusive programs for preschool children. They prepared themselves ahead of time and located and visited the various sites in which the county offered services. They also anticipated that the county may no longer agree to cross the county line and provide services in her current child care program, so they continued to search for a child care program in their county of residence, while requesting that the county continue to serve Theresa Marie in her current child care program. They asked our research project to write a letter indicating our views, based on our observations, of the appropriateness of Theresa Marie's current placement. They consulted a lawyer from a local advocacy organization, who came to the two transition individualized education program (IEP) meetings and advocated for the parents' perspectives.

From our point of view as observers, the district placement meetings revealed several essential ironies of the placement process. There was great emphasis on an apparently systematic process of assessment, then placement. Alexandra and Addison wanted Theresa Marie to remain in her preschool and continue to receive services there, so Alexandra began the meeting with this request. They provided documents, such as letters from our project and from the classroom teacher, to support their argument that Theresa Marie was doing well in an inclusive environment. As she told the service providers,

> The current placement is working very well. We tried to find a place that will accommodate the staff of the Infants and Toddlers program. We researched and researched and researched to find a day care. This is an exemplary school. We live on the dividing line of the county, but this is what is appropriate for Theresa Marie and my family. The school is working for her. Why would I change something that's working and we're seeing the changes that we want to see? Maybe the support needs to be delivered there. I realize this is nontraditional. But the IEP stands for individualized education program.

The chairperson's immediate response was that they could not discuss placement before discussing scores and intensity of services. This would seem to be a very rational process, but there were two aspects that undermined this idea. First, the process was impersonal in that the personnel in the meeting were entirely different from those who had conducted the assessments of Theresa Marie. These reports of her scores and the resultant placement recommendations, therefore, were being discussed by providers who had no personal knowledge of Theresa Marie. Second, the reports did not pass a simple reality check, as we explain.

After going through the test scores, the team concluded that Theresa Marie needed Level V services. This level represents the highest intensity of services, which are offered only in special education centers and usually serve children with severe needs. The team stated that Theresa Marie needed the small group size available at this level because the providers who tested her believed that she did not have a good attention span. Moni, observing this meeting and having conducted several observations of a very active and focused Theresa Marie, in her inclusive classroom, believed that it was obvious that Theresa Marie did not require Level V services and suspected that the professionals were recommending this level because this was, in fact, the only program that the district offered for this age group.

It was Theresa Marie's father and, ironically, Theresa Marie herself who clinched the argument. Addison, who had been silent during the initial part of the meeting, spoke up at that juncture, pointing to his daughter, who had been sitting quietly at the table, playing with her toys for more than 1½ hours. He asked the obvious question: "How could it be that this child was found to have a short attention span?" In response to his question, the chairperson looked down and sighed, and, for a while, no one said anything. The attorney who had accompanied the family then spoke up, supporting Addison's point. A decision was postponed for a second meeting.

In the second IEP meeting, the lack of logic in district recommendations was even more obvious. After much discussion, the service providers suggested that, if the family would like, Theresa Marie, then age 3, could be placed in her neighborhood school. Because the elementary school did not have a preschool section, this meant that Theresa Marie would be placed in the kindergarten, with children who were 2 years older than she. The family had no choice but to refuse.

With no decision made, Alexandra and Addison decided to take matters into their own hands. A child care program where they had put Theresa Marie's name on a waiting list called to say that they had a place for Theresa Marie. Alexandra and Addison registered her quickly and decided to go directly to the school district to request that services be provided at this center. Alexandra put together a portfolio with all of the documents, wrote a cover letter, and personally handed it to the director of special education. She did not make an appointment; rather, she asked the office staff to allow her to deliver the packet herself, as it involved her child. By doing so, she got the attention of the director, who instructed the county personnel to provide services in the preschool that the parents had chosen. This action resulted in Theresa Marie's being classified as Level III and receiving itinerant services in her inclusive preschool program.

It was interesting to note the differences in Alexandra's and Addison's advocacy styles. The couple saw their respective styles as complementary. For example, in IEP meetings, Alexandra always took a book in which she had recorded her conversations with various people in the school system. She usually made the opening statements and described the situation and told the service provider what they wanted. As we saw in the foregoing example, Addison typically waited until there was a problem and addressed the issue directly. According to Alexandra,

> I'm more of the talker. I'll talk, and my husband will say, "We need to stay with the point." So I'll get off the phone because I am all frustrated and my husband will take over and say, "Listen, this is why we called. The child needs so-and-so. We have 30 days to do it. If it hasn't been done in 30 days, then you should have contacted us and said, 'Well, we're still working on it,' or something, but you haven't done anything."

This couple's success in getting the services and placement that they wanted for their daughter encouraged them but also made them painfully aware of the need to be "on the ball." As they said, they "no longer took 'we can't do this' as an answer" from the county. Their approach was to help the professionals to focus their attention on the child, saying, "We know this is not traditional, but that does not mean that it cannot be done." They would try to work with the system in getting the services that their daughter needed. In Theresa Marie's preschool, they continued to monitor Theresa Marie's services carefully, including frequent observations of her classroom and her therapy sessions. Alexandra emphasized that their approach in their school visits was very constructive, their intention being to become part of the school team, not adversaries.

Theresa Marie's progress at her preschool program was excellent, and, 2 years later, in our follow-up interview with Alexandra, we found out that Theresa Marie was in a general kindergarten and was receiving services on site. She was getting ready to go to first grade in the same school. We wondered, how did this come about?

Did the family have to engage in another struggle with the school district to gain this inclusive placement? The answer was far more simple than that.

Theresa Marie's psychological evaluation as she approached the age of 5 revealed that Theresa Marie was capable of going to a general education kindergarten with only speech-language services from special education. There was no need for debate or discussion, no need for independent evaluations. Theresa Marie, apparently, had simply developed from a child who was perceived as warranting Level V status to one who warranted speech-language services only, to be delivered in a general education public school. Her parents went to her home school, observed all of the kindergarten classes, and requested that the school place Theresa Marie with the teacher of their choice. The school agreed, and the teacher turned out to be as good as Theresa Marie's parents expected.

During the kindergarten year, Alexandra volunteered to work in Theresa Marie's kindergarten classroom; as a result, she was able to find out about what was being taught and also to build a positive relationship with the teacher. This proved very effective in creating a collaborative relationship with the teacher and was entirely to Theresa Marie's benefit. For example, during one of the tests in the class, Theresa Marie was not able to respond appropriately to the questions, although the teacher realized that Theresa Marie actually knew all of the answers, so she contacted Theresa Marie's parents and explained what the problem was. Theresa Marie's parents worked with her on the tasks, and when the teacher gave her another opportunity to do the test, Theresa Marie excelled.

Theresa Marie's status as a full member of her school community was now established. However, we noted that Alexandra and Addison's thoughts on inclusion were not restricted to the classroom; they thought about inclusion of their children in the society at large. They tried to make sure that both Theresa Marie and her brother had the skills that they needed to fit into society. For example, they enrolled the children in a special reading program to give them a good foundation. They also enrolled them in ice skating and gymnastics lessons. They realized that many of Theresa Marie's peers participated in these activities, so they provided the same experience for their daughter so that she would be able to participate in conversations about ice skating and gymnastics. Addison clarified that the aim was not to push them to fit at any cost but that they wanted the children "to be aware of the social surroundings, to be knowledgeable about their social surroundings."

In our update discussions with Addison and Alexandra, they said that professionals in the county in which they lived were now well aware of their advocacy skills and treated them with respect because of their knowledge and advocacy strategies. Alexandra told us that they are still very focused on matters of education for both of their children. Although they are committed to the philosophy of inclusion, they do not rely solely on the school's input for their child's development. As always, Theresa Marie's progress reflects the tremendous personal effort and persistence of her now highly empowered parents. As Alexandra said,

> I know what my priorities are. We're still here with the same old furniture you saw us with when you came here 4 years ago, and my 16-year-old Volvo finally died last month. Those are not priorities for us. We are focused on our children. Last year, we paid for private tutoring for both the children, and during the summer these sessions cost us $200 a week. The tutor was using a reading method called "Reading Recovery," and Theresa Marie made fantastic progress. Now, imagine, this year, she's going into the first grade and the teacher told me they're going to be using that same program. So I said, "Okay! Theresa Marie can do that!"

For Alexandra and Addison, Theresa Marie's progress is nothing short of an "absolute miracle." According to Alexandra,

> She now has no lasting effects that we can really see. She does have several scars from the hundreds of needles she received, like on her heels and her navel. When she first noticed them, she asked what they were and I explained it all to her. I tell her all about the things that happened to her. Recently, there was a preemie reunion at the hospital where she was born, and I took her. The staff were all just amazed at her progress. Then just last week, her teacher asked the students to bring things about themselves to class, and I gave her her baby album to take. There's a picture of her lying next to a pen, and she and the pen are just about the same length. The teachers and her classmates couldn't believe it. I always tell her that she is very special, truly a special delivery!

VISIONS OF THE FUTURE

When we asked Alexandra how she and Addison envisioned the future for Theresa Marie, she replied,

> Just like any other child! We don't expect her problems to be any different from the usual problems parents have with their typical children. We have to keep on being totally involved in their lives, both Patrick and her, because this is how children succeed, with parental support. Our daughter is an African American child in a society where

there is still a lot of discrimination. My experiences as a Black person immigrating from the Caribbean and my husband's experiences as an African American are a great source of motivation for us. We are determined that our children will not be placed at a disadvantage. We have to do everything in our power to bring Theresa Marie up to be the very best she can be. And she will be!

APPLYING THE POSTURE
OF CULTURAL RECIPROCITY

1. *Professional conflict of interest:* Imagine that you are a service provider for Theresa Marie as well as her service coordinator. Her parents expect that you will advocate for her needs. They believe that she needs OT, but there is a shortage of such providers in the county. The parents' private evaluator has determined that she does need OT, but the district does not agree. What course of action is open to you?

2. *Working with strong parent advocates:* When they started out, Alexandra and Addison were, in their words, "blind" regarding the system. By the time our research team met them 2½ years later, they were well versed in special education law and in strategies for advocacy. Charlene, a worker from The Arc, and Ruth Coates, another parent advocate, played a critical role in this family's learning to be advocates. How might you feel as you approach your work with these parents? Use your personal identity web (see Figure 3 on p. 9) to examine your feelings about parent advocacy and about how you would react to parents such as these.

3. *The placement process:* When Alexandra and Addison went to the placement meetings, they already knew what they wanted for Theresa Marie. Alexandra started with a strong statement of their wishes and offered documentation to support it.

   a. Imagine that you are a service provider at the meeting. How would you react to her statement?

   b. The chairperson indicated that placement could not be discussed before the reporting of scores and a decision regarding intensity of services. What are the assumptions underlying this process? By contrast, what are the assumptions underlying the parents' view of how placement should be decided? Can you think of an alternative process that would be more congruent with the parents' perspectives on how decisions about placement should be made?

   c. Using your personal identity web (see Figure 3 on p. 9), identify your beliefs about quantifying the abilities and needs of a child. What is the role of these numbers in developing an IEP for Theresa Marie? Do you think that special education is or should be an exact science?

4. *Parent advocacy and the language of the system:* Alexandra and Addison explained that learning the language of the system was an essential part of their effective advocacy. They suggested that the parent must use not only "educated" language but also the jargon of the field. What are some of the cultural underpinnings of this? We believe that much of special education language is based on a belief that the more "objective" the language, the more accurate and professional it is.

   a. How do you respond to parents' language? Does the "educated" quality of their speech affect you? Does their ability to use special education language or jargon affect you? Use your personal identity web (see Figure 3 on p. 9) to examine the sources of your attitudes to language, both socially and professionally.

   b. Think of your own professional training, and identify some words and phrases that are commonly used in the profession, then translate them into the language that you think would be used by parents. Identify also some terms or phrases that may seem acceptable to professionals but might be offensive to parents.

8

Rafael

"La Alegría de la Casa"
[Our Family's Happiness]

Felita, Rafael, and Felix

In this tightly knit Dominican American family, the eighth of nine children has Down syndrome and is seen by his parents as "just like the others" yet "the center of the family." The case study describes Rafael's development as he moves from elementary to middle school. Service providers will be challenged to reflect on advocacy for a family whose sense of "rights" differs considerably from American views.

Allá donde vivíamos, todo el mundo lo conocía, y lo quería. Todo el mundo pasaba, llamando, "Arjeni!" Decía yo, ¿quién esta llamando? Y era personas que pasaban llamándolo a él. Cuando salimos para acá, en la comunidad en donde vivíamos, en el barrio donde vivíamos, había gente que lo querían muchísimo, y ese día ni salieron a mirarlo que él se fuera, porque no querían verlo cuando el salirera.

A él le gusta mucho la música—salsa, Americana, todo—le gusta bailar. El es muy amistoso con todo el mundo, todo el mundo lo quiere, porque él es muy amistoso. Los hermanos lo quieren mucho y se lleva muy bien con ellos. El no es un muchacho malcriado. No es un niño que no puede hacer nada. El sabe lo que hace. Es un niño obediente, no es agresivo. Tiene muy buena forma de vida. El lleva una vida normal, igual que los demás.

El no puede leer todavía . . . porque lo llevan muy lento en la escuela . . . pero conoce los colores, las diferencias. El es normal, en el quehacer es normal. En el físico tiene sus problemas y tiene dificultades para hablar. El es muy inteligente.

[Over there where we lived, everyone knew him and loved him. Everyone would pass by, calling, "Arjeni." And I would ask, "Who is calling out?" And it was people passing by, calling out to him. When we left to come here, there were people in our community who loved him so much that on the day we were leaving they could not come to see him off because they did not want to see him leave.

He loves music—salsa, American music, everything—he loves to dance. He is very friendly with everyone, and everyone loves him because he is so friendly. His brothers love him very much, and he carries himself very well with them. He is not a [spoiled/badly brought-up] child. He is not a child who cannot do anything. He knows what he's doing. He is an obedient child, not aggressive. He has a very good kind of life. He leads a normal life, the same as the others.

He still can't read . . . because they go slowly with him in school, but he can distinguish colors. He is normal, in the things he has to do (life functioning), he is normal. His problems are physical, and in speech. He is very intelligent.]

UNA VIDA NORMAL

I first interviewed Felix and Felicita Ignacio in December 1993. It was a Sunday at approximately 4 P.M. As I entered the L-shaped living/dining room of their three-bedroom apartment, there were three boys watching television while Rafael sat at the dining room table, eating. Rafael, who has Down syndrome, was 11 years old at that time. Felix and Felicita greeted me very cordially, introduced me to the boys, and invited me to make myself comfortable. The boys turned off the television, and, as the parents and I began some preliminary conversation, all three left the apartment. Felix and Felicita told me that the boys were going upstairs and to their cousins' but that Rafael was slow to eat and had to finish his supper before he could go.

We began our interview, which proceeded in a very sponta-neous and informal manner. Approximately 20 minutes into our in-terview, Rafael finished his dinner, ran into the kitchen and tossed his dish into the sink, and rushed out of the apartment without say-ing anything to anyone. I asked Felix and Felicita where he had gone, and they replied that he had gone to join his brothers. I asked whether he was always able to go about so independently, and they replied, *"¡Sí! Tiene una vida normal. Éles lo mismo cómo los demás."* [Oh, yes, he has a normal life. He's just like the others.]

That first interview revealed the Ignacio family's strong desire to use every opportunity for Rafael to continue to develop *"una vida normal"* [a normal life]. Felix and Felicita explained that they would be very glad to participate in our project because they saw Rafael's social development as very important. They expressed the concern that when he becomes an adult, his limitations will be more evident and he will have to fend for himself because his sib-lings will become more involved in their own lives. Despite Rafael's full integration with siblings and neighbors, Felix and Felicita be-lieved that additional activities with a wider community would be good for him because he was shy and tended to be withdrawn with strangers. Also, they thought it important for other children to learn that he is "just like them." In terms of the future, they expressed the hope that he would be able to do everything that everyone else does.

For Felix and Felicita, Rafael (or Arjeni, as he was usually called at home), was *"el centro de la familia"* [the center of the fam-ily] and *"la alegría de la casa"* [our happiness]. The entire family consisted of seven boys and two girls; the first five were grown and living in the Dominican Republic, and the last four boys lived in the United States with their parents. Felix and Felicita explained to me that their family is very close and that they are in constant touch with the family in their native country. Rafael, they told us, is a fa-vorite of the entire family but particularly so of the oldest son, who lives in the Dominican Republic and is married. Within the family household in the United States, Rafael's favorite was Felito, the old-est of the group of four. As our relationship with this family devel-oped, we gained increasing insights into Rafael's place and role in this large yet very close-knit extended family.

Four years later, Felix and Felicita still affectionately referred to Rafael, at the age of 14, as *"nuestro bebé"* [our baby] but quickly ex-plained that this did not mean they treated him like a baby but rather he was their baby *"en el cariño que tenemos para él"* [in the love we have for him].

During the 4 years of the project, Felix and Felicita remained consistently open to new suggestions for Rafael's social development and for his inclusion in school- and community-based activities of youth without disabilities. They also remained consistent participants in the educational planning conducted by Rafael's teachers. In the subsequent section, we describe the keen interest and participation displayed by these parents regarding their son's education and general development.

PARENTAL PARTICIPATION: THE CHALLENGE OF ADVOCACY

On the issue of parental participation, this Dominican couple displayed unwavering support of and interest in their son's educational planning. Although they certainly had their own ideas about what was good for Rafael, for the most part, they saw their role as to support and approve the recommendations of the professionals in charge of Rafael's education. Their respect for the school was evident, and their tradition of deference to school personnel showed in many ways.

For 4 years in a row, our research team observed Rafael's annual review conferences, which were always attended by either or both of the parents. On these occasions, Felix, in particular, always began by expressing the hope that his son was well behaved and respectful to the teachers. The importance of Rafael's being *"un muchacho bien educado"* [a well-brought-up child] was evident, as was his parents' consistent expression of respect for the school personnel. Even when they did not see eye to eye with school personnel, their disagreement was expressed only privately or by subtle, nonverbal messages, such as the raise of an eyebrow, a gentle shrug of the shoulders, or a mild grimace.

Another aspect of deference was the parents' assumption that they could not successfully challenge school district decisions. One such concern for this family was the school placement. In 1993, when we met the Ignacios, Rafael was in his first year in the district's least restrictive environment (LRE) program. He was bused to this school. That June, the parents received a letter from the school district advising them that, in the coming school year, Rafael would be moved to another LRE program at another school. The letter explained, "The reason for this move is that . . . Elementary School is an accessible, barrier-free school with room to allow for the LRE program's growth." Rafael had been at his current school only 1 year, and we knew that in just another year's time he would have to be moved to middle school. This would mean a new school in each of 3 consecutive years for Rafael, whose teachers had had a hard time recognizing that his apparent "babble" was actually meaningful, though rudimentary, Spanish and who, at the end of that school year, was finally beginning to be understood by his classmates and teachers.

Felix and Felicita received that letter in the first week of June and worried over it privately for almost 2 months. Toward the end of July, they told me about the letter and expressed their worry about the disruption that this would cause to Rafael's progress. The next day, I made a telephone call to a senior administrator whom I knew in the district's special education office and explained the effect that this decision would have on the Ignacio family. The fact that the matter was resolved in a matter of an hour revealed the arbitrariness of the school district's decision to make this move. A week or so later, the family received a letter from the school district "correcting" the previous one. The letter was copied to me.

In the following year, the Ignacios decided to move to the neighborhood of Rafael's school because that would allow Jason, the youngest brother, to attend the same school as Rafael. They wanted to move anyway because the apartments there were better and more reasonably priced. The parents were very pleased to see their two youngest sons walking just across the street to school together. Their pleasure was short lived, however, when they were informed that Rafael's middle school placement for the following year would not be in the neighborhood; rather, he would be bused to a school with an LRE program approximately 10 miles away. Felix and Felicita were disappointed about this decision also, but, as Felix explained, *"Nosotros no íbamos a hacer fuerza . . . a tratar de luchar que lo dejaran ahí. . . . Porque ellos son los que saben. . . . Ya cuando los niños hay que mudarlos a otra escuela, uno no puede oponerse."* [We weren't going to put any pressure . . . to fight for him to stay there. . . . Because they are the ones who know. . . . If kids have to be moved to another school, one can't be opposed.]

Yet another issue for potential disagreement was Rafael's formal assessment. This had been requested soon after we began working with Rafael, when concerns about his being in a monolingual English environment led to the discovery that the only psychological report in the file was a cursory summary done by a monolingual psychologist. As a result of this, in February of that year, the teacher put in a request for a bilingual evaluation, which was reiterated by his parents, and was emphasized as a priority in the annual review meeting held in April. The assessment by the bilingual psychologist was conducted a year later, in February 1994.

The arrival of the long-awaited assessment date also dovetailed with the family's concerns over Rafael's move to the far-away middle school. The psychologist had conducted a complete evaluation, including a parent interview, and he had given a brief summary of his findings to the parents. On one of my visits to their home, I asked Felicita what the psychologist had said. With a shrug and a mild grimace, she replied that he had concluded that Rafael was at the mental level of a 4-year-old. Her disagreement was unspoken but clear.

Soon afterward, we attended the annual review meeting at the new middle school. Most of the meeting was conducted by the two teachers who would be in charge of the mixed sixth- and seventh-grade classroom in which Rafael was to be placed. An administrator joined us later. The younger of the two was a recent graduate, beginning her first job, and the older was obviously very experienced and established that she wanted to ensure all parental rights. I had spoken on the telephone to the younger teacher about the parents' disappointment in the placement, and we began the meeting with a reminder of this. The older teacher said that she would like us to have an open discussion about the entire matter, although much of it would have to be "off the record." Felicita expressed her disappointment that Rafael's school was to be so far away because they had no transportation, and this made it hard for them to come to the school, as well as hard for Rafael to participate in any after-school activities.

The teacher took this opportunity to explain to the parents the relation between the recent bilingual evaluation and Rafael's middle school placement. She explained that Rafael's IQ score was 45 and that a score between 55 and 65 was considered "borderline." She also acknowledged that he was probably functioning at a higher social level than this score represented. Felicita listened intently to this conversation, nodding urgently when the teacher referred to the possible underestimation of Rafael's social skills. Nevertheless, the teacher continued, with this score, Rafael would be eligible only for the "Level 5" placement, and the only such class available at his home school was a Level 4 class. However, she went on to explain some other options: First, there was such a thing as a Level 4.5 class, which the district was thinking of starting at Rafael's neighborhood school but that he would have to be reevaluated and qualify for that level in order to be placed there. The teacher believed that after a year of working with him on his educational goals, he might qualify for a higher level placement. Another possibility, she said, was that the district might start an LRE program at Rafael's home school, and they suspected that this might be in the making. After explaining these possibilities, the teachers stated that they believed that it could be worth the parents' making a formal request for home school placement, but that would not be likely to happen right away.

At the end of the meeting, when the IEP was to be signed, the administrator pointed out the various options that Felicita could sign regarding the placement decision. One option was to disagree but waive her rights, which, the administrator commented, seemed inappropriate. The second would require that Rafael remain in his current placement until a decision was made. The third option would allow him to move to the recommended placement until a change could be made. Felicita asked whether they would really set up a new program, and the school team acknowledged that they could not be sure but that if enough parents asked for it, it probably would happen. He added that there were several students from Rafael's area in this program and that those families would probably prefer a home school placement but had not requested it. Felicita chose Option 3, and the team leader advised her to write that she "agreed to the placement but not the location." Felicita did so.

On reading over the document, I noticed that all three options required "a hearing," and I asked whether this meant that they would actually have to go through a hearing. The teacher replied that hearings are very rare and that these cases usually are handled unofficially with some kind of compromise. Most likely, the family would receive a telephone call from the department requesting more information. My field notes on this conversation read as follows:

> I feel sure that the Ignacios would not want to become engaged in any formal and adversarial procedures and feel a little uncomfortable at the possibility of encouraging them into a situation they would be unhappy with. However, the attitude of these two teachers is clearly that this is the family's right and that they are not doing anything particularly adversarial by signing this option.

I prepared a letter for the family to send to the school district requesting an appropriate program in Rafael's neighborhood. Several weeks later, Felicita handed me, with a shrug and raised eyebrows, a packet of papers that had come in the mail from the school district. The papers were a request for a hearing on the question of

Rafael's placement. The front page advised the parents that they were entitled to get a lawyer to assist them in the formal appeal. She and Felix said simply, "We don't have time or money for that. We have to work."

There was no further follow-up on the topic, and Rafael was placed in the recommended program that his mother described as *"tan lejos"* [so far away]. A year later, however, the program was moved to a school that was closer, and Rafael's parents were pleased. They were also happy that the teacher who had started Rafael in middle school also moved with the program, because they believed that she was very good and Rafael had become very attached to her.

A "4-YEAR-OLD" CUTS SCHOOL

In the following year, there was one more occasion that, for many parents, would have been grounds for serious argument with the school. Rafael's first year in middle school was going along quite nicely, except for one key factor: transportation. The busing arrangements presented a difficult logistical problem for the family because the morning bus typically arrived at some uncertain hour after 8:30, at which time every other member of the household was already on his or her way to school or to work. An appeal to the teacher yielded no results because transportation scheduling was done by the transportation system, not by the school. In typical fashion, the Ignacio family did what they could to make the best of a bad job. Rafael, dressed and ready for school, was equipped with a little purse with his own key, and, when the last family member left the apartment, Rafael was to stand in the foyer of the apartment building and look through the window for the bus.

One day, Felicita was alerted at work by her brother, who had passed by the Ignacios' apartment and noticed a broken window. Upon entering the house, he found Rafael there alone; he had apparently broken a window by throwing his school bag at it. Felicita hurried home and was told by Rafael that the bus had not come for him. So she took him to school, only to be told by the teacher that he had been absent for 4 days. Felicita spoke with the bus driver, who insisted that he had come and had not seen Rafael anywhere. It seemed that Rafael had decided to skip school, slipping back into the apartment after the last family member had left. According to Felicita, during those 4 days

> *Se quedaba ahí, comiendo, y vaciaba la refrigeradora. Pero él sólo no, él trae amiguitos. Entraban amiguitos de él de por aqui. Y comenzaba*

a brindarles sandwiches, y soda, y cosas así, y todo esto que había aquí se lo comieron. Y yo decía, y en tan poco rato los muchachos se comieron, se bebieron el pote de leche, se tomaron todo el jugo, y yo pensaba que eran los tres que se lo tomaban. Y después, fue que nos dimos cuenta que era él que hacía sus fiestas! [He stayed right here, eating, and emptying the refrigerator. But he wasn't alone, no! He brought in some little friends from next door. They came in right here and set about making sandwiches, getting sodas and other things, and they ate up everything that was here. And for a while, I thought that it was his brothers who were eating it all and drinking the jugs of milk and juice. And then we discovered that it was him giving his parties!]

Rafael got a good spanking from Felicita, who concluded that this event justified her disagreement with the psychologist's assessment of Rafael's mental level. As she said, the next time his favorite brother, Felito, came in asking affectionately for his little *"chiquito"* [little boy], *"No vaya a decirle ningún chiquito, que no es ningún chiquito. . . . Que no es gracia lo que él ha hecho, quedarse sin ir a la escuela."* [I'm not going to call him any "little boy," he's no little boy. . . . This is not very nice, what he has done, staying home instead of going to school.]

Felix joined in:

El tiene mucha inteligencia y todo. Hace unas cosas, le digo, "Quién hizo esto? "Ah, eso fue Fulano. No fui yo!" Y no hay quien le venga a decir que sí, que fue él. Y esas no son cosas de un niño de 4 años. De una mentalidad de 4 años. [He's very intelligent in everything. He does things, and when I ask, "Who did this?" he says, "Ah, it's 'whoever.' Not me!" And there's no one to say that it was really him. And these are not the behaviors of a 4-year-old. Of the mentality of a 4-year-old.]

The event led to a compromise with the school transportation system: The bus, from then on, arrived promptly at 8:30 A.M. (but still leaving Rafael to wait approximately 5 minutes on his own). His teacher, meanwhile, agreed that whenever Rafael was absent, she would call his aunt's home (neither parent could be reached by telephone on their jobs), and his absence would be verified by a note from his parents the next day.

RAFAEL AT SCHOOL

Rafael began school formally for the first time in September 1991, at the age of 9, when he and Felix came to the United States to join Felicita, who had migrated here 4 years before. In the Dominican Republic, Rafael had started off at a "little school" near the family's home, but he did not seem to like it much because he would not stay in school; he just kept coming back home. The teachers said that it was all right for him to stay, but everyone in the family, as well as the family physician, agreed that he should not be forced to stay if he did not want to.

Rafael's first year in school in the United States was in a special center for Level V children—that is, students with severe disabilities. His parents were happy with this school because the teacher loved Rafael very much and Rafael was very attached to her. They said that she went beyond the call of duty in her work; for example, she accompanied the family to a medical conference and explained to the doctors all that she knew about Rafael. At the end of that year, however, the teacher recommended that he be moved to a more advanced class in a general school (the district's LRE program) because he was the most advanced in his class at the center and she wanted him to move on. The parents had mixed feelings about this because they agreed that he needed to progress but knew that Rafael would miss this teacher. At first he did, they said, but he gradually became accustomed to the new school where the teacher was also very nice.

Our school-based data yielded rich information regarding Rafael's social interactions. In his special education classroom, we conducted numerous in-class observations of Rafael, including his group speech-language therapy, which was offered in the classroom twice per week and led by an English as a second language (ESL) teacher and/or a speech-language pathologist; his daily schedule of life skills and preacademic activities; and an occasion on which a Spanish-speaking "buddy" from a general fourth-grade class played with Legos with Rafael. Over the course of those 2 years, Rafael was increasingly exposed to mainstream environments, and we observed him in the following environments: a school awards assembly, a general fourth-grade music class, a general physical education (PE) class, a general fourth-grade homeroom, and the playground at recess.

Overall, we found Rafael to be an initially shy but very sociable youngster, who responded readily to initiations by peers and initiated interaction with peers whom he knew. However, he also stood up for himself very well and did not hesitate to refuse invitations in which he was not interested. In a new group activity, Rafael learned the rules by watching and imitating what his peers did. Sometimes he "spaced out" or played quietly by himself until someone actively prompted him to participate; at that point, he usually observed and imitated or followed a direct instruction. The following sections offer a detailed portrait of the sociable yet shy, fun-loving Rafael whom we came to know over the course of the first 2 years.

RAFAEL AND HIS PEERS

During the first year of our observations, we watched Rafael become a favorite with his peers without disabilities at school, although his participation in general education school life continued to be relatively marginal. Part of the classroom schedule was a buddy system, which had a couple of key features. One aspect was 30 minutes in which peers without disabilities from a fourth-grade class came to do activities, usually play with Legos or some table game, with the students in Rafael's class. Another aspect was that those students who were being mainstreamed for special classes such as PE and music or who participated in a general fourth-grade homeroom were picked up at the special education classroom by their "buddies," who took them along to the class. That year, Rafael was mainstreamed into PE and homeroom, and the buddy plan turned out to be an important bridge for Rafael to a more inclusive level of participation in school activities.

The PE teacher explained to us that the purpose of Rafael's having a buddy was to help him "blend" into the class and feel welcome. Our observations of Rafael in the PE class indicated that everything depended on two factors—what the activity was and whether the teacher or a peer advocated for accommodations for him. For example, we watched him participating in hockey and noted that the teacher sometimes paused the game to allow Rafael more time to swing, in which case he sometimes hit the ball and his peers sometimes cheered, "Yeah, Rafael!" Much of his time in this session, however, was down time for him, and he filled his time by twirling the hockey stick, making believe it was a gun. He tuned in sporadically to the game.

In basketball, Rafael competed much more aggressively and with more skill, although it was clear that he still depended on accommodations from his peers. Moni's field notes on one such observation gave a vivid picture of Rafael's interactions in such environments:

> When Rafael's group was about to start the [practice session], one of the boys gave the ball to Rafael, put his hand on Rafael's back, and pointed him towards the basketball net and told him to shoot. I'll call this boy Jerry. . . . Rafael shot it and it went through, and then the other boys caught the ball and started playing. Rafael was standing at the edge of the court most of the time when the boys played. He did not really get in and try to get the ball and play. Sometimes he did try to get the ball, and he would move toward them, and then he would move back, and he would shout something at them. At one point, the ball went out of the court and Rafael ran after it and brought it back. One of the boys

tried to take it from him, but Rafael said, "Not!" and managed to hold on to the ball and tried to shoot it. From time to time, Jerry would take the ball and give it to Rafael, take him towards the basket, and tell him to shoot. This happened quite a lot of times. No others seemed to make such a special effort to include Rafael in the group. Jerry was the only one.

The game had built up momentum, and Rafael had been asking for the ball for a long time, but no one ever gave it to him. He was standing at the edge of the court again . . . and he turned and watched the boys playing in the other court. He then turned facing the basket of his own group, and he shouted something. The boys continued to play. Rafael sighed, folded his hands, and had a frown on his face. He watched for a while, walked out of the court, and sat down in the corner against the wall. The boys were still playing, and they just continued to play. It was really hard for me to stand there and watch him sitting down quietly with a frown on his face and not intervene.

Jerry was playing. He looked at Rafael and went out of the court, and he sat down on his knees and said something to him. He took Rafael's hand and helped him up and then brought him into the court. He had his hand around Rafael's waist. He stood on one side of the court and yelled to the rest of the boys. All of the other boys stopped playing and stood around and listened to him. Jerry was yelling, but I couldn't hear because there was so much noise in the gym . . . but I heard him say, "Rafael." When Jerry finished talking, another boy said, "Okay, okay," and another boy passed the ball to Rafael. Rafael shot at the basket and it went through, and the boys started playing again. Later, another boy had the ball, and he passed it to Rafael. Rafael shot it into the basket. Even though it went into the basket, the boys did not applaud or anything. They were very involved in the game, and they just continued to play. During the whole game, Rafael shot at the basket about eight times, and out of the eight times, the ball was usually passed to him by Jerry. I think Rafael made a basket three times. Once, Rafael caught it by himself, and one other time, another boy passed it to him.

Finally, the teacher blew a very loud horn and told all the children it was time to leave. The boys started to line up near the door, and Rafael was standing in a line near the wall. A boy was standing behind him, and Rafael turned around and pretended to punch him. I will refer to this boy as "Tom." Tom pretended to get hurt. He was kind of holding his stomach. Rafael laughed and pretended to punch him harder. Tom leaned against the wall and pretended to be hurt. He was frowning and had a pained expression on his face, and Rafael pretended to kick and punch him at the same time, and Tom closed his eyes and slowly sat down on the floor, pretending to be totally knocked out. Rafael laughed really loudly. Tom was sitting on the floor with his eyes closed for quite a while. Then Rafael sat down and looked at him, kind of stared at him, and Tom suddenly opened his eyes and burst out laughing. Then he held Rafael's hand and stood up. The teacher told them it was time to leave, and they all left the gym.

I went to thank the teacher before leaving. He said that [the boys] fight a lot among each other, and they're very tough, but where Rafael is concerned, they're very gentle with him and they show the others by example. He also referred to Jerry, who has a twin brother. He said that Jerry and his twin fight a lot but that when it comes to Rafael, Jerry is very different with him. (November 17, 1993)

Both the advocacy in basketball and the play fighting observed on this occasion were noted frequently in Rafael's interactions with his peers without disabilities. Moni's observations also noted that assistance, as well as playful interactions at recess or on the way to classes, consistently came from Jerry, as well as two others. Rafael's responses to initiations from these peers were consistently positive, but we concluded that he was quite selective about his friends: We saw several occasions on which he responded in the negative to other peers, such as refusing an invitation to go onto the playground, saying, "No way!" or refusing to follow the instructions of a class peer.

The following excerpts from Moni's observations of Rafael in the general fourth-grade homeroom offer a detailed picture of Rafael's strategy of watching, imitating, and, thus, "fitting in," as well as of his selectiveness about his responses to his peers. In both excerpts, there is also a hint of the impact of the researcher's presence.

Rafael walked into his [special education] classroom. He was wearing a colorful jacket and a very colorful cap. He picked up his worksheet and walked out, down the hallway and entered the homeroom. . . . He entered the room and sat down at the first table on the right side. He took a corner seat and put down his pack and took off his cap and started taking off his jacket. . . . There were two other boys sitting at the table at which Rafael was going to sit. There was one boy on the right side of Rafael (I'll refer to him as Z) and another sitting diagonally across from Rafael. After Rafael took off his cap, he was taking off his jacket and he looked at Z. Z looked back at him, and both of them looked at each other for a long time. It was as if there was a competition going on and they were trying to see who was going to break the gaze. Rafael took off his jacket and hung it on the chair, and then he flexed his right hand, kind of showing off his muscles, showing off his biceps. Z laughed at him, and then looked at me and laughed again. Then he got back to his work. Rafael sat down, and he had already put the worksheet on the table. He took out his pencil, opened his book, and started writing. . . . At one point, he took out two cassettes from his pack and put them on the table. . . . He pulled at the sleeve of Z, who was sitting at the right side. Z nodded but continued with his work. During the whole session (about 25 minutes), he was writing and erasing a lot. But I'd say, from the position of his hand, he probably wrote a line or so. I'm not sure how he got to know that it was time for him to leave, but at a certain time he just got up and packed his cassettes and his book into the bag. He put on his jacket and tried to zip it. As he pulled the zipper right up to his neck, something had gone wrong so that the zipper was open. Rafael noticed this and pulled the zipper back down and tried again, and again the same thing happened. He tried again, and his face was getting red and tense, and he shouted, "Yaah!" just like that; he almost kind of screamed. . . . Then Z said, "Do you need help?" Rafael said, "No," with a lot of emphasis, and he pointed his thumb towards himself—sort of indicating, "I'll do it." He tried again and succeeded in zipping it correctly. Then he took out his cap and put it on his head backwards. He picked up his pack and left the room. (November 19, 1993)

On another occasion in the homeroom, Rafael showed his resistance to instructions from certain classmates and his acceptance of others:

Rafael entered the class and sat in his usual place near the rear. A boy was sitting on his right side. There was a girl sitting on his left. . . . Rafael took out his exercise book and put it on the table. He kept looking into his bag. E asked him, "What do you want?" Rafael replied, but I couldn't follow his speech. The boy said, "Here, take my pencil." He took out a pencil and gave it to Rafael. Rafael started his work. He had to match items in two columns. The girl next to him said, "Wear your glasses." Rafael continued to work. She repeated very slowly, "Wear your glasses." Rafael said, "No!" She said, "Ms. C wants you to wear your glasses." Rafael said, "Shut up!" Then a boy joined in, "Rafael, wear your glasses." Rafael did not reply but continued with his work. The boy took away Rafael's pencil and said, "Wear your glasses." Rafael took out his glasses from his backpack and wore them. The boy gave back the pencil, and Rafael continued to work. Rafael was closing his book, when the girl next to him pointed to an item he had missed and said, "You're still not done." Rafael completed it. She told him, "Write your name." Rafael wrote his name on the top of the paper. He put his book in his bag and returned the pencil to the boy, who then asked him, "Do you want to keep it?" Rafael said, "Ya." The boy threw the pencil playfully towards him. Rafael picked up the pencil from the desk and said, "Thanks." The boy looked at me and smiled. I'm not quite sure why he smiled at me at that point. (May 18, 1994)

The latter comment points to an issue of which we were constantly aware—the extent to which our observations influenced the children's behavior. Despite the possibility of this, Moni did conclude that interactions between Rafael and his peers in the homeroom had increased tremendously since her previous observation in November.

Over the course of those 2 years, Rafael's school popularity grew. Periodically, the school held awards assemblies, at which students from each class were given awards decided on by their teacher. Rafael always received some award. On these occasions,

Rafael rose quickly upon hearing his name, hurried up to the platform for his award, and returned to his seat, slapping the outreached hands of several peers on the way back and showing off his award to the students seated next to him. In the final assembly before he was to graduate to middle school, Rafael received an award for "Most Popular Student."

At the end of that school year, we were able to arrange an interview with Dennis, one of Rafael's special buddies, regarding his perceptions of Rafael. As a volunteer "buddy" for students in Rafael's self-contained classroom, Dennis visited every morning and assisted him with some of his school work, such as tracing and writing. He spontaneously played with Rafael at recess also, and they were in the same PE class. When asked whether he usually made special accommodations for Rafael in PE class, Dennis acknowledged, "We pass him the ball . . . and we tell him, ya know, like, 'Yeah Rafael, Yeah! Come on, come on!' Or, 'No! No!'" In playing football, he explained, sometimes someone stood behind Rafael and told him when to go. Dennis explained, "Everybody likes him [because] he likes to be in the group. He's always trying to fit into the group. You know, he wears his cap backwards." When asked what other kids could do to help Rafael "be in the group," Dennis said that if one kid befriends him, so will others. He explained that Jerry (whose advocacy in the PE class we described previously) had been the first to befriend Rafael and that Jerry's friends soon followed suit.

RAFAEL AT SUMMER DAY CAMP

At the end of the first school year, we talked with Rafael's family about possible activities for him during the summer. Because Felix and Felicita seemed so open to letting him try something new, we decided to investigate the county parks and recreation summer camp program. We located the community center for Rafael's area and spoke to the director, who was very open to including our students (we suggested three students for their 9–11 age group). We took the program materials to Rafael's parents, and, after a visit to the center, they readily agreed that Rafael could go and asked whether his younger brother, Jason, then 10, could also go. We said that he could and told them that we would pay for Rafael and try to get a reduced fee for Jason. Felicita knew the bus route from their home to the center and said that she would send Felito with them on the bus.

The week before the program was to begin, I picked up Rafael, Jason, and Felito one afternoon and took them to the center to meet the directors of the camp. I had also invited the director of the county's special programs, with whom I had talked several times on the telephone and who had agreed to offer the program personnel any guidance or support that they might need in including Rafael and our other students. The meeting went well; the special programs person assured the two camp directors that they would not have to make any special accommodations for Rafael.

One outcome of the meeting was that the director, on the spur of the moment, offered Felito a volunteer position in the program for the summer! Felito was delighted. Another interesting feature was the director's reluctance to agree to the boys' being escorted to camp by Felito. They explained that camp policy required an adult to accompany and sign in all children, and it was not until Felito and I had two or three times reiterated that they did not have a car and that their parents were out of the home at work from 6:30 A.M. until 6:30 P.M. that the camp personnel finally agreed that it would be all right for the boys to come with Felito.

The summer camp ran in 2-week sessions, and Rafael and Jason attended for 4 weeks in all. During that time, our research team observed eight times, one of which was videotaped.

One of the key issues in including Rafael was deciding in which group to place him. In the first session, he was placed in a group according to his age, which turned out to be children who were already 11. In that group, Rafael's small stature and evidently lower competence made him stand out among the 11-year-olds. We had initially discussed this with the director, suggesting that although the idea of age-appropriate grouping had some strengths we believed that Rafael would be able to relate better to smaller kids and would not stand out so much from the rest of the group. Although the director acknowledged the difficulty, he decided that the counselor in that 11-year-old group would be best with Rafael. Also, on the first day, they had put Rafael and Jason in separate groups but had placed Felito as an assistant in Rafael's group. This resulted in Felito's playing a role of personal supervisor for Rafael and in Rafael's turning to him for guidance throughout the day. We mentioned this to the director, and he moved Felito to another group the next day.

In the second 2-week period, the camp personnel decided to change Rafael's placement to the lower age group of children, who were more his size. This was an important change, which did result in better peer interaction for Rafael. Overall, during the first 2 weeks, he tried to participate in any large-group activities that required imitation of what peers were doing, but we believed that his main difficulty was the obvious difference in size and skills be-tween him and his peers. The second session was much better: Rafael was much more included in small-group activities.

Observing Rafael at the summer camp, we noted the following features of his learning style:

- Rafael learned by watching then imitating. For example, in team games, such as "potato sack race," in which he could watch those ahead of him, he waited his turn, then took his turn cor-rectly and enthusiastically, and returned with a flourish to his place, vigorously slapping the hands of his teammates.
- Rafael was successful in joint play that did not require system-atic rule following, provided that he was playing with a peer of similar physical skills. For example, at summer camp, he played ball spontaneously with peers his own size (who were probably a few years younger than he), passing the ball to his peer, shad-owing him to retrieve the ball, and shooting into the basket. No rejecting or excluding behaviors were observed among the peers.
- In activities that were based on team interaction and knowing the rules of the game, Rafael participated well when he received explicit assistance and instruction. For example, in a game of Bingo at summer camp, he was assisted by Felito. He followed instructions regarding moves, waited and took his turns appro-priately, but did not realize when he had won. However, because he was able to match some numbers correctly, we believed that more practice with this game would enable him to understand and enjoy the entire game.

At camp, as at school, in situations in which Rafael was playing with others more physically competent than he, such as in basket-ball, he was consistently left out unless a peer advocated for him or assisted him. At camp, however, we did not observe any peers emerging as consistent advocates for Rafael's inclusion. It seemed likely that the short time span did not allow for that development, and we concluded that this was one area in which we should inter-vene more proactively to create peer supports for Rafael.

This led us to continue our summer work with Rafael, enrolling him in summer camp again the subsequent two summers but with more explicit preplanning of appropriate conditions with the camp staff and peers. Although this seemed to result in the emergence of certain peer support for him, a more important trend became evi-dent: Rafael's increasing confidence in making his own decisions. This showed itself in his developing an increasing tendency to choose his friends and his activities very deliberately. When his favorite counselors or peers were around, he hung out with them and participated in the activities in which he was most competent; otherwise, he withdrew and created his own solitary activity. Team games, such as soccer, were simply beyond him, and he flatly refused to play.

In summary, our observations of Rafael at summer camp and in school suggested that he was very motivated to learn the social behaviors of his peers and that certain behaviors and characteristics of others were conducive to his being able to succeed in the group: the size and competence level of the group in which he is participating; assistance from peers, siblings, or adults in knowing what to do or actually performing a task; and support from a particular individual who advocates for his inclusion.

RAFAEL AND HIS BROTHERS: "HE CAN'T REALLY PLAY"

Our first-year observations led us to another idea that we hoped would help us understand the process of true inclusion. We reasoned that if we could have more insight into how Rafael was included at home, then we might learn some principles of more successfully including him in peer groups outside the home. We recognized, of course, that there would still be one missing ingredient: At home, he was already loved and accepted unconditionally. For example, although he liked to play with the Nintendo set, his brother, Jason, observed casually that "he can't really play," meaning that Rafael did not know the rules and was not able to make the right decisions about moves. In these situations, his brothers allowed him to join in to the extent that he did not deter the others from their play. It seemed to us that no special accommodations were made, but none were needed because he was already an unconditional member of the group. Another way of thinking about this is that unconditional acceptance was the primary accommodation made. Conversely, we knew that in situations outside the home, where our goal was to create acceptance, more attention would have to be paid to creating a supportive environment.

We asked Felix and Felicita whether they would allow us to spend a considerable amount of time observing Rafael and his brothers at play, either in or out of the home, to document in greater detail whether and to what extent the boys modify their behavior, the setting conditions, or the behavior of others to ensure their brother's inclusion. With the permission of Felix and Felicita, we then broached the question with Rafael's siblings, Felito, Andre, and Jason. They readily agreed to participate, and all that was left was for us to work out the logistics of how to accomplish this aspect of our study.

The logistics, however, were more challenging than we had envisioned. We wanted the study to consist of a series of naturalistic observations of the brothers' play interactions. Our overall plan for data collection was that Moni, who was an unusually youthful-looking 30-year-old, would simply "tag along" with the brothers on various informal occasions. The difficulty was that the brothers' play was always spontaneous, and it was only Felito who could be relied on to call Moni and invite her to go with them. We had agreed that she would go by invitation only because any other approach would have been too intrusive. However, because the brothers did not call frequently, Moni sometimes called them to find out what they were doing. Obviously, this turned what should have been a spontaneous event into something rather contrived, as well as something that possibly influenced the way in which the brothers behaved because they were being observed.

Despite these constraints, Moni was able to accompany the boys to the neighborhood park or basketball court on three occasions. In addition, she arranged for two outings that included Rafael and Jason along with three other children, two with disabilities and one without. Two of these occasions were videotaped. Moni's approach was to be mainly an observer, but she participated when appropriate. Spontaneous conversations between her and the brothers also provided valuable information. Rafael and his brothers all were accustomed to her presence because she had collected data at the summer camp and had visited their home on several occasions. At the end of September, I conducted a tape-recorded interview with the brothers, telling them our interpretations of what we had observed and inviting their comments.

Not surprising, the main thing that we found was that Rafael's three siblings played distinctly different roles in relation to him. Overall, the oldest brothers' roles were consistently marked by what we called "big brothering" and, to a lesser extent, "facilitating." By contrast, Jason, the youngest, showed a clear pattern of predominantly "parallel play" and a lesser pattern of "reciprocal play."

Big Brothering

In the first 3 years, the majority of the protecting, advising, helping, and reprimanding behavior came from Felito, the oldest brother, and occasionally from Andre, the second in line. Rafael's parents explained that this pattern was an established part of the family structure, whereby authority and responsibility were explicitly given to the siblings by order of chronological age. For Rafael and his youngest sibling, however, the usual order was reversed because Jason, although a year younger than Rafael, was the more competent.

Throughout those 3 years, Felito was Rafael's favorite. His parents explained that Rafael slept with Felito, was very affectionate with him, and cooperated with him in any situation, whereas Andre carried out his responsibilities regarding Rafael but was not as close to him. However, when Felito graduated from high school and began to move away from the family center, the parents reported that Andre seemed to take his place in Rafael's affections and to assume more responsibility for him. In the fourth and final summer of the study, we saw yet another change as Jason, who was then 14 and taller than Rafael, began to display more of the big brothering behaviors previously typical of the older siblings.

Rafael's brothers responded positively to family expectations of responsibility and authority. For example, in the second summer of our project, when Felito was offered a full-time job as a camp counselor at a site different from the one that Rafael attended, the parents readily delegated responsibility to Andre for escorting Rafael and Jason to camp. This proved beneficial for Andre in that the camp directors offered him a position as a volunteer for the summer. Both older brothers' big brothering of Rafael was low keyed and matter of fact, and Rafael accepted their authority readily. At camp, in particular, it was noticeable that whereas Rafael frequently ignored the instructions or reprimands of his peers, he typically acquiesced to his brothers' authority.

We also noted a more subtle type of big brothering that all three siblings displayed, which we called "keeping an eye out." This was a kind of peripheral watching, whereby the brothers would go ahead with their own play yet would seem to be instinctively watching out for Rafael. They would spot and resolve any momentary needs of Rafael, such as running to retrieve his ball when it traveled outside the usual bounds of their play or calling out to him to come back when he appeared about to move too far away. In the first 3 years, this was the only big brothering behavior that we consistently observed Jason displaying.

Facilitating

We saw some but not a lot of "facilitating" behavior by Rafael's brothers. They usually made explicit accommodations for including Rafael in play only when they were in a specifically supervisory role, such as at the summer camp, or when they were being observed by us. The brothers told us that they frequently made accommodations, such as "giving him a turn" if they were playing a game or play fighting with him "gently" so that he would not get hurt. In our member-check interview with them, however, when they were asked to elaborate on their "giving him a turn," they said that they would often give him a turn early in a game to ensure that he *would* have a turn. It seemed to us that the brothers often began by facilitating Rafael's participation in a game but that they did not always continue this as they became engrossed in their play and that Rafael spontaneously dropped out as the demands of his siblings' pace excluded him.

A clear example of this pattern was an occasion when Moni went to the park with Andre, Rafael, and Jason. On their arrival, Rafael spontaneously began solitary play with the soccer ball, until Andre instructed him to participate in a game of baseball and directed him to his place first as catcher and later as batter and then as pitcher. Rafael participated, doing better at pitching than at batting, until a point at which Jason hit the ball quite far and Rafael started after it. When he was quickly surpassed by Jason in his attempt to retrieve the ball, Rafael stopped, watched Jason pick up the ball, and then turned to playing by himself with the football. When Andre called out to Rafael to rejoin them, Rafael ignored him and continued to play by himself, while Andre and Jason resumed their game of baseball without him.

As far as Jason was concerned, we seldom saw any spontaneous accommodations for Rafael. That he was capable of this, however, was evident on one occasion, when we observed him adjusting his pace so that Rafael could keep up as they played on a slide at the park.

One common way of facilitating Rafael's participation was by interpreting his meanings or wishes to others. This was usually in response to their being asked what Rafael had said or when they were directly involved in a conversation in which someone did not understand Rafael's communication. Thus, their interpreting seemed very pragmatic rather than indicating a feeling of having to advocate for him. Indeed, their interpreting behaviors were distinct from advocacy, and when we asked the brothers whether they found that they had to advocate for Rafael outside the family environment, they said no, explaining that everyone in the neighborhood knew and liked Rafael, so they saw no need for advocacy. This feeling of not having to advocate for Rafael was further strengthened by the fact that most of the family's socializing was done within a large extended family in which Rafael was an integral member.

Parallel Play

Rafael's youngest brother's interactions were predominantly "parallel play." The two were interested in similar activities, but their levels of play generally were so different in terms of use of equipment and skill in accomplishing goals of play that they usually played side by side yet separately. This seemed to be the established and accepted way that these two played when in each other's company. For example, upon going to the basketball court, each carried his own ball and immediately set about playing separately; Rafael often practiced kicking the soccer ball into the air while Jason shot baskets. Similarly, when playing on jungle gyms in the park, they simply played in a parallel fashion on the same equipment.

At summer camp, Rafael and Jason were always placed in separate groups. On occasion, Rafael looked to Jason for guidance, but because one of his older brothers was usually present, he most often relied on them.

Reciprocal Play

Occasionally, Jason and Rafael engaged briefly in spontaneous interactive play that did not require significant accommodations by Jason. For example, as the boys set out to return home after about 20 minutes of parallel play on the basketball court, Jason initiated a game of reciprocal kicking of the ball to each other across the court and the roadway as they walked, and Rafael joined in readily. Also, there were occasions when the two played in a reciprocal fashion with the basketball, and each tried to obstruct the other or take the ball in a teasing manner. Jason inevitably won these rounds, but that did not seem to upset Rafael or to spoil the friendly nature of this teasing interaction. In our observations, we saw no examples of unkind teasing of Rafael by Jason.

The differences in the brothers' skill levels meant that their attempts at reciprocal play did not last long. Usually, Jason took over, to which Rafael responded either by giving up or by playing alone, with no show of annoyance.

RAFAEL'S REACTIONS: ACQUIESCENCE, RELIANCE, PARTICIPATION, AND WITHDRAWAL

As far as we could see and as reported by the parents, Rafael cooperated well with the family pattern of sibling authority. Although he was always seen to be outgoing and comfortable in the family environments and social situations arranged by our project, he was much less confident outside these familiar environments. His parents confirmed that he was shy with strangers, and our observations in public situations indicated that he seemed to rely a lot on his brothers for a feeling of security. For example, at summer camp, we noticed that he relied on Andre to assist him with putting on a T-shirt that had gone askew, whereas we had seen him put on a T-shirt at home, with no difficulty. In his first summer at camp, Rafael's participation was very much facilitated by Felito, who often coaxed him into participation or guided him through a game, such as Bingo. Rafael was less willing to join in when Felito was not around.

In our observations, Rafael always joined in willingly when invited or facilitated by his brothers. Conversely, when he could not keep up with the group or when they moved on without him, he turned to his own play, apparently unperturbed. When playing away from home, he was always the first to say that he was ready to go home. This dramatic difference between Rafael's comfortable response to being excluded from his brothers' play as compared with his response when he was excluded from play with his peers at school was intriguing.

Rafael's family members interpreted much of his behavior as his own choice: He often decided not to go outside with the others because he did not like to be too far away from home and liked to return home sooner than the others. All family members agreed that Rafael seemed happy to play on his own with things that he liked, such as his guitar, video games, television, or weight-lifting apparatus, which he became increasingly fond of as he grew into a teenager.

PARENTS' VIEWS OF SIBLINGS' ACCEPTANCE

As we watched Rafael with his brothers, we wondered what feelings he might have gone through to come to the realization and acceptance of not being able to keep up with his brothers. We speculated that this might have been a painful process for him, but when we asked his mother, she said that she could not recall his ever seeming to feel left out in the family. As she said, *"Nunca lo pusieron en menos—o lo hicieron sentir mal."* [They never put him down— or made him feel bad.] In fact, she said, she thought that Rafael probably saw himself as the same as the others, and she gave this example:

Siempre pensaba que podía igual que los demás. Por ejemplo, Jason lo agarra y le pone en el piso, pero Rafael le da una vuelta y lo agarra y le hace ver que "Yo también te puedo agarrar!" [He always thought he was the same as the others. For example, Jason grabs him and puts him down on the floor, but Rafael turns Jason over and grabs him as if to make him see that "I can get you too!"]

I then asked Felicita how she explained to the brothers about Rafael's condition. Shrugging and looking somewhat puzzled, she replied, *"Nunca preguntaron. Si ellos jugaban demasiado fuerte con él, yo les decía, 'Tengan cuidado porque tiene el cuello muy delicado.'"* [They never asked. If they were playing too roughly with him, I would tell them, "Remember to be careful, because of his neck."] (Her reference to his neck reflected a warning that the family doctor had given them regarding a common weakness of the neck in individuals with Down syndrome.)

I asked her whether she had ever explained Rafael's *"problema"* [problem] to his brothers, but she said no. As she spoke, her attitude suggested that there was only a need to refer to Rafael's condition if a problematic situation arose. She went on to tell me a story of an occasion when a boy in the neighborhood had deliberately burned Rafael with a cigarette and Andre got into a fight with the boy. On discussing this with Andre, Felicita emphasized that Rafael was not to be blamed for his condition because God had made him that way. After that, Andre made a point of taking Rafael into the neighborhood every day, as if to show his peers that "this is my brother." Overall, all of our work with this family suggested that Rafael was a youth whose unconditional acceptance and wide range of activities within his family made it possible for him to have his own place and his own *"vida normal."*

VISIONS OF THE FUTURE

Two years after the completion of the project, we conducted an update interview with the Ignacios. A lot had happened in that time; some of Rafael's brothers went through their own changes and challenges, but Rafael's place in the family remained the same. He was still *"el centro de la familia"* [the center of the family].

By the time of our update interview, Rafael had completed his first year in high school and was placed in the same LRE program in which the older students in our project had been. The Ignacios were pleased with the teacher, just as the other parents in our study had been. In the year to come, Rafael's program would become more intensively vocational, with which, once more, his parents were pleased because they saw him as increasingly independent and saw paid employment as a reality for him in the future.

One aspect of their satisfaction with Rafael's progress related to their decision to immigrate to the United States. This had worked out well for Rafael in particular because, they explained, the only opportunity for employment that he would have had in their native country would have been in a "rehabilitation program." However, one intriguing aspect of their comparisons between the United States and the Dominican Republic was the different ways of defining *disability*. When we asked Felix and Felicita whether Rafael would be called "disabled" or "handicapped" in their native country, they answered simultaneously, but Felicita exclaimed, "Yes," while her husband exclaimed, "No!" As we explored this a bit, Felicita clarified that she was using an American definition because she knew that in the United States "even a person with a limp" would be called "handicapped." In their native country, despite the lack of opportunities for Rafael, his condition would not be serious enough to warrant such a label.

The Ignacios' vision of Rafael's future was tied to the family. Throughout the years of the project, their strong emphasis on family unity had been consistent. For example, the project held a Christmas get-together for the families every year, and in the final summer, we held a picnic. On all of these occasions, the entire Ignacio family attended, including all four siblings and usually a sprinkling of uncles, aunts, and cousins, bearing delicious, home-prepared Dominican dishes. When we arranged for a videotaped interview with the family, the parents required all four brothers to be present. The parents also spoke frequently of their relationship with the five adult offspring in their homeland and explained that Rafael was a particular favorite of the oldest son.

Felix and Felicita placed their full faith in this family structure. They were confident that in the event of their deaths, Rafael would live within the biological family. The couple, speaking sometimes simultaneously, sometimes alternately, outlined their expectations for him in the following words:

> *Que él pueda trabajar—trabajar para sobrevivir. . . . No espero algo grandioso para él, porque hemos aceptado su condición. Pero espero que va a estar bien independiente entre la familia. . . . Mientras nosotros estemos vivos nunca saldrá de nosotros. . . . Y después— bueno, mis hijos grandes no lo dejaría nunca. Digo los grandes, porque estos todavía no saben ni lo que quieren. . . . Pero estamos seguros que no será nunca abandonado de sus hermanos porque ellos lo quieren mucho.* [That he'll be able to work—work to make a living. . . . We

don't expect anything grandiose for him because we have accepted his condition. But we hope that he'll be quite independent within the family. . . . As long as we're alive, he won't leave our side. . . . And after—well, our older children will never leave him. I can't speak for these younger ones because they don't even know what they want to do yet! But we're sure that he'll never be abandoned by his brothers and sisters, because they love him very much.]

APPLYING THE POSTURE OF CULTURAL RECIPROCITY

1. *Inclusion as a cultural philosophy:* We believe that values such as equity and individualism underlie the philosophy of inclusion. However, although these values are cornerstones of American culture, they are by no means universal values. The idea of the equal importance of each individual is not universally held. In fact, there are societies in which the concept of "value inequity" is accepted; that is, it is accepted that differential value will be placed on individuals according to factors such as social status, biological limitations, age, gender, or other factors. Describe your own concept of equity, and figure out how it influences your view of inclusion. Using your personal identity web (see Figure 3 on p. 9), examine the source of this view. Then ask yourself, "To what extent were Rafael's summer camp program and schooling adequately inclusive?"

2. *The implications of inclusion:* Rafael had a certain place within the sibling hierarchy where his dependence was expected and accepted. Does this conflict with your definition of *inclusion*? To what extent can an individual be seen simultaneously as equal to yet less competent than others? To what extent does it matter that that person most likely will not be able to reciprocate the help of his peers in similar ways? To what extent are you comfortable, as were Rafael's parents, with Rafael's preference for play with children who were younger than he? Use your personal identity web (see Figure 3 on p. 9) to explore the sources of your responses to these questions.

3. *Psychological assessment—parental versus professional perspectives:* Rafael's parents displayed a keen interest in Rafael's educational planning. They always attended his annual review conferences and supported the recommendations of the professionals who were in charge of his education. When Rafael finally had a bilingual evaluation, his parents believed that the assessment had underestimated Rafael's abilities; they thought it ridiculous that he should be described as being at the level of

a 4-year-old. However, they did not oppose the school when this assessment was used to justify placement in a self-contained class in the middle school. Rafael's parents had been satisfied with his previous placement, which was essentially the same program to which he would now be moved at the middle school level. Their dissatisfaction with the assessment was more a matter of objecting to Rafael's being seen as so low—not recognizing his strengths; they were not really worried about the kind of program placement in which it resulted.

Imagine that you are one of the professionals, perhaps a teacher or a psychologist, working with Rafael's family. Examine your own beliefs on the issue of the accuracy of a psychological assessment. Using your personal identity web (see Figure 3 on p. 9), examine the source of your definition of intelligence and how it affects the value that you place on formal psychological assessment. Then figure out how you would explain to the family the professional view of this psychological assessment.

4. *The power differential in parental participation:* Identify in the Ignacios' dealings with the school system some specific events that indicate how the power differential between the family and the school system worked against the family. What are the cultural underpinnings of those events? How could professionals change these patterns?

5. *Deference versus equality in parental participation:* This family's participation style is very deferential to authority. It was evident that the Ignacio family knew a great deal about including a person with a disability, and they had distinct opinions about Rafael's intelligence and skills. However, because of an ingrained deference to school authorities, they tended not to express their opinions. They were aware of their responsibility as Rafael's parents to be involved in his education, but they were unaware of two taken-for-granted beliefs that are embedded in special education law: a) that parents are expected to be partners and that their knowledge about their child is, ideally, perceived to be as important as professionals' and b) that if parents do not agree with professionals' recommendations, then the onus is on them to advocate on behalf of their child for an appropriate education, even if it results in an adversarial relationship. The Ignacios, however, believed that the professionals knew best and deferred to them, even when they did not like a decision. At the same time, the professionals were operating within the traditional model of positivism, which values profes-

sional knowledge more than parental knowledge—contradicting the partnership expectation of the legal mandate.

Imagine that you are an advocate for Rafael, provided by a private (non–school-related) agency. Using your personal identity web (see Figure 3 on p. 9), identify those aspects of your own value system that might affect your view of this family's participation. Then work through the steps of the process of cultural reciprocity to assist this family in becoming more effective advocates. Specify some actual events on which you would work with them.

6. *The sibling study—equality versus hierarchy:* Sibling interaction in this family revealed full acceptance of Rafael, within a hierarchical family structure. We saw this as an "equitable hierarchy" in which Rafael's position of dependence was a privilege by virtue of his disability, just as his older brothers' responsibility for and authority over him were a consequence of their respective positions in the family as well as their perceived competence. Conversely, the taken-for-granted belief that is embedded in inclusive schooling, based on the ideal of equality, is that being dependent is a devalued position. What is your own reaction to these differing perspectives? What can the sibling study teach us about equity and hierarchy in peer relationships?

7. *The sibling study—unconditional acceptance and inclusion:* The portrait of unconditional acceptance that emerged from our study of Rafael's family was underscored by Felicita's assumption that there was no need to explain Rafael's condition to his siblings. Except on occasions when some particular need arose, the family's acknowledgment of Rafael's differences was mostly implicit. Against this background, we see Rafael accepted yet frequently "excluded" from his siblings' play. How do you interpret the brothers' patterns of play with Rafael and the difference between his response to being excluded from their play and his response to being excluded from play with peers at school? Is unconditional acceptance possible outside the family? What can the sibling study teach us about facilitating inclusion among peers?

8. *Visions of the future:* Felix and Felicita's view of Rafael's future is based on the conviction that Rafael's siblings "will never abandon him." This suggests that anything less than full commitment from his siblings would constitute "abandonment." How do you react to this perspective? Imagine that you are a service provider working with this family on the issue of transi-

tion planning for Rafael's adulthood. Work out with the family a hypothetical series of interactions that would reflect the four steps of the posture of cultural reciprocity.

9. *Definitions of disability:* The Ignacios' explanations of cultural differences in defining disability reflect that the parameters of what is considered "normal" differ according to cultural expectations. What is your own definition of *disability?* How disabled does an individual have to be to be called "disabled" in your personal view? How does your view compare with the official definitions used by the special education system? What implications might differing definitions have for your communication and interaction with families from diverse cultural backgrounds?

Epilogue

Personalism and Responsibility in Researcher–Family Relationships

As you have seen from the range of these case studies, our participatory action research with the families meant a level of personal involvement and commitment that is not a part of the traditional, positivist research paradigm. Indeed, this kind of study generally is seen as representing a new paradigm in research methodology. We believe that this approach yields more practical, more in-depth, and more valid information because of its close-up lens and collaborative approaches. This type of work also has its challenges, one of which is the increased personal responsibility that comes with increased involvement.

We have mentioned in the case studies the differing interaction styles of the various families with whom we worked. All of the families were welcoming to us and were supportive of and cooperative with our efforts. Obviously, however, we experienced a range of personal interaction styles, some of which can be interpreted in terms of traditional cultural patterns and others of which probably represent purely individual and unique styles. Although we always caution students to avoid stereotyping families, it is certainly true that most cultural groups exhibit interaction styles that reflect certain values that are held by that culture. Families within that culture may adhere greatly, a bit, or not at all to those traditions.

One of the features often cited in descriptions of traditional Hispanic interaction style is an emphasis on what has been called *personalism*. This refers to a preference for very personalized interaction, which takes into account the status of each individual yet which also moves beyond that status to seek an increasingly personal level of communication, which, ideally, comes to be based on *confianza* [trust] and *respeto* [respect]. Let us take, for example, our relationship with the Ignacio family.

We found the Ignacio family to be very representative of these traditional Hispanic patterns. We were welcomed into their home in a friendly yet very respectful manner, which gradually became increasingly personalized, lively, and hospitable. By the end of our first year, it was close to impossible to pay a visit to the Ignacios without sharing a meal with them or, if it was nowhere near meal-time, being offered some special treat. We came to know several of their extended family members through their frequent presence during our visits and through their participation in our project's social events. Similarly, the Ignacios came to know some of our family members, and Beth would sometimes take along her step-son, who would play with the Ignacio boys while the interview proceeded.

For the three team members who spent a lot of time with the Ignacios (Beth, Moni, and Cecelia), these interaction patterns were very comfortable because of a sense of cultural compatibility with our own cultural backgrounds and personal styles. The personal quality of the relationship also led to an enriched understanding of the family's experiences and perspectives regarding Rafael. The only downside of the entire relationship was the difficulty in with-drawing our project's support when our time and funds were up. Of course, this was not the only family about whom we felt this way, but the more personal the quality of the relationship was, the greater our sense of responsibility was. In this family, this feeling was also strengthened by the fact that our interventions had as-sisted the family in unexpected ways, such as inadvertently intro-ducing opportunities for Rafael's brothers to get summer employ-ment. Smaller contributions included frequent assistance to the family in transportation to school events, support for the family's advocacy needs, and attempts to assist Felicita in gaining employ-ment.

If you were engaged in a research project of this nature, how might you answer some of the following questions:

1. With which kind of interaction style would you be more com-fortable and why?
2. What kind of limits do you think you would want to set as you offered assistance to the family?
3. How might you try to provide assistance that would ensure the continuity of your efforts after the project ended?

4. What kinds of assistance would be most likely to offer the families skills that they could use after your project ended?
5. Can you think of any ethical dilemmas that likely would have been challenging for you in your relationship with any of these families? If so, for one last time in reading this book, use your personal identity web (see Figure 3 on p. 9) to explore the sources and implications of your answer to this question.

References and Recommended Readings

REFERENCES

Apple, M.W., & Beane, J.A. (Eds.). (1995). *Democratic schools.* Alexandria, VA: Association for Supervision and Curriculum Development.

Banks, J.A., & McGee Banks, C.A. (Eds.). (1997). *Multicultiral education: Issues and perspectives* (3rd ed.). Needham Heights, MA: Allyn & Bacon.

Bender, L. (1946). *Bender Gestalt Test: Cards and manual of instructions.* New York: American Orthopsychiatric Association.

Harry, B. (1992). *Cultural diversity, families, and the special education system.* New York: Teachers College Press.

Individuals with Disabilities Education Act (IDEA) of 1990, PL 101-476, 20 U.S.C. §§ 1400 *et seq.*

Individuals with Disabilities Education Act Amendments of 1997, PL 105-17, 20 U.S.C. §§ 1400 *et seq.*

Kalyanpur, M., & Harry, B. (1999). *Culture and special education: Building reciprocal family–professional relationships.* Baltimore: Paul H. Brookes Publishing Co.

Kincaid, J. (1990). *Lucy.* New York: Penguin.

Meyer, L.H., Park, H.-S., Grenot-Scheyer, M., Schwartz, I., & Harry, B. (1998). *Making friends: The influences of culture and development.* Baltimore: Paul H. Brookes Publishing Co.

Skrtic, T.M. (Ed.). (1995). *Disability and democracy: Reconstructing (special) education for postmodernity.* New York: Teachers College Press.

Wechsler, D. (1974). *Wechsler Intelligence Scale for Children–Revised.* San Antonio, TX: The Psychological Corporation.

Wechsler, D. (1981). *Wechsler Adult Intelligence Scale–Revised.* San Antonio, TX: The Psychological Corporation.

Woodcock, R.W., & Johnson, M.B. (1977). *Woodcock-Johnson Psychoeducational Test Battery.* Boston: Teaching Resources.

RECOMMENDED READINGS

Ballenger, C. (1994). Because you like us: The language of control. *Harvard Educational Review, 62,* 199–208.

Banks, J.A. (1997). *Teaching strategies for ethnic studies* (6th ed.). Needham Heights, MA: Allyn & Bacon.

Banks, J.A., & McGee Banks, C.A. (Eds.). (1997). *Multicultural education: Issues and perspectives* (3rd ed.). Needham Heights, MA: Allyn & Bacon.

Billingsley, A. (1992). *Climbing Jacob's ladder: The enduring legacy of African-American families.* New York: Simon & Schuster.

Bowers, C.A. (1984). *The promise of theory: Education and the politics of cultural change.* Reading, MA: Addison Wesley Longman.

Chen, D., Brekken, L., Chan, S., & Guarneri, G. (1997). *Project CRAFT: Culturally responsive and family focused training* [Videotape]. Baltimore: Paul H. Brookes Publishing Co.

Dorris, M. (1989). *The broken cord.* New York: HarperCollins.

Fadiman, A. (1997). *The spirit catches you and you fall down: A Hmong child, her American doctors, and the collision of two cultures.* New York: Farrar, Straus, & Giroux.

Groce, N.E., & Zola, I.K. (1993). Multiculturalism, chronic illness, and disability. *Pediatrics, 91,* 1048–1055.

Hall, E.T. (1981). *Beyond culture.* Garden City, NY: Anchor Press/Doubleday.

Harris, M. (1974). *Cows, pigs, wars, and witches: The riddles of culture.* New York: Random House.

Harry, B. (1992). *Cultural diversity, families, and the special education system: Communication and empowerment.* New York: Teachers College Press.

Harry, B. (1992). Developing cultural self-awareness: The first step in values clarification for early interventionists. *Topics in Early Childhood Special Education, 12,* 333–350.

Hill, R.B. (1993). Research on the African-American family: A holistic perspective. Westport, CT: Auburn House.

Ingstad, B., & Whyte, S.R. (Eds.). (1995). *Disability and culture.* Berkeley: University of California Press.

Kalyanpur, M., & Harry, B. (1997). A posture of reciprocity: A practical approach to collaboration between professionals and parents of culturally diverse backgrounds. *Journal of Child and Family Studies, 6,* 487–509.

Kleinman, A. (1980). *Patients and healers in the context of culture.* Berkeley: University of California Press.

Lynch, E.W., & Hanson, M.J. (Eds.). (1998). *Developing cross-cultural competence: A guide to working with children and their families* (2nd ed.). Baltimore: Paul H. Brookes Publishing Co.

Marion, R. (1981). *Educators, parents and exceptional children.* Rockville, MD: Aspen.

McGoldrick, M., Pearce, J.K., & Giordano, J. (Eds.). (1996). *Ethnicity and family therapy* (2nd ed.). New York: Guilford Press.

Meyer, L.H., Park, H.-S., Grenot-Scheyer, M., Schwartz, I.S., & Harry, B. (Eds.). (1998). *Making friends: The influences of culture and development.* Baltimore: Paul H. Brookes Publishing Co.

Reese, L., Balzano, S., Gallimore, R., & Goldenberg, C. (1995). The concept of *educacion:* Latino family values and American schooling. *International Journal of Educational Research, 23*(1), 57–81.

Rueda, R., & Martinez, I. (1992). Fiesta educative: One community's approach to parent training in developmental disabilities for Latino families. *Journal of The Association for Persons with Severe Handicaps, 17*(2), 95–103.

Schön, D.A. (1983). *The reflective practitioner: How professionals think in action.* New York: BasicBooks.

Serpell, R. (1997). Critical issues, literacy connections between school and home: How should we evaluate them? *Journal of Literacy Research, 29,* 587–616.

Singh, N.N. (1995). In search of unity: Some thoughts on family–professional relationships in service delivery systems. *Journal of Child and Family Studies, 4*(1), 3–18.

Skrtic, T.M. (Ed.). (1995). *Disability and democracy: Reconstructing (special) education for postmodernity.* New York: Teachers College Press.

Spindler, G., & Spindler, L. (Eds.). (1997). *Pathways to cultural awareness: Culture therapy with teachers and students.* Thousand Oaks, CA: Corwin Press.

Tapestry: Weaving sustaining threads [Newsletter]. (Available from Grassroots Consortium on Disabilities, Post Office Box 61628, Houston, TX 77208.)

Tharp, R., & Gallimore, R. (1988). *Rousing minds to life: Teaching, learning, and schooling in social context.* New York: Cambridge University Press.

Tobin, J.J., Wu, D.Y.H., & Davidson, D.H. (1989). *Preschool in three cultures: Japan, China, and the United States.* New Haven, CT: Yale University Press.

Turnbull, A.P., & Turnbull, H.R. (1997). *Families, professionals, and exceptionality: A special partnership* (3rd ed.). Upper Saddle River, NJ: Merrill/ Prentice-Hall.

Valdés, G. (1996). *Con respeto: Bridging the distances between culturally diverse families and schools: An ethnographic portrait.* New York: Teachers College Press.